CONCERNING
INTELLECTUAL
PHILANDERING

CONCERNING INTELLECTUAL PHILANDERING

Poets and Philosophers,
Priests and Politicians

Marion Montgomery

ROWMAN & LITTLEFIELD PUBLISHERS, INC.
Lanham • Boulder • New York • Oxford

ROWMAN & LITTLEFIELD PUBLISHERS, INC.

Published in the United States of America
by Rowman & Littlefield Publishers, Inc.
4720 Boston Way, Lanham, Maryland 20706

12 Hid's Copse Road
Cumnor Hill, Oxford OX2 9JJ, England

British Library Cataloguing in Publication Information Available

Library of Congress Cataloging-in-Publication Data

Montgomery, Marion.
    Concerning intellectual philandering : poets and philosophers,
priests and politicians / Marion Montgomery.
        p.   cm.
    Includes bibliographical references and index.
    ISBN 0-8476-9200-0 (alk. paper)
    1. American poetry—20th century—History and criticism—Theory,
etc. 2. Eliot, T. S. (Thomas Stearns), 1888–1965—Knowledge and
learning. 3. English poetry—History and criticism—Theory, etc.
4. Pound, Ezra, 1885–1972—Knowledge and learning. 5. Knowledge,
Theory of, in literature. 6. Creation (Literary, artistic, etc.)
7. Reality in literature. 8. Analogy in literature. 9. Authorship.
I. Title.
PS323.5.M64   1998
811'.5209—dc21   98-7792
                                                                      CIP

Printed in the United States of America

⊖™ The paper used in this publication meets the minimum requirements of American
National Standard for Information Sciences—Permanence of Paper for Printed Library
Materials, ANSI Z39.48–1984.

The asserted likeness of the practical intellect to God is one of proportion; that is to say, by reason of its standing in relation to what it knows (and brings into existence) as God does to what He knows (creatively). But the likeness of the speculative to God is one of union and information; which is a much greater likeness.

—St. Thomas Aquinas, *Summa Theologica*, I-II, Q3, 5

Contents

Acknowledgments

Once more I am grateful to the Earhart Foundation for its continuing support of my work and especially once more to David B. Kennedy, president, and Antony T. Sullivan, director of program. Their encouragement has been sustaining.

Permissions: Excerpts from "Animula" in *Collected Poems 1909–1962* by T. S. Eliot, copyright by Harcourt Brace & Company, copyright © 1954, 1963 by T. S. Eliot, reprinted by permission of the publisher. I am grateful to New Directions for permission to use an excerpt from Ezra Pound's *Gaudier-Brzeska,* copyright © 1970 by Ezra Pound. Used by permission of New Directions Publishing Corporation.

Introduction:
Getting Beyond the Cartesian Bubble

In *Thomism and Romantic Confusions of the Good*, to which this is something of an addendum, the concern was for what we called the "Romantic" poet, and though we concentrated on some of those poets usually associated with that "movement" in the history of literature—Wordsworth, Keats, and in our addition to them T. S. Eliot—our concern was rather with a common inclination we considered trans-historical, in one aspect perhaps pre-historical. We argued that those 19th century "Romantic" poets were given to the intuitive inclination of intellect, but that such an inclination is common to intellect and not peculiar to either a time or a place. The theme developed was that, insofar as an intellect tends to disjoin its intuitive gift from its rational gift, it becomes endangered by a confusion of the nature of the Good, just as that intellect which disjoins its rational gift will do if it eschew its intuitive gifts, becoming in our epithet a "Romantic rationalist." When those gifts are ordinate in intellects's engagement of reality, we contended, intellect is enabled to distinguish its mediate ends from its ultimate end and so come to an accommodation with the truth of things created—with creation in general. In this manner it may come to an accommodation of its own journeying through creation toward its proper end, which is the perfection of the soul called Beatitude.

As for that "Romantic" intellect moved intuitively, and especially if that intellect's local calling—its practical office in time and place—is that of the poet: we suggested that the labor of its making brings it into a community with being in the world, though it does so through the offices of rational intellect. By song, intellect accedes to the nature of reality, both to the reality of its own given nature as a particular thing in itself—

this *person* with this *calling*—and thereby to that reality larger and more inclusive of its own particularity, that reality we call Creation. But (our argument ran) because art is an activity of the practical intellect, it is crucial that the rational intellect is centrally operative in any singing raised as art—indeed to any making. *Making*, we said, is the significant (the *signed*) aspect of human existence in time. This was the argument's turning point, since it seems evident in the history of diverse "Romantic" minds—Romantic "poets" or Romantic "rationalists"—that, with the impulse of the intuitive, it is the poet who is particularly susceptible to errors of intellectual action through unreasoned use of signs. (By comparison, the "Romantic rationalist" tends to deny his initiating dependence upon the intuitive.) Those signs, to borrow from Wordsworth's formulation of "poetry," are "feelings" that are adequately "recollected"—collected and ordered by practical intellect—in that "tranquility" which reason may bring to the support of the intellect's intuitive vision of the truth of things.

Words, our argument held, may be therefore forced either to exceed the limited authority of sign or to fall short of the limits possible to sign in sign's capacity to move intellect to an understanding of existence. That difficulty is complicated by intellect's temptation to attribution, whereby it prematurely imposes signs as if an action upon things, misleading itself in the limits of its own authority in respect to the truth of things. Because intellect by its nature responds through the senses to things other than itself, and inasmuch as the senses engage the accidents of things in themselves, it is *through* that sensual engagement of things in themselves that the *essence* of the thing perceived, as Thomas says, is possessed by intellect *before* its conceptual action. But intellect's orientation to what it knows and how it knows it is easily confused. For, until it *understand* in what sense it already knows *essence* before its conceptual actions, it is easily inclined to dwell in the accidents of things as perceived. That dwelling in accidents is the arena of fancy which, for instance, Coleridge was concerned to extricate from the imagination to safeguard a vision of reality.

Put another way, when intellect becomes aware of itself, it becomes aware (if given to reason's reflection) that it is already in possession of knowledge. Intellect as a knowing agent of the soul cannot reach a point in its memory of itself at which it might say that at this point it did not already know something. This is a truth of intellect, we argued, which sets the Thomistic Realist apart from the Cartesian Idealist. And we considered that the dominance of Cartesian thought in recent intellectual history made it extremely difficult to the Romantic poet to recover that realist's position. To have recovered the realist's position is to set out in song with a quite different perspective upon reality. It means that, though the inclination to attributive analogy continues, there comes to the support and modification of that analogy, under the auspices of reason, a deeper understanding of existence whereby analogy is grounded in the structure of reality. That is the analogy of proper proportionality which St. Thomas Aquinas opens to us, especially in his treatise *On Being and Essence*.

The distinction between these species of analogy is crucial to our understanding of our intellectual actions, whether we happen to be poet or philosopher or whatever local calling, and regardless of when we live— whether in the thirteenth or the twentieth century. And so, though we considered the distinction to some extent in *Thomism and Romantic Confusions of the Good*, the consideration is of such importance that we are justified in exploring it further. For if attribution is the strategy of intellect in its first response to the wonder of existence itself, and is in fact intellect's first movement toward beholding the structure of reality, it becomes important to intellect to contain and direct that inclination, lest intellect itself end up isolated from being by its becoming hopelessly embroiled in the accidents of being. By attribution, then, we mean an action in which the sign of an intellectual action (the word or the poem) is insufficiently related to the structure of reality itself, which is the structure of *being* made manifold in discrete beings. That structure yields insight to intellect when intellect is properly oriented, when it sees proportionately in relation to *being* itself, as opposed to that limited seeing through perception of accidents of *being*.

Thus joined in reality, the joined intellect (intuitive-rational) acts according to the limit of intellect's authority. Thus it neither fails nor exceeds its power of vision of the nature of things. That such concerns haunt the poet, however he may speak of them, is evident, and we shall be exploring some poet's awareness of this concern. We do not intend thereby, of course, to suggest the problem unique to the poet. Such is the concern of any intellect, because of its given nature. But perhaps the poet's "poetic" concern for the problem, particularly his concern with analogy, may serve to concentrate the concern to our general benefit. Some of the poets—indeed most of them—are the ones we considered in the earlier work. Our consideration here is with a somewhat different emphasis, but it is probable that the two works complement each other, or so I intend them to be complementary.

1

Sign: The Fruit of Intellect

Intellect, failing its limit of action, imposes sign upon the truth of things, confusing the sign with truth and thus violating reality at the expense of its valid vision. Such violation of reality is through the poet's will to order reality by the concert of the power of his will and his intellect as instrument to the operation of that power. It is in this relation of intellect to reality that *attribution* deludes intellect into supposing itself the cause of order by the very action of attribution. Here we should understand that, from our intended Thomistic perspective on the problem, *sign* is understood as an outward display signifying not only the concept as held by intellect, but signifying as well the very nature of that intellect which holds and advances the sign toward other intellects. A mind signifying to another mind speaks through its signs not only of something not itself but of itself as well. One knows an intellect by its signs, whatever else of truth may be revealed by that intellect's ordering of its signs. Signs are the fruit of intellect, so that however sharply the fruit may be separated from the tree, a continuing presence of the tree is implicit in the fruit. This is an observation we shall have to consider again in relation to the troublesome question of the poet's relation to his poem, as representative of any maker's relation to the thing he makes. This is that complexly ambiguous problem of the relation of *person* to the thing the person makes, whether poem or system of thought, or social order.

And so: intellect, through its act of conception within reality, bears as offspring of that conjoining of itself and some other a sign of some sort, more or less proportionately ordered to its "fathering" in reality. It is in this relation of intellect to reality that the poet can but speak figuratively, as he has done from the beginning of sign in relation to intellect. Athene, the poet says, sprang full grown from the head of Zeus. The difficulty, and a confusion in such figurings in signs, is that sign cannot speak either clearly or fully of its progenitors. Still, this action whereby sign is begotten implies that double nature to intellect. For Zeus, the God-Father, has borne Athene the Wise One, not simply through a "full term" in the analogy as based in natural begetting. Athene springs fully grown, fully armed into the world. Setting aside that mystery of the suddness of Wisdom after its hidden maturation, there is yet that other mystery: the myth suggests intellect itself as "feminine."

Certainly the poet, attempting to understand himself as a maker, discovers through long thought about the process of his making which issues in signs that he cannot escape a certain "feminine" aspect in his intellect, however vigorously "masculine" his deportment through the making of sign. One might helpfully remember the dramatic representation Dante makes of this mystery of the poet's intellect. Virgil, after his patient preparation of the pilgrim poet's rational intellect on its journey through Hell and up to the top of Purgatory Mountain, surrenders his office of intellectual guide to Beatrice at the edge of the earthly paradise. It was Beatrice, of course, who initiated the poet's journey of rescue in the first place, her help hinted at along the way, though Dante as pilgrim is not prepared to understand those hints until fully exercised intellectually. It is the *rational* intellect that is in training under Virgil's tutelage in the first part of the journey, a preparation for Dante's coming into a fullness of *intuitive* vision through speculative intellect. If we put the point in St. Thomas's terms, the practical intellect develops until it is worthy of its speculative gift. Our epigraph from St. Thomas puts the relation carefully in relation to the analogy of proper proportionality. "The asserted likeness of the practical intellect to God is one of proportion; that is to say, by reason of its standing in relation to what it knows (and brings into existence) as God does to what He knows (creatively). But the likeness of the speculative [intellect] to God is one of union and information; which is a much greater likeness" (*Summa Theologica*, I-II, Q3, 5). This analogy of proportionality is central to and pervasive of the *Summa*, dependent in that belief central to Christianity which says that God created man in his own image.

It should not be surprising then, given the long history of the poet's figurative attempts upon the mystery of man as maker, to find him accepting himself as somehow the nurturing, no less than the conceiving, agent to his begotten offspring, his "word." What remains mysterious is the nature of the inception. One need but read in the lyric poetry of that most masculine of Ages to which we attach a woman's name: the Elizabethan Age. Such is the irony in our figurative language, but it may in the end prove paradox beyond irony.

One encounters a philosophical concern for understanding the nature of intellect itself, put in figurative ways by the poet at the time of Queen Elizabeth. A famous instance is that of an aggressive soldier poet, Sir Philip Sidney, who also wrote a "Defense of Poetry" attempting to incarnate Platonic Idealism in relation to art. Not that treatise is our source, however, but Sidney's famous figure with which he embarks upon a love-making sonnet sequence, *Astrophel and Stella*. The poet's ravagement by Love is the fictional strategy of that sonnet sequence.

The sonnet signs speak of a fanciful agony of conception, nurturing, delivering as they are at first unnaturally responded to by the poet, and then naturally by the poet in his mothering verses. Sidney speaks in the famous opening figure of being "great with child to speak, helpless in my throes." Nature, having seeded his heart through his beholding Stella, seems then to have quite abandoned the poet. The figurative strategy casts that poet in the role, not of Lover, but of an abandoned Beloved. Clearly, Sidney violates the sonnet's expected music in respect to the metrical form of the sonnet, though that form is not yet severely fixed in English prosody in the rigor of the iambic pentameter line which Pound complains overtakes and arrests English prosody. Even the grammar of Sidney's attempt is highly tangled, as is the rhetorical structure. The octave is a flood of verbals clustered about the central labor ("I sought fit words. . . ."). And within that clever confusion of borrowed metrical form, concepts from classical rhetoric are caught struggling out of his memory as well: expressed or implied, the terms *conception, invention, disposition, elocution* are summoned, but fruitlessly. The Alexandrine line breaks down into dangling modifiers, centering always on the laboring poet and coming to issue in the sestet, a smooth issue at last in the concluding line: " 'Fool,' said my Muse to me, 'look in thy heart and write.' " That smooth issue prepares a "natural" birth to the sonnets which follow. But we must not be careless here. We must not suppose that Sidney's message from his Muse means what our own age inclines to make of his message. He is not being advised to say what he "feels," or to "tell it like it is," by which we mean usually what it *seems* like, nor what "it" is in "its" actuality. Sidney, as maker, is assuming a reasoned relation to the thing he is making (for otherwise there could not be such a dramatic order to this imitation of intellectual disorder). Rather certainly he means that as poet he must *look* to a restoring of intellect to its proper midwifery offices, devoted to the consort of heart and mind in the making of the thing.

Thus, though the poet declares himself "great with child," it is a more complicated figure as it emerges from beneath the confusions of forms—metrical, grammatical, rhetorical—that hold Sidney's attention as he

makes. We may, from the figure, begin to reflect that nature as a somewhat indifferent father of the poem is the nature of intellect itself, the
given nature of a spiritual creature, the poet himself. The actions of maker
are complex because the given nature out of which such making proceeds
is complex, not easily reduced to the formulae of classical rhetoric. So
that figurative *looking* may prove more revealing, in that it puts rational
ordering of what is seen—the execution or making of a thing, the poem—
into a sounder perspective in relation to the reality of intellect itself. The
possibility of a proper "wedding" constituting a unity of intellect, a new
oneness, might well put the concern figuratively, in relation to the sexual
act and the resulting progeny. For figurative language appears to the poet
the most suitable access to the mystery in such matters. And so in this
respect *mind* as "masculine," *heart* as "feminine," comes as no surprise.

Intellect is thus seen to prosper in a "family way," as it were, when the
intuitive "heart" and the rational "head" are in happy union, on an analogy not simply biological but of that sacrament of marriage whereby man
and woman are made one.[1] Now in that sacrament, man and woman are
made one in a consummation mystical: the sexual act becomes ritualisti-
cally transformed by sacrament beyond the merely bestial level. Thus a
family becomes itself spirit and flesh, a new being incarnate. But what we
are by way of saying here is that it is the poet's "heart" that has been
made "pregnant," subsequently becoming "great with child," over which
the solicitous head as puzzled "husband" seems determined to force a
birth by inducing false labor. Head is anxious for issue, impatient of
term—unable it seems to abide the proper course of nature. In looking
into the heart in that manner which the Muse counsels, head comes to
understand a proper relation of its act as governed by those finitudes of
intellect that are its given nature. The issue, the birth of the poem, becomes natural, relative to the "nature" of intellect. By being "still" before
such a looking, one is nevertheless "still moving," as Eliot might say to
the point. When Sidney is at last so stilled, the issue becomes the final
line, his labor relieved though not ended.

One might, without great violation of Sidney's figure, say that what is
seen in looking into the heart is a proper relation of rational and intuitive
intellect in the bringing forth of the sign. It is a proper relation of "heart"
and "head" in that ancient figurative naming of the relation. Nor do we
violate the truth hidden under the figure to add that one has here a recovered recognition of "nature's" relation to art which may be put Thomistically. If the intuitive intellect is that mode whereby one "sees into the
life of things" by an openness to things—or in Thomas's as opposed to
Wordsworth's words, "sees the truth of the thing in itself"—then it is the

intuitive which is more nearly the "feminine" in our figure, to which the active rational intellect must be brought into a husbandly service. Of course the "rational" may find itself somewhat shocked to discover its bride to have already conceived.

Thomas, we are reminded, emphasizes that knowledge of *essence* is in intellect prior to the rational recognition of *essence*. The truth of the thing in itself is already possessed in the "heart," to put the point figuratively. And it is a point the poet holds to again and again, though he seldom sees it in the terms the philosopher would use. It is in deference to the poet's inclination, then, that we consider the *ratio* and the *intellectus*, the *rational* and the *intuitive*, under the aspects of "feminine" and "masculine," of "lover" and "beloved." There is that monumental work which does the same, Dante's *Divine Comedy*, a work that owes a great deal to St. Thomas, whose understanding of the nature of the intellect is figuratively narrated in that intricate relation of Dante to Virgil on the one hand and to Beatrice on the other. Closer to our own time, we might remember William Butler Yeats struggling with such question, complicated by his imaginative response to Maude Gonne. Eliot's own question of his "lady," ambiguously present from "Prufrock" to *Little Gidding*, is significant to the mystery of the nature of intellect itself.

Those figures, and others we supply from memory, bring us back toward Sidney. We reflect that the shock to fathers-to-be is a standard comic element most anciently, an element which Sidney touches upon playfully. That shock of the poet as father-to-be is often enough accompanied by doubt, by a suspicion that somehow the poet has been secretly "had" in one way or another, perhaps by some "Muse" if not some dark incubus, some "devil in the ink pot." And such is the wonder of the *word* as child of intellect that the poet might well be uncertain of his intellect's participation, whether as passive or active participant, whether "feminine" or "masculine." Analogues to this wonder we encounter here and there, the poem itself bearing that ambiguous wonder on occasion. A sort of analogue, perhaps, might be that subtle moment at the court of King Nestor, when Nestor asks his young guest Telemachus, "Are you indeed the son of the great Odysseus?" To which, Telemachus: "My mother *says* I am." I propose the analogue—Telemachus as the "word" of Odysseus and Penelope—because Homer takes great delight in making Odysseus the great "Poet," especially at the court of the Phaeacians. That very present poet Homer, whose accustomed place is near the wine bowl and next to the king, becomes the honored fabulous king who sings his great deeds at Troy and beyond.

There is another instance of fatherly doubt, of the poet (in our figurative borrowing) concerned for his relation to the word, his child in the limits of his fathering, a poem closer to Sidney. In the lovely "Cherry Tree Carol," Joseph is rebuked for his sullen response to Mary's request as they walk in the cherry orchard. Mary asks, "So meek and so mild: 'Pluck me one cherry, Joseph, / For I am with child!' " To which, Joseph, "With words most unkind: / 'Let him pluck thee a cherry / That brought thee with child.' " Such is an early instance of that festering shock to the father over the mystery of conception. Intellect knows it participates in conception, actual or figurative, but knows even less certainly in the figurative. How or in what capacity does it participate in fathering forth through concept? There is nevertheless a strong suspicion that at some level there is a concert of union *in* being, out of which comes the blossoming, whether word or actual fruits of actual wombs. For even Sidney is not merely fanciful in his metaphor which deals with the conception and execution of a poem, such is the mystery of the life of the mind. In our day, so advanced are we in this mystery of the blossoming of being, that there is much clinical evidence, not without its own comic dimension, of the husband's experiencing false pregnancy, even false labor. Enough to make one wonder, then, whether there may be a unity in creation such that *all* touches *all*, beyond fancy's attribution. If so, the making of poem may even bear analogy beyond mere fancy as related to the making of a marriage. Surely Sidney touches upon that possibility, which is to say that there is a seriousness beneath his playfulness, though the spectacle of his play hides it somewhat. Deep down, the mystery of the word and the mystery of one's actual child may touch each other in ways mysterious, may indeed touch upon the mystery of the Word which is the cause of all the children of being. That is the poet's intuitive suspicion, but it is at last St. Thomas's rational argument.

Christ's rebuke of Joseph from the womb in "The Cherry Tree Carol," his commanding the cherry trees to bow down to Mary, is not unlike that rebuke to the modernist's position on intellect which St. Thomas presents long before we began to think of ourselves collectively as "modernists." For Thomas insists that intellect is already pregnant with the essence of things as beheld through the senses in a pre-conceptual way, whereupon *conception* ensues in intellect, issuing at last in outward signs. Indeed, that is the precise point of Thomistic Realism's rebuke of Cartesian Idealism. That Idealism is far from the mystery of the complexity of the existential complexity, and is an outcast from its own possible fullness in the mystical wedding of the rational and intuitive. Idealism's signs, given intellect's self-exile, come halting forth, crippled, but nevertheless bearing even in their misshapenness implications of reality beyond the false labor forced by the distorting intellect. That is a realization, we have remarked, that a poet like Eliot comes to at last, rescuing him to a new openness to realism out of intellectual exile. (On the differences between Thomistic Realism and Cartesian Idealism, see E. Gilson's *Methodical Realism*.)

That Sidney's poem lends itself to such a reading, which we have perhaps ourselves somewhat labored, is suggested by the very randomness of the sonnet's form, as we have seen. The poet's rational intellect at first, though with best intention, becomes in its desperateness almost a philanderer, because it lacks, is "wanting Invention's stay." *Invention*: that rhetorical term applied to figurative conception, from which follows *disposition* (ordering of the figurative conception) and *elocution* (diction, the actual tropes). And all these must proceed not only from conception, but from perception, from insight which is the "inspiriting" of intellect. The process of growth toward birth begins for the rational mind from its first looking into the heart, wherein lies the mystery of intellect's conception governed by the nature of things, some of which are already held there. But lacking "Invention's stay," our poet impatiently ravages "others' leaves," a raiding of other poets' offspring, which leads only to misshapen premature offspring not even his own. For in that attempt, "words came halting forth" into the world as flawed art. The proper concern for the good of the thing made by rational intellect, for the poet's offspring that threaten to burst forth awkwardly if so forced, requires a term quite other than the terms of classical rhetoric or the stolen parts of other poets' inventions. What is required is an ordering of the poet's intellect toward making, to an action of making, in which his family faculties, the rational and intuitive, are companionably wedded in a proportion proper to the nature of reality. And the nature of reality here means the poet's own intellectual nature first, whereby it may turn to nature at large, the enveloping "house" as it were which is called Creation. In realizing this necessity at last, the poet's words cease to come halting forth, in consequence of which he can turn to his "Stella" in that actual enveloping world of nature, and to the sequence of sonnets following thereupon, now addressed to his heart's desire as a man of the world to a woman in the world.

2

The Mystery of Fathering Forth

It is from these reflections upon Sidney's text, and upon our own experience as makers, whatever our particular making, that we say figuratively
that intellect by its "conceptions" bears forth sign as the issue of intellectual action. What we recognize with guarded attention is that such a figure
of intellect's "fathering forth" is an echo of its cause (as being created in
the "image" of God) very nearly bordering on the attributive, fanciful
misappropriation of proportionate analogy. The inclination to excess is
intellectually titillating, even though intended toward the truth of how
things stand beyond the weakness of our attributive signs. It is an inclination in Sidney which, a few generations later, becomes such an established
manner of literary making that it is given a formal name, "Metaphysical
Poetry." Dr. Johnson, we recall, rebuked the Metaphysicals for an excessive fancy which he took to violate the structure of reality precisely because it was attributive. But then if Dr. Johnson is right, it follows that
those poets are less truly "metaphysical" than the term implies.

Intellect, when so excited by its attributive inclination, easily overlooks
the reality of its limited relation as a mediator, through sign, of reality to
other intellects. It tends to "conceive" an existence as if the action and
the existent thing that is an effect of that action were independent of actual
existences. Of course, the poet's "fathering forth" is more complex to
understand than allowed by our somewhat fanciful analogy. That analogy
presents intellect's "begetting" as occurring by the *con-fusion* of intellect
with itself, the melding of intuitive and rational intellect, in relation to an
in-fusion of essence consequent to an encounter by complex intellect with
natures separate from itself. But there are enlightening correspondences
spoken of in such figuring, which the proper metaphysician may speak of
more precisely, the poet as philosopher, such as St. Thomas, as we shall
presently consider. Meanwhile, we observe differences. In "nature," in

that gathering of *things* in the ground of *being*, the gathering we call Creation, a finite begettor is conspicuously dependent upon a recipient of some "masculine" action at a physical level. A *thing else* is in general a necessity to progeneration. The consequences to natural coupling is a begotten, quite another *thing else*, though one which is itself also limited within the finitudes of Creation. And parents as medium to the begotten are themselves mediate of being itself *a priori*, and so in no sense absolute cause to the begotten. The poet in his myth of Zeus's fathering forth of Athene, or the sea's bearing Aphrodite, realize the limit even as through such mythological figurings he attempts to escape it.

Intellectual creatures such as poets or philosophers may mistake or overlook the inescapable dependence that is implicit in the circumstances of existence. Creatures who are themselves less than gods cannot do otherwise, which may be one reason the poet in particular is so ravenous of being, and easily mistakes himself as being's god. The limits of actual animal existence within the perspective of being per se are adhered to "naturally," of necessity, by animal existences, which is one source of intellect's sense of its superiority to subordinate existences. Still, the additional gift to man of intellect to his material, biological existence proves both a blessing and a burden, making man's conduct toward natural existence complex and confusing. He may even be envious (if one is Donne) of poisonous minerals and lecherous goats, for in those things there is no rebuke to fatal or lecherous properties. Still, intellect fails to advance a sufficient indictment of God for such unequal distribution of properties. In that failure, one might well wish at least to have been a pair of ragged claws rather than a social lounge lizard such as Prufrock finds himself. And thus Donne's angry envy decays to Prufrock's pathetic envy.

Nevertheless, it is through that gift which these poets take as burdensome, the gift of intellect, that the rational soul may discover the limits of its finitude, the parameters of its actions and its possible effects in Creation, whether in respect to the making of a natural child or of a poem. For it is through rational intellect that the soul discovers its limited power to create, despite its dependent nature. It may resent at first, but may also at last come to accept the limit joyfully: it makes only *with* the made, and discovers a pervasive made as shared with all existence. All is dependent in *being*! The recognition of this limit comes initially through the "heart," St. Thomas says, though heart is not his explicit term. As an image of the Maker of all, man is dependent, but more complexly dependent than accounted for by a rational summing of his mineral, vegetable, animal natures—the constituent elements to his life which the rational intellect describes through its variety of "sciences." One might even say that the range of intellectual freedom is revealed through the freedom of attribution possessed by intellect. Since there are limited properties in support of that freedom, intellect's summations of life are always less than comprehensive, inadequate to the fullness of life as it knows it intuitively. That is why, in the plumage of pride, a person as "scientist" may insist on rejecting any spiritual dimension to life, the necessity we have argued to any gnostic manipulation of being. For the scientist no less than the poet wants full credit for his making, wishing to be independent of muse or Holy Ghost. Having said as much, we may declare the importance of distinctions such as that between a limited knowing and the pretense that one's knowledge is fully comprehensive of the thing known. We may then feel more comfortable in other distinctions, as between one's natural child and the child of the imagination, the poem. For in such distinctions lies the guide to our understanding of the very limit of finite understanding. It is thus that one arrives at wisdom. More immediate to discrete actions of intellect, one may the more readily assent to the limits of his powers of making in the dimension of "nature," and thence to the limits of intellectual authority over being. One easily grants genetic determinations of being in the natural child (which is not the same as *determined* being in a mechanistic sense). Over that species of determinations, the will is powerless beyond event itself, when to us a child is born. The body is most persuasive of our dependence in existence in a range of ways, though about such realities intellect may be careless or indifferent. For the body's dependence exacerbates the will's desire for intellectual freedom, a ready cause to Manichean dualism in the secularized intellect we label "modernist."

When one considers himself in regard to his intellectual acts of fathering forth (as of a poem), he may therefore be less content with being merely a participatory "creator," since fundamentally participating *through* being even in his making, and furthermore doomed to participate through the senses. He would prefer to be not a creator, but *the* Creator of his little world, even if it is only (as Frost says on one occasion) some little man-made form of order. That is the inclination we observe in Wallace Stevens as poet, which he exploits by making what he terms "supreme fictions." And we observed Joyce giving us a portrait of the artist, the "Romantic" poet Stephen Dedalus, who justifies his position as Creator by appropriating and distorting from St. Thomas's *Summa* the arguments about the relation of art to intellect. In short, while a natural father is less likely than the poet as father of the poem to forget himself as merely involved in an inception, a conception leading to an issue in the child, not so with the poet. Of course domestic concerns abound in which the parent would relive himself in the offspring, as sometimes the poet would do, as in Dylan Thomas's "Fern Hill." The point is that the natural manifestation of the child confronts the father, as the intellectual manifestation of the poem through the sign does not confront the poet in the same manner of immediacy. The poet the more easily forgets himself as mediate, and in a dependent way, in the inception and issue of the poem. A natural father will, often enough and in response to difficulties with the child that are notoriously immediate, look to the child's parents and kinsmen, to his ancestors, to discover the limits of his own causal relation to the child. Or he looks to society or to the schools or to some present cultural participant that might possibly leave him exonerated. Few are the poets who readily consent to the poem's causes as ranging beyond the poet himself. That is the difficulty of the individual talent's coming to terms with its tradition and it is most troublesome. For the poet, if untempered in his intellectual nature, is likely to want absolute credit for the making, even willing to be worshipped for his originality. Little wonder, then, that the poet will be antagonistic to Socrates's argument in the *Ion*, or that the poet's bored or impatient fellows responding to his pretense of being "orginator" will use Socrates' argument there to put the poet in his place, reduce him from his pretense to godhead.

The poet as maker may mistake the limits of his finite intellect in relation to his power to generate his offspring, the poem. And since he does so by failing to distinguish attributive analogy from analogy based in the principle of proper proportionality, it becomes necessary that we explore that distinction if we are to serve the poet as critic. The distinction turns in the poet's gift which Aristotle declares peculiar to him, his gift of seeing likeness in unlike things. Our attention is to Thomas's understanding of proper proportionality as affecting concept. What is at issue is, first, the poet as maker in relation to the thing he makes; and second, the dependence of both poet and poem *within* the structure of reality, to which structure neither the poet nor reality itself is sufficient cause and therefore not sufficient principle in the order of that structure. The evolutionist poet such as Darwin and his followers, of course, attempt to make existence self-begetting in respect to this point. Therefore we must repeatedly insist, given the pervasiveness of the assumption of this half-way point as if the point of origin, and because of that reluctance consequent upon our fallen nature to be beholden to anything beyond the self: *maker* and *made* are dependent upon the *given*. The Darwinian determinist and the reluctant poet as Cartesian Idealist resist the obvious content of personal experience, lest metaphysical questions put theory and intent to flight. For a content independent of intellectual action as determinate is always waiting its recognition within intellect itself, waiting only intellect's recognition of that particular given.

And so our insistence: the poet's intellect bears no absolutely fundamental originating role as cause, anymore than the universe is itself uncaused cause. Therefore the poet's is no absolute creative act, however much he may celebrate or be celebrated, or wish to be celebrated, as "original." Acting from a given nature, he acts within temporal circumstances proper to that given nature. He cannot issue a "supreme fiction" as above reality, as Stevens tends to suggest possible till questioned closely. The poem is not a "world" sprung from intellect by the art of willing, an "Idea" beyond the entanglement of the artist as person in creation, or beyond the incarnational service rendered to art by creation in general through things as they exist in themselves. Or, more accurately, such attributive figures are just that, attributive, though they may by careful, rational exploration reveal analogy founded in being itself beyond mere attribution. It is thus that analogy reveals a truth beneath the figure. In an act of folly, Stephen Dedalus dreams to make a world actual rather than figurative, from which as its supreme God he would turn in a bored indifference and thereby escape both creation in general and his own created "world," which he takes as but a particular occasion to his professed indifference. The poignancy in the attempt we come to at the end of Joyce's novel: Stephen is writing cryptic notes to himself, isolated from the world and hardly productive of things as poet. Stephen's is a clever violation of reality by attribution, the action fancifully seductive to intellect, his own particularly but, judging from the sentimental affection for Stephen among his readers, ours as well. For one must respond beyond that initial "suspension of disbelief" that Coleridge counsels us to practice toward art, toward the made thing, if we are not ourselves to become victim to art through sentimentality.

As participant, whether poet or reader, we are susceptible to distortions of the limits of art. And never more than when the particular made thing seems most to reflect ourselves as makers—that is to say, when the artisan has been most concerned with himself as cause of the made thing, whereby we as reader the more easily identify our response in a tacit analogy of ourself to the artisan. The difficulty lies in our finding an ordered, proportionate response to our gifts as makers, whether in the active role of poet or passive role whereby we participate in "making" as audience. What is fundamental to art is its role in our recovery or discovery of our diverse gifts as makers. But given our freedom as makers and the temptation to become fascinated with ourselves as maker, the shifting of intellectual attention from the reality restricting that freedom to intellect itself may obscure both the diversity of persons as makers and even the complexity of this discrete, particular person—myself as maker. For the false sense of freedom of intellect as an unlimited freedom distorts intellect's sense of reality, at the expense of intellect, not of reality. The dilettante in art is a caricature of this error of disproportionate manipulation of art in the interest of the manipulator as artist, as creator. It will not follow that in such dislocation certain gifts in certain artists do not sometimes result in works which in themselves are good. For we remember once more that the good of a work of art lies in itself as a made thing. Were the poet indeed absolute in his power as maker, then the good of that thing would reside primarily in the poet, as the good of creation in general lies primarily in the good of its Creator God. Indeed, its very being would lie in the poet as its cause, out of which alone would rise its particular being. It is this dilemma to the poet, tacitly recognized if not overtly recognized, that complicates his coming to terms with "tradition" in relation to his "individual talent."

The implicit presumption by intellect of such an absolute relation of poet to poem is in the argument we cited earlier by Robert Frost, the good of whose made things is not to be gainsaid. Frost argues existence to be chaotic, with an immanent force in existence that pulls to nothingness. It is the ordering act of human intellect that Frost praises as a rescue of consciousness, the only being he cherishes. That "background in hugeness and confusion" which we have been calling "creation" Frost sees as "shading away from where we stand into black and utter chaos." Against the terror of despair at such a prospect, Frost turns the very prospect toward the self as maker: "*against* the background any small man-made figure of order and concentration," and any "little form" asserted "*upon* it" becomes salvational of consciousness. The italics are mine, to emphasize the sense of separation in the speaker from that which is not his own form-making intellect. It is to be "considered for how much more it is than *nothing*," the only alternative in this view. It is significant that Frost concludes his argument: "If I were a Platonist I should have to consider it, I suppose, for how much less it is than everything."

What one cannot escape here is a gathering sense of pathos in an intellect gradually losing its battle against finitudes collectively termed *chaos*. Man as creator, independent of all save the power of intellect itself, concedes at last a limit to that power, for as creator there seems possible only some "small man-made figure of order and concentration," momently engulfed by chaos. But this is nevertheless a recognition sufficient to the good of certain things made with craft that escape chaos, if but for the moment. For art as reason in making, as Thomas describes it, may not always be a reason directed to proper or final, but only to mediate ends. In this respect, such an art—as I think Frost's poems do—truly reflects *a* mode of intellect's response to creation within the freedom of its nature. That is, they are a true reflection of human nature within the range of its possible or probable potentialities. As drama, a poem like "After Apple-Picking" or "Mending Wall" or "Birches" bears a true witness of the possible, which is not to conclude that the witness is of the truth of reality in general. That is, intellect in its freedom is capable of responding to its own given nature, to the givenness of inclusive creation as if dark and rolling clouds of chaos, against which it projects its attempted order. The order *in* made things though out of such a dark vision, constitutes a goodness in that made thing, insofar as it reflects the action of that intellect which is caught up in such a dark vision. One is required to value the "art" of such a thing, but not required to accede to the witness implied, as if it were a revelation of the truth of being when it is only a witness of the distortion of the truth of being as possible to intellect through that dimension of its gift we call free will.[2]

If we are susceptible to self-deception in relation to the limits of our nature as maker, which deception we may not charge to the things we make in expiation of our misjudgment by practical intellect, we may in some degree find protection in the wisdom of such a thinker as St. Thomas. Art itself is never the cause of our confusion, but rather a failure of our own understanding of the nature of art. It is in this interest that St. Thomas, on the subject of the gift of understanding to intellect (*Summa*, I–II, Q8), proves reassuring. The *understanding*, he says, as distinguished from *knowledge*, "implies a certain ultimate apprehension." That is, the term *intelligere* (to understand) is as if it were rather "*intus legere*," *inwardly read*. Such an apprehension is to be distinguished from *sensitive* apprehension, which is an operation of intellect under the "natural light" of its given nature as created intellect. This understanding that is penetrative and reads the thing inwardly "penetrates to the essence of things." It sees "what is." *Seeing* here is of visionary import, and it is this seeing which is the beginning of knowledge. It is an effect in intellect whereby intellect finds itself already possessed of some knowledge as the preliminary necessity to its action as rational intellect, its action of thinking. That is the crucial point distinguishing Thomistic realism from Cartesian idealism, a point already considered in our precedent work on *Romantic Confusions of the Good*. It was to this point that we introduced Wordsworth's recollection of the circumstance to intellect in which he saw "into the life of things." It is Wordsworth's difficulty in discovering a relation of his *thought* as a consequence to this preliminary gift to intellect that disorients him, for he does not welcome a relation between the two in a growth out of intellectual potency. He rather fears an antipathy, as if the intuitive and rational modes were antipathetic. St. Thomas opposes this assumption of antipathy, which is a "modern" burden since Descartes. Thomas speaks of the operation of intellect upon this given knowledge as an operation out of intellect's "natural light," in a progress toward *understanding*.

Here "natural light" is of "finite power," says Thomas, and so requires a "determinate something" toward which to act. Thus such a "something" exists precedent to the act of knowing. That something is being itself, made known to intellect from those "somethings" that exist independent of intellect. That is, being is made known to intellect through sensitive apprehension of those somethings that constitute creation. We are here prepared to distinguish a "natural light" of intellect from a "supernatural light" given intellect, a distinction Thomas makes. It is well, then, to observe in doing so that in our intellectual address to existence as philosopher (as opposed to an address as theologian), intellect inclines to a dependence more or less restricted to the "natural light" of intellect, being cautious in regard to any power separate from or even superadded to its natural power. Thomas is to be distinguished in this respect from such a thinker as Eric Voegelin, in that Voegelin would, as philosopher, move *toward* a faith by a cautious, intellectual action of "natural light," whereas Thomas moves *from* a faith, himself cautious of the limits of the rational "natural light." By the gift of his "natural light," St. Thomas would rationally certify what he has already accepted by faith.

In this distinction lies another: St. Thomas's concern as philosopher is for souls other than his own, a concern to support other intellects by his faith in Christ as Incarnate God. Thus he devotes himself to a rational justification of faith, fulfilling through signs (such as the *Summa*) those rational powers proper to man by virtue of his existence as a rational, created creature. Voegelin's concern at its most fundamental level seems rather to be first, and properly so, for his own soul and its rescue to a faith yet to be embraced through rational intellect. The distinction here does not intend so much a subordination of intent on the part of either thinker, for it is certain enough that Voegelin exercises a charitable concern for souls other than his own. The distinction lies rather in the degree of certitude supporting each intellect in its exercise of the rational faculty. Thomas, for instance, is supported by an intellectual community and by the Church in his certitude. For Voegelin, that community of intellect is in considerable disarray, the Church itself seemingly become at best peripheral to that community. Voegelin as intellectual pilgrim attempts a recovery from exile, a restoration to citizenship in a country long since generally abandoned by the intellectual community through perversions of reality which affect any intellect in the modern world, though that world may not be said to affect it decisively.

I pose Voegelin to St. Thomas here since Voegelin represents the modern mind in its journey toward a recovery of reality, a mind which must deal with the historical accidents of modernism. Modernism is a sediment accreted and hardened in Western thought since the abandonment of metaphysics—that is, since St. Thomas's day. Voegelin must undertake a considerable archeological excavation to recover intellect. Initially, as one comes to an awareness of being lost in the dark wood of modernism, intellect seems to itself at first a victim to the accidents of recent intellectual history. Its first task is a recovery out of the general intellectual wreckage, a recovery by Voegelin testified to by an impressive body of work. For that reason, Voegelin's address to the possibility of our recovering a metaphysical vision is additionally fruitful in relation to our concern for the "Romantic" poet. We might, without too great a violation, consider Voegelin a "Romantic" philosopher. This is a complex aspect of Voegelin's thought that I must explore separately, and especially in relation to what I think a central difficulty for him in his pursuit of faith, his difficulty in coming to terms with the reality of grace.[3]

3

The Poet and Natural Light

Consider, in this association of Voegelin with the Romantic poet, our representative figure, William Wordsworth. Wordsworth attempts to arrive at a faith in existence through his experience of determinate "somethings" encountered in his personal experience. He guards himself as best he can against leaping to a conclusion in a faith which might prove in the end but a projection of wishful thinking, an attempt to satisfy a discomforting desire in intellect. Wordsworth's was a deportment which, incidentally, irritated the younger Romantics when they thought they discovered in him a surrender to conclusion. He seemed to have joined himself to the "Establishment," through such a display as that of the easy Platonism of his "Intimations Ode." From Shelley and Keats to Browning a protest is made, as it was made by Eliot initially against Wordsworth. It continued an irritant to Ezra Pound long after his youth, Pound never quite reconciled to "olde shepe Wordsworth." Keats speaks, and hardly approvingly, of "the Wordsworthean or egotistical sublime" in suggesting Wordsworth's growing distance from things. (It was a disposition which Wordsworth had already recognized in himself and spoken of: he had been too much "at distance from the kind.") Shelley produces a merciless parody of Wordsworth's "Idiot Boy," Wordsworth's bathetic attempt at a negative capability that might overcome that distancing. And later the young Browning, at a more superficial level, complains that the older Wordsworth, now become the English Laureate, has surrendered: "Just for a handful of silver he left us."

One might more perceptively find the causes of that change in Wordsworth lying in his disappointment at the seeming failure of his "natural light" to bring him to an accord with that "supernatural light" he believes himself to have lost soon after *Lyrical Ballads*. The "natural light" of intellect requires determinate things, and an immediacy of intellect's relation to them, in order to set intellect on its way toward its true end through the operations of practical intellect. But there is, St. Thomas says, also a "supernatural light," an added gift of grace both to and in the nature of intellect. "Supernatural light" is a gift of the Holy Spirit in this view, operative at particular moments of the soul's temporal existence. The will may command natural light. It cannot command supernatural light, though by a right will, operative through the actions of natural light, the will may at least remove obstacles to that operative grace. We might add that, as natural light stirs practical intellect (though not an exclusive office), supernatural light stirs speculative intellect (though not its exclusive office). For in the aspect of finite intellect taken as a unity, as a *simple* existence in the scholastic sense, there is a mutual stirring, each of the other. It is this simple union of which we spoke in figurative language: the "wedding" of the intuitive and rational, the "head" and "heart."

One sees in this distinction of intellectual lights a relation of the "natural light" to that mode of intellection of the *ratio* and of the "supernatural light" to that mode called the *intellectus*.[4] St. Thomas distinguishes these operational modes, proposed for reflection in *Quaestiones disputate de veritate*, 1, 1: "Although the knowledge which is most characteristic of the human soul occurs in the mode of *ratio*, nevertheless there is in it a sort of participation in the simple knowledge which is proper to higher beings, of whom it is therefore said that they posses the faculty of spiritual vision." It is in the mode of the *intellectus* that the person shares in *simple knowledge*, intuitively as opposed to discursively. That is the mode of knowing characteristic of the angelic mind.

If we have abandoned St. Thomas's terms, we nevertheless recognize a distinction in modes of knowing from our own experience as knowers. We "see" a thing, responding with wonder to the suddenness of our recognition of it. And we are likely to characterize such an act of knowing as having occurred through *intuition*. There has been a lively and diverse attention to this operation, especially in those speculations about the relation of the "subconscious" to the "conscious" and in the extensive exploration at the level of physiology concerned with seats of particular receptions, and reactions to receptions, in the geography of the brain. The intricate extrapolations from data gathered by mechanical means, the readings of that data, attempt to establish empirically the reality of modes of knowing other than rational or analytical discursiveness, with that always curious difficulty of any objective measuring of this particular thing, since the thing measured is itself the measurer. Usually this scientific attention anchors our intuitive or rational knowing in material-temporal ground as necessarily the primordial ground itself. But that ground is not

justified by the desire in intellect itself for a causal ground more fundamental. Intellect seems incapable of coming to rest itself in a merely
material-temporal ground as if it fears origin in an uncaused cause, mechanistic existence. The procedures, however scientific, are further handi-
capped by the necessity of discursiveness, which means that the attempt
is temporally circumscribed: first *this*, then *that*—not always a procedure
of recognition which is recognized as a limitation upon the simple nature
of intellectual action of any science. It is a dilemma to the science of
thought whose parallel in particle physics we associate with Heisenberg's
uncertainty principle.

The point intended here is to remind us that knowledge as possessed
by intellect can never be inclusive of the thing about which intellect
knows certain truths. That recognition is nowhere more important than
when we are attempting to account for intellection itself. What we tend
to hold as *certain* knowledge is knowledge nevertheless short of the full
truth of the thing that is held, as the historical evolution of particular
sciences, physical or biological, reveals. In such a term as *certain* we must
rather understand *particular* as more appropriate. Our supposed certainty
must yield again and again to additions of particular knowledge. From
Ptolemy to Newton to Einstein: our recollection of these great thinkers
reveals the difficulty of separating the true from the false, whereupon we
discover ourselves possessing "certain" truths yet to be fully reconciled
to the fullness of reality. Today's certainty yields to tomorrow's, perhaps
on the following day to return to today's.

St. Thomas's speculative proposal about the nature of intellectual action
may be said to speak toward a truth larger than any scientific specificity
possible to finite intellect in its signs. But Thomas does not consent to
claim his arguments on any point absolutely conclusive in its rational
claim. He recognizes the rational as severely limited in the pursuit of
truth, since he recognizes the finitude of intellect itself. Intellect cannot
fully understand even itself. It is this recognition which makes him most
valuable to us. It is this recognition out of piety founded in his faith that
governs the whole of his rational speculation in pursuit of truth. He is
thus governed by his visionary recognition of ultimate Truth, out of a
faith beyond reason. It is by this address to the mystery of intellectual
action that makes him a good guide now. We may say with some confidence, short of certainty, that it is by the enlargement he allows through
his precise arguments understood in their limits and submissive to the gift
of "supernatural light" that we may orient our own pursuit of truth
among contending claimants to certainty.[5]

It is through the *intuitive* mode, the mode of *intellectus*, that one knows the "thing itself," knows an *essence* to be inbiding an *ens* according to St. Thomas. And one "knows" this *essence* in a preconceptual way through the perceptual gifts of one's own nature. It may also follow that Thomas's *intellectus* is companionable as a term to our more usual *intuition*, in that both terms attempt to name an actual experience of the intellect. Indeed, Jacques Maritain attempts to rescue the term *intuition*, which is much decayed through popular abuse, to a Thomistic respectability in his influential *Creative Intuition in Art and Poetry* (1953). But such have been the confusions in respect to intellect that at least since the Enlightenment the term *intellect* has been commanded as a term designating the reasoning function of mind, the intuition having been disjoined from mind or relegated increasingly toward, at best, an aspect of animal rather than intellectual nature. Maritain, to some extent in his earlier *Art and Scholasticism* (1920) and more particularly in such chapters of *Creative Intuition in Art and Poetry* as "The Pre-Conscious Life of the Intellect" and "Creative Intuition and Poetic Knowledge," is supportive of our pursuit of analogy as stirred intuitively. That analogy is anchored in that truth which intellect perceives, through its reflection, as the structure of reality, a reality independent of intellectual perception.

As modernists, we tend to feel less offended by the term *intuition* since psychology has given it a certain respectability as related to our animal nature. In that orientation of the term we find ourselves more comfortable with the actuality we are dealing with than we might be if urged to consider it as in an *angelic mode* rather than *animal mode* of knowing. Indeed psychological intuition grounded in physiology very easily accommodates *instinct* as a synonym to *intuition*. The two terms become entwined increasingly through our partially digested Darwinism.[6]

However we term this experience, honest reflection upon actual personal experience of some event to intellect, some instance of our "knowing," will say to us that we gain a knowledge of something, of some *thing*, in a way independent of that immediate labor of intellect which we designate as rational discursiveness. It is this sort of knowing that Thomas is speaking of when he says that intellect perceives the essence of things, knows the thing for what it is, in a preconceptual act of intellect. Long after Thomas, we hear Wordsworth testifying to those moments of knowing in which, freed of discursive reflection, freed of "thought," he remembers having seen "into the life of things." But it is also an experience testified to long before Thomas, by an ancient philosopher recently popular among modern poets, who speaks of "listening to the essence of things." It is this philosopher, Heraclitus, who supplies the initiating epigraphs of Eliot's *Four Quartets*. The first one Eliot chooses shows that a modernist such as the young Eliot is already more ancient than he thought at the time of his "Prufrock": "Although the *logos* is common, the majority of people live as though they had an understanding of their own."

In Heraclitus's day or in our own, we need not be surprised when the "Romantic" poet, moved by intuition, responds though lacking the intellectual maturity required of such response. The maturity I mean is one gradually accumulated, a durational maturity through discursive activity of intellect which is our more common and natural mode of intellection. Such is a recognition interestingly borne out by an experiment at Cornell University. Fourteen "students" took a poetry course. The students were professional scientists: a chemist, physicist, engineer, and so on. The poets studied were Chaucer and Wordsworth. What some of the students discovered from writing papers explicating poems is that, as the engineer said, "It was impossible to sit back and knock off a composition. You actually had to sit there and think about it." The chemist complained, "I just don't like thinking in vague terms. I like working in concrete terms where there's an answer and not just an opinion." But what most of these special students came to realize is that the intellectual action of humanistic study was very much like that of graduate science courses, and even more, like the conduct of their own research. "We really don't know what the important points are [in our research]. We really don't know exactly what to look for." (The literature course was conducted at the undergraduate level for these select students.) What their principal instructor came to, as his summary of his experience in teaching scientists who had been long alienated from the humanities, bears very much on the necessity of duration if *knowledge* is to be *understood*: "where scientific information of an objective kind is in question all beginners are pretty much on the same footing, whether they are 19 or 45. . . . But in the case of literature, the difference between 19 and 45 fundamentally affects a reader's approach to the material" (*Science News*, Dec. 22 & 29, 1990).

One might say, in respect to this durational aspect which seems a necessity to understanding beyond the mere appropriation of knowledge, that in both science and literature a certain elementary level of knowing, acquired through discursive rational procedures, is a necessary preliminary. It is that level of knowledge held by intellect which has been traditionally spoken of as the knowledge of *grammar*, whether in respect to the chemist's "concrete terms" or the formulaic grammar of any subject. The students of the Cornell experiment, as reported in *Science News*, experienced, indeed, something of a recollection of earlier childhood. One remembered "old frustrations and feelings of inadequacy." But another declared "It was fun." Another: "It made me remember the literature courses I had enjoyed so much in my college days. . . . I wish I had more time to pursue that kind of thing." We might summarize as common to these responses by professional scientists, after their encounter with Chaucer and Wordsworth, their sense of wonder, whether raising nostalgia, frustration, or even irritation. If we put it metaphorically, the analogy is to that state of encounter with the world as Wordsworth experienced it on revisiting the banks of the Wye. What is also evident is that these scientists, no longer 19, bring with them a *durational* advantage, conspicuous to their teacher in contrast to his usual undergraduates.

One may, if remembering intently, recall that early state of intellect in which one begins to emerge from a wonder at existence into a fascination with the grammar as an intellectual necessity to the pursuit of wonder. G. K. Chesterton speaks of this relation when he says that "A child of seven is excited by being told that Tommy opened a door and saw a dragon. But a child of three is excited by being told that Tommy opened the door" ("The Ethics of Elfland," *Orthodoxy*). The grammar of dragons at seven has not entirely supplanted the wonder of existence. It is the door through which the intuitive sense of being leads on to dragons or angels and even on to particle physics or chemical certainties. Nor does the intuitive moment die completely in the light of common day but is always in some degree present at points when we know and *know* that we know a something or other. *Knowledge* recognized as a possession has concomitant effect upon the intellect. It regains, if but fleetingly, a sense of the very youthfulness of intellect itself, through understanding grown of a duration of such knowledge, an enduring of knowledge. It steadies youthful enthusiasm so that wisdom itself seems to require a metaphor related to years. It is no accident that the epithet runs "old and full of years." But old or young in years, the intuitive continues present as a faculty to intellect, however much overlaid by the active consciousness of the rational, discursive faculty operating in intellect. The ancient meditative intellect, indeed, seems to hold more steadily to intellect's intuitive support. That aspect of an intellect's bearing in and toward the world we are likely to describe as "mystical," whether as pejorative epithet rejecting it or approvingly in support of visionary "seeing."

Old or young in years, in the intuitive moment of wonder at knowing, that intuitive action seems not subject to time nor to the labors of discursiveness, that labor of thought that moves from *this* to *this* and to some conclusion. Except as we may set aside that rare mystic who seems to have been born old, who seems never to have been burdened by reflective discursiveness but is blessed with a contemplative immediacy, we may conclude that the maturity of intellect which we call *wisdom* comes not on the instant but through long, long thought. But even in rare instances of "premature" wisdom, seemingly exceptional because seemingly unrelated to a maturing through intellectual duration, we might notice that duration is not only acknowledged but insisted upon by the mystics. (As for those instances of "premature" wisdom, we might suspect in them the operation of that grace of "super-natural light" St. Thomas speaks of, overriding the intellect's "natural light.") The mystic reminds us of a necessary patience of intellect as we wait the floodlight of understanding. Such a mystic may even formulate procedures leading from reflection to meditation, as does St. John of the Cross, procedures through which one may arrive at a contemplative state, thus enabled to dwell within "the life of things" mysteriously.

That indwelling is mysterious, since it is an experience of existence untouched by those severities of time and place with which the practical intellect must deal so steadily in finding itself through knowledge. It is perhaps of some helpfulness here to remember what St. Thomas says about the relation of knowledge in relation to a vision of reality, both knowledge and vision dependent upon habits of intellect, though habits differing in the intellect's access to truth. In his "Prologue" to the *Summa Theologica*, II-II, Thomas speaks of those possible habits to intellectual action. "As for the intellectual virtues, one of them is prudence, which is contained by the cardinal virtues and numbered among them. . . . The other three intellectual virtues, namely wisdom, understanding, and knowledge, share their names with certain gifts of the Holy Spirit."

The duration which we are attempting to characterize may be said to be (in the light of this remark) intellectual discipline which becomes intellectual habit under the governance of prudence. Through those habits, obstacles to the gifts of the Holy Spirit may be removed. These virtues are not related to each other sequentially, although a hierarchical relation exists, we may say, whereby knowledge feeds the enlarging possibility of understanding, and understanding allows at last a sufficient openness of intellect to truth so that wisdom is granted. Since we are concerned in this relationship with the capacity of intellect afforded through the gifts of the Holy Spirit, it is evident that we cannot mean by *duration* a capacity in intellect to see truth as determined in any way by either time or place, for this would anchor those virtues in the accidents of time and place inasmuch as time and place are accidents accruing to the nature of the created soul. Through virtues initiated by prudence, intellect is enabled to its enlarged potential, but since the gifts to intellect under the auspices of the grace of God, exercised through intellect by the Holy Spirit, neither the cardinal virtues *in* themselves and *through* themselves, nor a mere duration of the soul in time, are sufficient warrant to those gifts. One may say only that by the intellect's pursuit of those virtues, obstacles to the those gracious gifts are displaced. That is why the person "born old" and the person who comes to wisdom only when seen in the accidents of his personhood as "old and full of years" are but ways of speaking of the mystery of wisdom as a gift revealed through the accident upon personhood, time.

Let us recall an instance out of history, a person remembered as growing in wisdom. To talk of this person necessarily requires reference to the accidents of her personhood which we term autobiographical history, although our concern is to penetrate beneath those accidents to substantive concerns. I mean Dame Julian of Norwich, who was born some sixty years after the death of St. Thomas. Her *Revelations of Divine Love* give an account of a vision experienced as she turned thirty, leading her to become recluse, an anchoress, practicing a discipline of intellect thenceforth. She thus pursues a disciplined way of life to come to an understanding of her vision. But it is not till twenty years afterward that she becomes content in understanding that earlier vision. The circumstances of the vision: at the point of death, last rites having been administered, her parish priest left a crucifix before her, expecting no doubt that by morning she would be dead. There occurred to her, by her explicative account of them later (this is the matter of her *Revelations*) sixteen "showings," upon which she meditated in the following two decades toward understanding. It is that score of years that mark her patient enduring of the "showings" in relation to her continuing existence in the world. Her intellect is opened more and more to the fullness of those granted revelations, received on her death bed as she fixed her eyes on the crucifix, though she was not to die for another 40 years.

Now that early gift of vision proved increasingly complex in her enduring of it by her finite, natural gifts of intellect. But paradoxically, as the revelations opened to her, through intricate intellectual explorations, they became more simple. Dom Roger Hudleston, in his "Introduction" to her *Revelations*, remarks this duration in relation to the emerging reward to her understanding of the mystical simpleness of her vision. She was able to come to that understanding, Dom Hudleston says, because "the wheel having come full circle—she finds herself back at the point from which she had set out upon her mystical journey, the mystery of the Love of God." It is this Love which is the mystical simplicity of which we spoke, an all-inclusive Love. One may well recognize in Dom Hudleston's words a seeming echo of more famous words, found at the end of Eliot's *Little Gidding*, though we must remark that Dom Hudleston's own words antedate Eliot's poem by many years, having been published in 1927 as Eliot is at work on his "Ash-Wednesday." Eliot concludes his *Little Gidding* with his recognition that "the end of all our exploring" is "to arrive where we started / And know the place for the first time." But this echo of Dom Hudleston is beside the point at issue. What we are remarking is Eliot's recognition of the parallel of his own spiritual journey to that of Dame Julian's—a journey made over many years (it is now also nearly two decades since Eliot's "Ash-Wednesday") but not affected by any measure of years.

Neither the journey nor the span of years signify so much to Eliot's newly-granted understanding as the marvelous opening of his intellect through vision. Eliot understands that opening as a gift not earned by the labored years of his journeying. He sees, as did Dame Julian, that "all manner of thing shall be well" because of that Love, that Calling, that Word. And that is a simple vision vouchsafed his journeyman soul. Eliot has discovered that in its journey his person, himself as created soul, is at the place from which he set out intellectually. And as poet, Eliot attempts to make this recognition apparent to us in his imagistic revisiting in this final poem of that world as imaged in his earlier poetry. The change is in his *seeing* of that world, a seeing of what that world had signified by its created nature all along. But only now is it available to the soul through understanding, increasingly enveloped by wisdom—by Eliot's wise seeing of reality afforded his intellect through those gifts of the Holy Spirit to intellect.

It is important to notice in Eliot's newly understood vision of reality that the created world as experienced through the senses reveals to him his own sensitive nature restored in relation to created things. In the early poetry, there is an uneasy address to the sensual aspect of his existence which is finally overcome at the end. For he now understands, through a new experiencing of reality, what is meant when we say that the soul is the substantial unity of personhood. That is, as *person* one exists through an *essential unity* which is indivisible. There had been an intellectual recognition of the point, based in psychology, which had made Eliot abandon his "Dialogues of Body and Soul" to write that more complex attempt to dramatize that limited knowledge of personhood in "The Love Song of J. Alfred Prufrock." But the advance upon his understanding of personhood from "Prufrock" to *Little Gidding* is for him now breathtaking, a phrase intentional in that "breath" is traditionally associated with the soul through metaphor in our poetry. Put in his own phrase, from "Ash-Wednesday," what is restored is a "salt savor" of reality to intellect, out of particular existences to which intellect responds in a new freedom through appetitive senses. Dame Julian in her long journeying discovered at circle's close that she had experienced vision in its variety, beginning with the initiating corporeal, imagistic encounter with Christ; leading on to an imaginative vision beyond, or beneath, image; arriving at last at intellectual vision. This intellectual vision St. Teresa also speaks of when she says "It is like feeling someone near one in a dark place." And Eliot, we have suggested, had had just such an experience in day light, seeing roses that "had the look of roses that are looked at" in that decayed English garden of Burnt Norton.[7]

One may know intuitively the desirability of wisdom without being therefore enabled by that knowledge to satisfy the desire for wisdom. It is in this difficulty to intellect that a temptation rises: the temptation to excessive conclusion on the authority of intuitive knowledge when intellect is no longer governed by prudence. To act thus excessively is to act as if that knowledge, prompting willful intellect to fulfill its desire for wisdom, were a visionary enablement rather than willfulness. Prudence in this circumstance of soul tempers desire's impetus to excessive conclusion. It does so in deference to those durational necessities attendant upon the soul's existence that are implicit in our saying that the soul is a created creature differing from the angel in its necessity to intellectual discursiveness. And it is this durational state of the soul which Eliot would seem to have in mind when he speaks of being "still and still moving," a description of endurance through hope, in anticipation of the gift to intellect of understanding.

We are speaking, then, of a maturing through the practical intellect that at least sometimes makes possible the poet's persuasive articulation of his vision of reality. We are not, as we have emphasized, set out to argue a maturity of soul effected *by* duration as if duration were prescribed by three-score-and-ten, even though the poet uses that description of duration as related to time again and again in his metaphorical structuring of poems, or in relation to the historical moment in his actual career at which he turns visionary. Dame Julian, we noted, had her initial vision on what she and her attendants believed her death bed, when she was just past thirty years old. And it was approximately midway his "earthly days" that Dante came to himself in his dark wood. So, too, Wordsworth in "Tintern Abbey." And so as well for Eliot in his *Waste Land*. Ezra Pound at thirty declares, as if delivered to him upon Sinai, that no poet is capable of writing significantly before he is past thirty. We remember as well the popular slogan of the 1960s: don't trust anyone over thirty, our young shouted. (That was a caution necessary if they were to summon Eden spontaneously into history.) The reality to which such figurative language is sometimes forced by literalness will not serve reality, of course. Thus Keats seems one of those wiser than his years, dead at 26. At least the older and wiser Eliot concluded as much of Keats, astonished when in his own mid-forties at Keats's early wisdom, especially in his letters. Eliot was then emerging from his own dark woods.

It is nevertheless true that Keats again and again in his actions of making poems, into which he enters so persuasively in a *personal* way, is left in despair at the end, though even his craft seems to belie his actual years. Keats as intuitive poet turns always to the question intellect must come to, but his art is such as to remind us of Thomas's insistence that "Art is nothing else but the right reason about certain works to be made." As maker, Keats must surely be concluded to have exercised right reason in much of his work, though much of it remains unfinished. That unfinished work, or so it seems to me, bears evidence of lacking not a suitable craft, but that *duration* of which we have been speaking. The sufficiency of craft to intent, as in *Hyperion*, may speak that failure, in that the object of intent is not clearly seen. His craft is sufficient to the shadow of despair against which he so directly responds in his great Odes.

The principle at issue about art as seen by Thomas surfaces among artists in this century largely through Maritain's *Art and Scholasticism*. (That work has influenced poets as diverse as Eliot and Flannery O'Connor.) The principle itself warrants further recalling here. In the second article of Question 57, Thomas argues that there are different kinds of knowable matter, therefore requiring different habits of scientific knowledge suited to the differences, among them the "science" of art. But, he adds, there is only one *wisdom*, which we might gloss here for our purposes as *understandings of things* made resonant by a vision enlarged toward embracing creation, the opening of the *in-wised* soul to the Cause of all being. In so putting it, we emphasize thereby the seeming slowness of wisdom as acquired by intellect in its finite journeying through finite existences. Thomas adds that speculative intellect, as opposed to art's practical intellect, is concerned with truth, both particular and ultimate. That is, truth may be known in itself and known through another. Here, the operative *principle* is knowing the thing in itself, a knowing which may be at once an understanding by intellect as it is a knowing of the thing in itself. *Understanding*, the habit of principles, perfects intellect for its consideration of truth through principles, and we add that the habit of intellectual perfection requires duration—implies an accumulated enlargement of intellect toward fulfilling its potential. It is this aspect of duration of intellect, necessarily within the accident of time, that becomes crucial to a wisdom whereby one exercises through signs an understanding of proper proportionality.

Truth, Thomas goes on, when known through another is known by means of reason's inquiry, in which respect truth is either the last in some particular genus or as an ultimate term in all human knowledge. This partial knowing of truth stirs the desire in the Romantic poet, we have suggested, and in the light of Thomas's words we might better appreciate Wordsworth's assertion in his famous "Preface" that poetry is the first and last of knowledge, preceding science and concluding science. Thomas concludes that *wisdom* judges all things and sets them in order as they are known to intellect, the judgement and perceived order based on first causes. Wisdom differs from scientific knowledge (including the knowledge of poetry as an art) in that scientific knowledge is dependent upon different habits of the different sciences. The different sciences are required because there are different kinds of knowable things. But wisdom as a "knowing" is singular. It is the habit which orders all knowledge in relation to the first Cause, an action which thus orders intellect itself proportionately to its Cause. But the intellect, if it lack wisdom, may confuse its possession of a certain science or sciences with the possession of a wisdom. In the instance of poets such as Shelley and Pound, such a poet assumes a prophetic role but one insufficiently anchored in wisdom. This does not obviate his possession of a limited understanding in respect to the particular science or sciences he professes knowledge of. It is when there is this confusion of a limited understanding as if it were wisdom that the poet—or any intellect—may assume or pretend to a position of intellectual power whereby he would command the structure of reality by his intellect, rather than conform intellect in its actions to the structure of reality. In brief, such is the condition of intellect whereby it assumes gnostic authority over being itself, a concern about which Voegelin has alerted us with his profound readings of this modernist presumption.

A further reminder seems pertinent in the light of the gnostic uses of the sign, one of whose species is art itself. For we must not consent to the abused use of sign, anymore than its ordinate use, as the cause of either error or rescue to the soul responding to such signs through intellect. The art thing is good or bad in and of itself, in accordance with the virtues of making as directed to the good of the thing made. It must follow from this that the poet or his reader is not either saved or damned by the poem in itself, for that is a concern separate from the nature of the made thing in itself. We have argued nevertheless that art is inescapably an imitation of the action of nature, and explicitly so as related to the nature of the human intellect, its maker. That is, the work of art is most basically an imitation of that action of being associated with our belief that the artist as man is a nature created "in the image" of God.

It is in this subtle distinction that one must unravel the relation of the maker as person. For as person he becomes a presence to and in the poem. But the poem is a "history" of the poet only at the level of accident, the distinction here very crucial to our argument. Perhaps it is a distinction implicit in Aristotle's concern in his *Poetics* when he distinguishes art as dealing with the "possible or probable" as opposed to history's actualities. It is art as autobiography that Eliot would escape by declaring that poetry must escape the "personal." Later he discovers a new sense of "personal" in the poetry of Keats and Wordsworth, wherein the possible or probable of human nature, because created in God's image, is a presence in the poetry. It is a presence as an imitation of the action of intellect in making. In virtue of this aspect of the made thing of art as an imitation of the artist's *person*, we said earlier that the first discovery to the poet, during or consequent to his making, is his recognition of himself as reflected in his poem. What is "reflected" is his intellectual action. The poem is not, consequently, the cause of his appetitive perfection, though it is a means toward it. It is in this respect, let us say, that art as an action of the practical intellect is one of the means to the perfection of intellect. Such is a distinction crucial to the agitated confusions of our moment over the effect of pornography in relation to the fate of discrete souls confronting pornography as art.

Since art is an action governed by the practical intellect, the visionary "seeing" granted through supernatural light requires the good offices of that practical intellect to an effective articulation. Failing to recognize this necessity, a poet may well err by a premature, and so inadequate, attempt to articulate a fleeting vision, though that vision itself be true. It is a spontaneous response to vision, to an "emotional" moment of experience, in which state we so often find the artist when a young man. A sufficient "right reason" often satisfies a lyric moment, the art required hiding the office played in the making by the practical intellect. It is through reason employed in the making of a lyric that it is perfected so that it seems the articulation coincides with the emotion at issue in the poem. It has the effect of being spontaneous, but it is the art in its making that gives an immediacy, as the proliferation of drafts of a given poem suggests. We have suggested the importance of duration, of the actual enduring by the poet of his own complex being, as supportive of that right reason required in the making of a poem, however spontaneous it may seem. (And of course on occasion the poem is actually spontaneous.)

Let us consider that, in respect to the art of the lyric poem as an instance of a thing to be made, a lyric poem must bear the force through its signs as of an immediate, spontaneous bursting out through those signs of a living presence in the signs, whether imagined or actual—whether the poet himself or some imagined personae such as have been particularly enticing to poets in our century. It is thus that a poem gives a similitude of that action of human nature as if the actual experience of a "lyric" moment, though effected by the practical intellect in the poet's making. We value the craft whereby such a poet has brought us his song as an imitation of an actuality. Craft here is the attention of that "science" we call prosody in the execution of a seemingly unrestrained voice. The voice in a good poem, we discover again and again, seems to speak as we encounter the words. This is not Keats in 1820, but a presence in this instant of our encounter of voice in the thing made of words. Indeed, how surprised we may be to discover of a favorite poem that it exists in a multitude of drafts, thus speaking the poet's labor of making and remaking. So fascinating is this aspect of poetic spontaneity that the various drafts of a single poem have been critical fodder to certain critics of the poetic process. Such critics Yeats dubbed "bald heads" who "cough in ink," and we add, periodically, given the proliferation of academic journals. They "cough" over what "young men, tossing on their beds, / Rhymed out in love's despair / To flatter beauty's ignorant ear." What Yeats fails to acknowledge is the laborious coughing of the craftsman himself, to which we are calling attention, Yeats himself among such poets. A multitude of revisions of whatever vision: that is more the rule to the making of poems than exception, especially when the poet is committed to the good of the poem he would make. Whether born of love's despair in actuality or only supposed as possible or probable to love's despair, the laborious making through the offices of the practical intellect is more common to good poetry than not. One might even venture that Yeats as voice in this poem in defending restless lovers conjures both bald heads and young men through rational strategies in order to simulate actualities. For his passionate cry is made long after his own hair is advanced toward gray and he himself no longer, in actuality, member of either party, the tossing young or the coughing old.

Some poems are indeed spontaneous. We know what happened when Keats first looked into Chapman's Homer, and even the gaff of Cortez as first European discoverer of the Pacific is as effective as if it had been deliberate. But an actual spontaneous response to vision is unlikely to effectively catch a moment if unsupported by a long exercise of craft under the authority of reason. One seeks "fit words to paint the blackest face of woe" (to recall Sir Philip Sidney's sonnet) through a labor of reason turned repeatedly to the necessities of art as defined by the nature of art. For that reason, Pound advises the apprentice poet to translate other poets as a preparation for that possible moment when the neophyte might indeed have something to say. But the preparation necessary is larger than the science of poetic craft. The moment "a skate's heel sweeps smooth on a bow-bend," or that arresting immediacy to the eye of "rose-moles in stipple" on trout quivering in clear water at one's feet; the fettling of the drayhorse's "bright and battering sandal": these are past moments arrestingly caught by image to a present through words managed by reason through craft. But such capture is possible only after a long labor—or rather an *intense* labor not restricted by time—of openness whereby one sees into the life of such things. The artist as a young man, however spontaneous (as Hopkins knew well) may not have sufficiently matured, whether in his craft or in his perception of things in themselves, to catch actual experience at the actual visionary moment; inclined indeed not to a similitude of action in such an event but to entrapment of art by that actuality itself. That is, in such moments of a "spontaneous overflow of powerful feeling" (as Wordsworth described it), the temptation to credit the accidents of the history of that occasion is likely to distort the aspect of the possible or probable, in which aspect lies the higher possibility of art in itself and therefore a higher tribute to the nature of reality through art.

In such a seeming empowerment of art by powerful feeling, the poet may forget the necessity to his simulation of the aspect of spontaneity through reason's control of the making, the proper deportment in his use of words as poem. A simulation of art is beyond any attempt to arrest the moment itself in amber. Reason will remind him, with the return of a tranquility, that art's proper capture is of that *action* of event as opposed to the event itself in its detailed history. Dr. Johnson may object, and perhaps to a degree justly, that a poet through the violence of his making may build a poem which suggests that the poet's "courtship [is] void of fondness" or his "lamentation of sorrow." But if by such violence we mean only the poet's violation of the actual history of his sorrow or courtship, we shall have confused the issue as it properly relates to the nature of art. The decisive violence by the poet is that against the possible or probable, not against those accidents of history reflecting the actual. In our valuing art in itself, we need not be overly troubled when we realize that John Donne in "The Flea" sits at his desk fiddling with words and meter rather than that the words burst forth as he touches his Beloved in an actual seductive encounter with her on a London sofa in the early 17th century. The virtue of "Lycidas" as a poem is a consideration apart from, though not necessarily inconsequential to, Milton's limited sorrow at the death of a schoolmate to whom he was never close.

In the light of these considerations of the relation of reason exercised in the making of a poem so that the poem may seem to escape reason's rule by its emotional immediacy, we may better understand the embarrassment we may have felt on reading a friend's very bad poem, to which he will always request our honest response as poem. Or consider that species of poetry which Mark Twain makes fun of through Emmiline Grangerford in *Huckleberry Finn*, a species of poetry still very much with us in weekly newspapers: a friends's or parent's awkwardly rhymed lament over the death of a loved child or friend or spouse. What is discomforting to us is not the absence of genuine grief, but the absence of art. Not that bad art certifies genuine grief—anymore than that good art certifies the absence of genuine grief. It is rather that the actual, the "historical," grief is not at issue, but the practical address of the maker to his poem which requires his concern to be primarily for the good of the thing he is making. But having said this, we must add that the good poem by its virtues does not lie about the genuineness of the poet in his personhood, in which grief and sorrow and affection are appropriate indication of his life as person. In this regard the good poem reflects by its very nature as a made thing not only a difference between the actual as history but the actual as appropriate to the limits of art.

Sorrow or affection are not themselves repudiated nor denigrated by the poet who practices a primary responsibility to the good of the thing he makes and not to its notations as history. We tend to recognize this, as critics, in distinguishing "occasional" poetry from "poetry." We may say further that, if the poem is to be good in itself, it may not distort the nature of the actual, though in avoiding the risk of a flawed making it may very well distort actual experience, the circumstantial, historical accidents of event upon which it depends. It would appear, for instance, that "historically" Keats's experience with the nightingale, from which he very quickly wrote his "Ode," did not occur actually at night in an English garden. But moonlight through shifting shadows suits the necessities of his poem, just as high noon suits the conditions caught in Wordsworth's "Tintern Abbey." Wordsworth's, we are told, is a direct record of the actual experience as reflected in the poem.

And so we may say that the possible or probable does not necessarily preclude the actual. The determining concern is always the good of the thing under construction, made by reason through craft. The problem for the poet who is committed to the good of his poem is most subtle in this regard. For all is not yet said in insisting that his commitment must be shifted from the restrictions of actuality such as he may have experienced and which may have initiated his poem. He is required, by the nature of his art, neither to pursue rigid correspondences of the poem to actual event nor to exclude such correspondences, the point we make in noting Keats's introduction of night as a more suitable condition in which to "hear" his nightingale or Wordsworth's appropriation of the actual noon-day setting of light to his exploration of the inland murmurings of memory.

On the other hand, this seeming freedom from the restrictions of actualities does not justify an assumption of poetry as a science of mechanics independent of actualities, as if laws following from that freedom are to be executed as determinate laws abstracted from reality. Put another way, the poet may not conclude that his exercise of "reason in making" is divorced from his nature as person, for by his created nature he is a "creator," though the thing he makes is at a level of creation which we must acknowledge as secondary. Secondary creations differ from primary creations in respect to that proportion whereby man as creator differs from God as Creator. Primary creation is dependent in being in a manner differing from the dependence of secondary creations, for the secondary are dependent in being through the actions of making of that primarily created thing, the poet himself. (On this distinction, see J. R. R. Tolkien's "On Fairy-Stories," which sets the "Primary World," creation, in relation to the "Secondary World," art.) Because of the poet's primary nature, his "science" of making may not be separated from that personhood which signifies him a made thing at a primary level of existence. It cannot be separated, though he often wishes a separation in the interest of his autonomy as maker. Because he may wish it so, he may therefore suppose it so. But not even the "science" of the chemist or the geometrician is so easily divorced from personhood. Indeed, it is increasingly notable at the close of our century that physicists and biologists in particular recognize their participation as persons in their practice of science, in contrast to what one would have discovered of their counterparts at the turn into this century. At that time a dogmatically insistent "objectivity" was being everywhere proclaimed by the new sciences, purporting to assure a separation of intellectual action from the object of that action.

Some poetry seems nevertheless made as if from such an objective science through the practiced reduction of the person of the maker through the rational intellect, in the interest of an "objectivity" in art. The possible fulfillment of the person as maker through his actions as maker is denied or kept at bay. Such a deportment by the artist may lead to a poetry technically brilliant, but it will also be a poetry dead through the very rigidity of its "objective" making. In the academy it results in that sort of writing that can be taught, as Flannery O'Connor observed—the kind

that we must then "teach people not to read." Its counter, now very much
a part of academic programs, is a writing more or less automatic, out of
spontaneous overflow of feeling supposed powerful because it is the feeling of the overflower himself, the art of which is the absence of reason in
making. (The advantage of this sort of writing is that one need not bother
to teach people not to read it, since it withers in the blossoming.) The
judgment registered against the studied, objective control of art is more
problematic in its continuing handicap to poetry, because we are by nature rational creatures and the rational dimension has therefore a purchase
upon our intellectual attention.

Let us remember Edgar Allen Poe as an instance of the poet as objective
scientist of making, a charge sometimes brought against him. I cite Poe
because Eliot was troubled for many years by a confusion in Poe of his
nature as maker in relation to the science of making, resolved at last in his
essay "From Poe to Valéry." During the years before *The Waste Land*,
Eliot read Poe intensely, being drawn to him in part because of Poe's
influence on livelier poets like Baudelaire and those French poets taking
poetic cue from Baudelaire's interest in Poe. Eliot had been much taken
with those French poets as he attempted to understand his own practice
in relation to a science of making. At the same time, however, Eliot was
reading not only Poe, but Hawthorne. He was taken with Hawthorne
because of what he called the "psychological" dimension of Hawthorne's
fiction, though this virtue in Hawthorne troubled Eliot (as it had troubled
Henry James). Hawthorne insisted on relating the "psychological" to
man's fallen nature, to "sin," and neither James nor the younger Eliot had
much patience with the concept of sin. They were, if the truth be told,
somewhat embarrassed by sin's repeated intrusion into Hawthorne's fictions, which were otherwise rather impressive. Still, Eliot saw that Hawthorne's sense of the "psychological" nature of man was a ground in
which the truth of man's nature must be located. Never mind that for
Hawthorne the psychological was understood to have spiritual implications (as of course it will come to have for Eliot later). Meanwhile, the
problem of sin was one which Eliot as modernist was reluctant to address.
And so his intense fascination with the rationalist Poe on the one hand
and the romantic Hawthorne on the other, in both of whom there is the
concern for a psychological dimension to be captured in the sign, the word.
The fascination suggests unresolved questions in Eliot about the nature of
the poet as maker.

Those questions increasingly demand attention by Eliot in that part of
his intellectual journey bounded by "Prufrock" and *The Waste Land*. In
that period he was concerned to purge art of the personal, so that his

version of "reason in making" art would be reason as understood by advanced Enlightenment rationalism, given a literary plausibility by Poe's arguments, Poe serving as mathematician to poetry. It is no accident of metaphor, then, when Eliot compares a chemical process to the operation of the poet's mind. He insists that the "progress of an artist is . . . a continual extinction of personality," made possible to the poet if he but recognize that the "mind of the poet is the shred of platinum," the catalyst whereby the poem (whose correspondence in the metaphor is sulphurous acid) is the effect of a controlled process of making. And it is in order to sever from that mind as operating catalyst all traces of that impurity "personality" that he is led to consider the importance of "objective correlatives." Those formulated word-presences would constitute the body of the poem, out of which body rises to the reader's perception those psychological effects upon the reader controlled by objective correlatives. Both the poet's personality and the reader's are disjoined from consideration in such an accounting.

Eliot's sense of the *personal* at this early stage of his journey as poet is far other than St. Thomas's sense of the *personal*. Eliot rather sees the significance of personality as limited to the accidents of the circumstances of the poet's life, and such a judgment obscures from him the significance to art of the deeply personal. For what he has succeeded in doing is to dissociate accident from essence itself, and particularly the essence to which accidents of "personality" accrue. It means he is left with no principle whereby to order accidents except that of the autonomous authority of intellect itself. It is thus that he prepares himself for that agony over the personal, out of which he emerges at last with a new appreciation of Hawthorne's concern for "sin" as an effect of intellectual willfulness, of which the pretense to autonomy is conspicuous instance. He will then come to see in Valéry as poet the dead end Poe's arguments led to. When Eliot comes at last to see such distinctions as we are proposing, he will come as well to insist on the fundamental importance of the personal to poetry. We see him doing so in his revised judgment about the Romantics, particularly Wordsworth and Keats, whom he elevates in his esteem.

4

The Wisdom of Leisure

Our age has had considerable difficulty deciding the relation between work and leisure. The difficulty follows the disorientation in our personhood through specializations by work. Attendant upon the precisions required by the emerging sciences of making, made feasible through technology, specialization is proved pragmatically effective, but it leads to a reduction of our intellect through its restricted concentration in the mediate end. Intellect becomes limited by the concentration. By the ritual habit of concentration upon a limited task, intellect becomes gradually dislocated from its journey through the world. It begins to stagnate. We easily recognize such dislocation as undesirable when we consider man and his servile arts. The worker on the assembly line is devoted through his eight-hour shift to setting a pre-made piece into another pre-made piece rolling along an assembly line—a refrigerator or washing machine or automobile. We know humanity well enough to appreciate how unsatisfying such tasks become to that desire in us to make a thing good in itself by making a *whole* thing ourselves, for only that way does it seem possible to see it in itself as good. A satisfaction of a wholeness in the thing as an effect of our making is hardly to be supplied by the labor of tightening this pre-set bolt—but don't touch that one next to it. Meanwhile, the thing a-making moves in a mechanical rhythm before the limited maker. As maker, he gradually atrophies.

What we do not sufficiently appreciate, however, is that this same set of mind through specialized gestures of making affects intellect beyond the merely servile arts now dominated by technology. There is beginning to appear some recognitions of the reductionism. A feature article in the evening paper gives us a sentimentalized visit to one of the last "family" physicians, a "general practitioner." The tonal gist in the account is that it is unfortunate that such a doctor has been outmoded by the progress in medicine. But, then, there has been such a proliferation of specializa-tions in the medical arts for the past half century that any general prac-titioner may hope to survive only if he becomes an expert himself, an expert in referrals. His task is increasingly reduced to being well informed on the specializations available.

An even more crucial problem to the reduction of intellectual arts through specialization is in the destructions to intellect practiced in the name of the education of intellect by the academy. Through program-matic emphasis in higher education upon the production of specialized experts, intellectual vitality is channelled more and more to concentrate upon a limited aspect of intellectual art. For a century now, that trend has led inexorably to our present extreme disintegration of intellectual *understanding* through the emphasis upon specialized *knowledge* as the highest intellectual virtue. Academic specialization now serves a structure of order in the body social which, in the interest of that order, has in fact changed our view of the social body. We see "society" more and more as mechanism, and higher education in response to its own view of society has more and more concentrated on producing the variety of social engi-neers needed to keep that mechanism operating, whether the engineer have a degree in economics, biology, sociology, history, languages. Never in the history of Western man has there been available to intellect, at the touch of a button, so much knowledge. And it is undeniably a knowledge of proven validity at the level of empirical precision. But one wonders whether, ever in the history of mankind, there has been a more conspicu-ous absence of common understanding of the nature of human existence in its social aspect. It is surely evident that society becomes increasingly centrifugal, with no balancing centripetal pull from its disintegration, no center to hold, though in proportion to the dissipation of the body social, the state has been urged as the myth necessary to its order.

Now it seems highly probable that the loss of *understanding*, growing from the elevation of *knowledge* as ultimate, is a principal cause of the general social chaos. And to that chaos we attempt to apply abstractions, such as those of *law* and *order*, whose justifying principle is the disinte-gration itself. The beginning and continuing unrest in the academy—since the 1960s into the 1990s—is from a recognition, at least intuitive, that neither nature nor society is sufficiently served by mechanistic, abstract paradigms purporting to be necessary to the order of reality, of existence itself. For such paradigmatic order is understood as necessary to the in-trinsic chaos of the existential world, rather than derived from the implicit structure of that world. It is applied by intellect to that world, an imposi-tion of form whose cause is intellect itself. Such is the gnostic condition of intellect in our moment, and nowhere more evidently so than in the bastions of secular gnosticism, the academies. It becomes all the more important, then, to recover at an elementary level the relation of *knowledge* to *understanding*, in the interest of an eventual *wisdom* that might prove more healing to the body social than all the "products" of our educational factory. As social, civil body, we lament increasingly that we are served by politicians, not by statesmen. But to recover statesmen requires more than an anxious bewailing, as if to complain would cure the disease.

One does not set aside those "products" from our specializations. Rather, one reflects upon them as they may or should relate to the well-being of the person, so that persons may begin some recovery within the body social. That is why Maritains's words are important to such a large concern:

> As an individual, each of us is a fragment of a species, a part of the universe, a unique point in the intense web of cosmic, ethical, historical forces and influences—and bound by their laws. . . . Nevertheles, each of us is also a person and, as such, is not controlled by the stars. . . . It is the human *person* who enters society; as an individual, it enters society as a part whose proper good is inferior to the good of the whole [of that *whole* constituted of persons, *society*. But] because of the highest requirements of personality as such, the human person, as a spiritual totality referred to the transcendent whole, *surpasses* and is superior to all temporal societies. . . . With respect to the eternal destiny of the soul, society exists for each person and is subordinate to it. (*The Person and the Common Good*, 39, 60–61)

The beginning of our recovery of our role as person in society is the understanding of the nature of intellect in the person. If intellect is reduced to a limit as governed by a "science" of some species or other through specialization, person is endangered by that reduction, becoming *individual* rather than *person*, and thus made subservient to the science, sometimes even to that modern science of imposed obeisance to the state as the individual's final end.

It is not that such "sciences" are not both necessary and apt to the conditions of person in the world; only that the necessity and the aptness are at last defined by that largeness of *person* beyond *individual* as Maritain relates the terms. And so, our argument does not intend to rule out of the social body the statistical expert or the radiologist or the geneticist, as Plato on one occasion seemed to rule out the poet from his *Republic*. (Indeed, Plato's concern was with a certain kind of poet—the poet as echo mechanic of reality, for on another occasion he elevates the poet as lover of beauty and harmony—another sort of poet—as equally desirable to society with the philosopher.) One does not, then, solve the excessive reductionism engineered by the sciences as the limit of person by counterposing equally excessive violations of person in denying the suitability of science, of knowledge, to the pursuit of personhood. This is the cautionary concern always needed against intellectual Luddites, their present manifestation conspicuous among the disoriented environmentalists. For one must insist that "science" is an appropriate and necessary conduct of intellect in its relations to reality. Like art in this respect, science is a good as an action of intellect when intent upon the good of the thing made by that action, whether social structure, medical wonder, or the like. What is undesirable is any science which becomes a fixed reduction of the intellect of the "scientist" himself by excluding the potentials of person in that scientist. For then science itself becomes the ultimate manner of intellect, understanding and wisdom made at first peripheral and then declared antiquated—antique concepts attaching to intellect only historically.

One can hardly overlook that Eliot, in the early point of his journey, is captive to modernism, his argument as to the nature of the poet's mind a mechanistic one, a deterministic one whereby the action of making is formulaic, requiring of the poet himself an indifferent detachment from his making. As poet, Eliot is very much a "scientist." For in such a view as he held, intellect is reduced to the limit of scientific process. What he has to say of the "objective correlative" in his essay on *Hamlet* would seem to lead necessarily to formulae controlling emotional response, as if art were largely dependent on Pavlovian psychology. One is dealing here with intellect as specialized to a limited end, in Eliot's case to the writing of poetry. This is not to say that such specialization, even in the poet, is undesirable in itself, for no less than science poetry requires specialized knowledge. That "science" of poetry is a good when governed by an intellect intent upon the good of the thing it makes through specialized action. Put more congenially, craftsmanship, whether practiced by particle physicist or poet, is crucial to any making of a thing if that thing is to be good in itself. Craftsmanship in *the fullness* of its action, we may say, is art appropriate to the particular science. Furthermore, a multitude of sciences are necessary to intellect in its pursuit of the truth of things, since things are multitudinous. That is a point St. Thomas is insistent upon. Poet or physicist, one must deal with *being* through a concentration whereby knowledge is acquired to intellect. But as we have said often, knowledge is not understanding, however much the two states of intellect may be confused by an intentional but disoriented will.

What is to be avoided, then, is not a science or sciences, but a willful fixation through any particular science as if it alone were sufficient to that faith whose province is the speculative intellect's, not the practical intellect's. By such fixation, however, intellect may become permanently reduced in such a way as to exclude the potential of personhood to itself, the possible fullness of the specific knowing soul. That such a reduction of intellect is at large in community is nowhere more evident than in the difficulty we have in deciding the relation between work and leisure. Specialization of intellect (and the description is applicable to the assembly line worker no less than to the specialized surgeon or physicist, we said) is practically effective because intellect is concentrated by the necessity to science of a reductionism of intellect in its focus upon a mediate end. Under the pressure of such reductionism, as in the name of "professionalism," the mediate end, good in itself, becomes for the specialized intellect its own ultimate end. It is only after a physical or a psychological collapse that one discovers the need of "leisure" lest one become "burned out."

Put another way (for so important is the concern that it must be put again and again), through specialization accepted as a calling, the gift of calling in the specific soul may transform the calling itself into an idol. It is thus that in the end craft consumes the craftsman. For, losing the understanding which is enlarged by knowledge, we lose a vision of our own potential being as person. That vision must see that we are fulfilled through the limited and limiting gifts of our discrete being as person, those limits which we must pursue by practical intellect *through* and not merely *in* craft's support of our specific gifts as maker. Specific gift reduced to an end turns one specialist, and one becomes consumed by craft until the craftsman himself becomes an "object" no less than the thing he makes. This aspect of the specialized self as an object woos the withering soul to worship it in the desperateness of its desire.

We have once more, it seems, arrived at that modernist state of the soul whereby it is alienated, in exile, from being, but most disturbingly from its own potential being. In returning to the point, we have once more underlined the intellect's distortion of the nature of art. In that distortion the discrete soul, as either poet or physicist, makes itself *the* creator of a world—in which it finds itself homeless. From assembly line worker to academic philosopher, then, the most common problem continues: how shall I accommodate myself as maker to the made thing without becoming enslaved to the thing or to myself as its god? How shall I discover a harmony of intellectual action in which the burden of work and a vague dream of leisure from work are reconciled? The answer to such agitated question is not far to find. It is articulated by many, including Gabriel

Marcel in *Man Against Mass Society* and by Josef Pieper in *Leisure: the Basis of Culture*. But what is required for such answer to truly signify to us is a response whereby the *music* of the answer vibrates beyond the limited intellectual encounter of the signs upon the page, vibrates in the soul and not merely registers in intellect as concepts. For signs are truly articulate only when they sound intellect to its depths. Short of the fortuitous intervention of grace, that duration we argued is necessary. We must live and live, struggling for that harmony. Otherwise, Keats would be right when, in a moment of panic, he requests a friend to recommend three or four books since he, Keats, discovers the necessity of a "metaphysical" system. The recovery of reality, alas, is no less difficult than the escape from it, and a ready-made metaphysics never proves sufficient. A "metaphysical" vision must be earned by intellect by enduring life.

If, then, one presume art—one's specialized address to existence—to be the end which alone reflects the value of the artist, then the fullness, the potency of *person*, is lost in a means as end. The artist's concern for the good of the thing made, his concern that it *be* in its own nature through his craft, becomes by that distortion a *specification* of the craftsman as the limit of personhood. In the social realm the loss through such specialization troubles the slumbering spirit with dreams of leisure. We observed how readily we see these symptoms so long as we concentrate on the practice of the servile arts, especially insofar as we blame such disorder in the social community as an effect of the industrial revolution, that easy and common excuse. But increasingly we must consider as well, as increasingly we are being forced to do, that the liberal arts suffer no less from the reductionism of person through the elevation of making as end rather than means to the fulfillment of the maker. In the academy the debate over the consequences of intellectual sin signified by the shibboleth "publish or perish" makes the judgment immediately. Meanwhile, the poet or painter, whether fleeing from or to the academy, if he succumb to an intellectual disorientation in the confused academic climate, will declare, though desperately, that beauty is truth, truth beauty. As person, man is by nature an artist of some calling, a maker. But he may lose his soul to his "art" through the intellectual error of elevating art as end. The pathos, if not tragedy, is that he may do so in attempting to escape a worldliness he intuitively resists. It is nevertheless such "Romantic" poets who recall us to the circumstances of our self-exile from reality through their intuitive resistance. The witness of their poetry raises the necessary question by the desperateness of the poets' presence in the things they make, the poems.

The maker is always larger than the thing made, unless he sacrifice himself to the thing made by idolatry. That is a principle one discovers out of a mystery: namely, our being created in the image of the Creator. And by our movement toward the Creator, through perfection of the soul, we move beyond our own makings, escaping that idolatry prevalent in any "system" whereby God is seen dependent upon his making, as if God were Himself idolater. Such are the closed systems, East and West, against which Christianity stands anciently and presently. As for the poet given to his art as end, he becomes less than his art. He may believe to the contrary. He may suppose his art his rescue to immortality, and indeed, though not an immortality, there is necessarily a presence of the maker in the made thing. Once more, by such a "presence" of the maker in his made thing we do not mean it at the biographical level, though that may be a part of that presence.

There is a deeper, more resonant presence beyond the biographical, whether or not he sees his art as an end or a means, and that presence will bear witness through the thing made as to whether he understands art as one or the other. It is a difference consequent upon his understanding of his own nature as maker. We are, in short, speaking of the poet's presence in his work as revealing his own belief as to his own proper end as person, a concern larger than the details of his biography can account for. What we come to see is his understanding of his own end in relation to the means of his becoming, the actions of his own intellect. If his art is an end, it will be for him a mirror to himself. If it is means to a larger end, it will be more nearly a window opening him to prospects beyond the local, mediate dimension of his art.

As for this resonant presence of the maker separate from the merely biographical, Keats does not know the urn-maker by any explicit, denotative reference, though something of the cultural circumstances to the urn-maker impinge upon the urn as Keats encounters it on a pedestal in a museum thousands of miles and hundreds of years away from its origin. Such urns, he knows, were often used not only to hold wine but to house the ashes of the dead, points of knowledge present to Keats in his encounter. The empathy of poet to urn-maker through the art of the urn is thereby enlarged, speaking the poet's awareness of sharing with the old artisan the dilemma to personhood in its necessity as maker. Such are the encounters of person and person in response to the made thing, the urn, separate from those accidents of biographical or cultural history. For both urn-maker and poet are responding to those accidents from a perspective counter to the accident of the biographically literal, the culturally literal. The shared response is a spiritual one, in which the dominant presence of the poet eulogizes the urn-maker by recognizing that the making is inadequate to the spirit's desires. The effect is that of pathos, since no release of the spirit beyond mortality seems possible to that eulogizing poet.

Without the presence of the maker of the thing in the thing itself, the thing can be but dead artifact. Its descriptive, factual label on the pedestal will be sufficient. For the "articulation" of art occurs only through the respondent's encounter of a resonance of presence. With that dimension, we recover a mystery common to our nature as persons, whatever the century or place that supplies biographical and cultural descriptions adjacent to the thing in its aspect as a residue of history. The mystery we perceive is that through our actions of making, under the guidance of the practical intellect as justified by the speculative intellect—through our exercise of our gift as maker—we move toward a fulfillment of personhood. And it is in this respect that the "audience" to the urn or poem participates as maker, though passively. The participation is that of our becoming, such as Rilke speaks of in his poem "On a Bust of Apollo." In the presence of that sculpture, says Rilke, "You must change your life." Thus we discover ourselves members one of another despite the vagaries and variousness of time and place or the limit of gift whereby each is yet *specific* in membership. We come to understand in the discovery of membership that our own making is not sufficient to our desire. It is in this recognition that one realizes the limits to art in the rescue of the soul, as Keats recognized it though he could not find what was a sufficient rescue. Hence, we have said, the pathos of his poetry, the melancholy, which is to us a vital witness through, not *in*, the art to a necessity of some rescue not afforded through our own actions of making.

In such consideration, perhaps, we come to understand more fully the intuitive inclination in the artist that leads him to make of the poem or painting or the sculpture or music a thing glowing significantly beyond itself with his own presence as anxious for transcendence of the self as maker, beyond the limits of art. It is this intuitive sense of art's relation to person that made Keats at first suppose art itself a possible means of transport beyond decay. He found, as we must, art failing, for the "viewless wings of poesy" are insufficient to the transport the soul requires. Yeats similarly, but overly confident of art as transport, makes of art an altar through which he would commune with the transcendent. The absolute he supposes may be made incarnate by the artist as priest. Eliot, seeing this presence of person in relation to the made thing in both Yeats and Keats, recognizes Keats the wiser poet—wise beyond his lyric years in that Keats knows, though he does not understand, the insufficiency of art as the rescue of person.

Yeats, our own century's most conspicuous Romantic poet, is significantly the poet as priest, but that is an office assumed by various poets at many points in history. Increasingly since the 18th century, however, we find the poet intent on a relation to society in this role. He thinks himself ordained by his imagination. Armed by that authority and moved by his intuitive concern for a recovery of reality, he becomes (in Shelley's characterization) the unacknowledged legislator of what is proper social order. One may understand how it comes to such a poet to suppose that his is a special power whereby reality is to be transubstantiated by art. His art is a ritualistic act, invocative of a transcendent authority of some sort. But as ritual, it requires a general consent if not general participation. The immediate difficulty to such consent is the ambiguous nature of that enveloping authority needed to give some spiritual dimension to social order. With the Church in rapid decay, its established clergy increasingly in disrepute through the sharp contrast of its affluency to the growing social poverty, such a poetic spirit as Shelley's could well suppose itself beneficiary of the spiritual inclination of the generality of Englishmen. God would seem, from that position, if not dead, then mortally wounded, evidenced by the corruption of the spiritual leaders on one hand and the growing geological and (soon to follow) biological underminings of the old beliefs founded in *Genesis*. Not Shelley, but Wordsworth, had already declared England "a fen / Of stagnant waters," the corruption general: "altar, sword, and pen, / Fireside, the heroic wealth of hall and bower" are decayed through a common selfishness, through which has been "forfeited" the common "English dower / Of inward happiness."

One notes Wordsworth's concern for an "inward happiness" now lost, his reformist inclination not so radically social and political as Shelley's. The failure of "altar, sword, and pen" for Shelley was institutional failure, requiring a general restructuring by an emerging intellectual elite, themselves made independent of traditional sentiments by the very power of intellect. But Shelley's "Intellectual Beauty" seems hardly a sufficient substitute for Christianity if he is to command a popular allegiance. Still Prometheus must be unbound from such time-accreted restrictions as Christianity to build a new city of man, neither that under the light of a Heavenly City nor like that city everywhere in decay through the general selfishness operative as authority in matters social and political. But to call on "Intellectual Beauty" to "free / This world from its dark slavery" through its "awful LOVELINESS" will hardly stir the factory slaves or the slum dwellers whom Dickens will presently bring to intellectual consciousness. As for that intellectual consciousness, wherever it might reside, the wild vagueness of Shelley could not supply direction or leadership.

The sordid problems, social and economic, attendant upon the explo-sive emergence of industry seem hardly spoken to by such invocative whistlings as Shelley's. Nor does Wordsworth seem to have countered the shifting poles of social, economic, political power. However paraded in robes of Church, state or traditional responsibilities in the halls of the withering aristocracy, Karl Marx will see in London much more clearly than that would-be vatic poet Wordsworth the shifting tensional poles in the social order, the emerging new lords of industry dominant over, not only the hoi polloi, but over "altar, sword, and pen" as the Empire ex-pands. Meanwhile, there were land and church reforms, but also potato famines and abject poverty and the like beginning to affect the public spirit, even as the populace—destitute or not—became increasingly mo-bile in its restlessness. Ruskin would write on that point very scathingly that, with the coming of cheap, rapid rail transportation, "every fool in Buxton can be at Bakewell in half-an-hour, and every fool in Bakewell at Buxton."

In the political history of England from the 1830s to this century's Irish troubles and World War I, the poet is less and less significant legisla-tor than he might either wish to be or think himself to be. The ritualistic act of poetry becomes isolated to enclaves, especially in the second half of last century. By the time of Yeats in his visionary phase of the 1920s, the poet appears isolated to practice his rituals in privacy, though he of-fers invitation to a popular support. It is a support, however, that he would have concentrate on the rescue of the separate self. Yeats had tried popular office, only to see it fail, with some bitterness his lot. Pound, looking at that early Yeats, recalls in the *Pisan Cantos* Yeats's disappoint-ment: "the problem after any revolution is what to do with / your gunmen / as old Billyum found out in Oireland" (LXXX). We notice that in Yeats's "Sailing to Byzantium" (published the same year as Eliot's "Ash-Wednesday") the concern is for the rescue of the singular soul by that soul itself, through art. There is no longer the hopeful forcing of the issue of the poet as legislator that one has in Shelley's "Hymn to Intellec-tual Beauty." Yeats's is no call for a program of conduct in social institu-tions under the authority of intellect. For Shelley, in contrast, intellect was to be defined by the poet, after the failures of philosophers and theo-logians.

There will follow after Shelley, a hundred years later, Ezra Pound's own attempt to recover the ground the poet has lost since Shelley. Pound, too, would reestablish the poet as vatic, but not in the sense of Virgil as vatic. For Virgil is the wise echo of a national spirit turned empiric. In-stead, for Pound the poet is to be central to the direction of the institutions of the state. Yeats (from Pound's point of view) had failed in that attempt in "Oireland" and had retreated into a strange mysticism divorced from pragmatic offices to poetry. He might as well have taken Eliot's route for all his effectiveness as poet—at least as it appeared to Pound in the late 1920s and 1930s. And so Pound attempts to move into a position of public authority as poet. Not that there was much support for Pound in his emphatic position, but the very opposition he encountered confirmed for him the rightness of his position. The "establishment" by its opposition recognized his threat as viable. All was not yet lost to the poet.

Meanwhile, there is that half-way position between Shelley and Pound as represented by Yeats (and in Pound's view, by Eliot, since Eliot's position appears also a vague, mystical sort of nonsense, Eliot now "Parson" Eliot to Pound). Art, Yeats insists in "Sailing to Byzantium," is capable of rescuing the soul, even as Keats thought it might, though Keats lacked the faith necessary to advance the mystical cause of art as Yeats set about doing. Pound, remembering Yeats, responds in the *Pisan Cantos* (LXX-VII): " 'Sligo in heaven' murmured uncle William." It is art that teaches the isolated soul to "clap its hands and sing" to compensate for the heart now "sick with desire" and "fastened to a dying animal," the body. Not the City of God is its destination, however, but "Sligo" imagined into "heaven" by the power of intellect.

As for that art thing, the poem, it always says much of the maker because it is an imitation of the creative act of the poet himself. It is that presence of Yeats in his words to which Pound responds, a presence we would recognize even if Yeats and his own biography did not intrude upon the poem as it does. It is a presence persuaded of its immortality as certified by art. This imitation of the action possible to a person in given circumstances, here the circumstance of exile in the created world, constitutes the presence of the maker. If we are able to separate the accidents of personality, the "biography" of the poet as opposed to that presence of intellect or soul that is inescapable in the made thing, we become acutely aware of distinctions in the sense of exile reflected in "Sailing to Byzantium" on the one hand and "Ash-Wednesday" on the other, whose coincidental publication in 1928 is of interest in the general history of the poet's quest for his personal relation to creation amidst modernist dislocations of the soul. By this presence of Yeats and Eliot as exiles, let us say once more, we do not mean that in this specific act of each "making" his poem at this specific point of time thereby transfers to the poem only the poet's present historical self. For if this were strictly the meaning of the poet's presence, the poem could never be more than a footnote in the history of our formal uses of signs. We mean a deportment of intellect in respect to its actions as the soul's agent, and these poets differ in these instances in their understanding of exile. They recognize that condition of exile as implying a spiritual dimension, however radically they differ in attempting to recover the spirit to community. They are closer to each other than either is to his mutual friend and would-be protector and champion Ezra Pound, whose own sense of exile is seen by the current establishment as a denial of his gifts of order to the secular city, his power through the word to recover, not the soul to a transcendent community, but civilization to the state.

5

The Authority of Voice in the Sign

By art, the poet would capture a spontaneous cry of anguish, a particular, possible agony of youth caught in the enveloping circumstances of love summoned through sign. The heart's cry is given a similitude as of a present actual moment, by the art of similitude hiding art. It is this necessity that requires of the poet a rational understanding, whatever his actual years in relation to the similitude of his voice in his signs. Thereby the made thing, the lyric or monologue or personae in a drama, resonates with an authority of duration proportionate to the voice in the signs. The authority of voice in the signs is a necessity, though not an authority corresponding literally to the degree of maturity in the poet, the maker. What is effected as the drama of the word, whether lyric or epic or dramatic word, is the craft's control of the journey of intellect which is simulated, suited to the degree of understanding in the journeyman, the agent speaking the words. And at issue here is an analogy proportionate to the reality simulated in the art, a persuasive imitation of the possible or probable intellect as projected through sign, a voice speaking as if in actual circumstances. This is so, whether the simulation is of a person caught up in a moment of passion's despair or the soul more largely coming to itself in a dark wood. This is to say that the word as art requires a reasoned control by the poet of the level of maturity in the agent. The poet, through practical intellect, manages an articulation of that degree of maturity proper to an imagined state of intellect in the agent. It is this concern among others that Aristotle speaks to in proposing that art must be concerned with the "possible or probable" as distinct from history's "actual."

This aspect of the possible or probable voice in words is the concern about which so much criticism has been written in our century under the rubric of "point of view." It leads Eliot, in "Hamlet and His Problems"

51

(1919), to his term "objective correlative." He finds Shakespeare's play flawed because "Hamlet [the man] is dominated by an emotion which is inexpressible, because it is in *excess* of the facts as they appear." The weakness in the play, in Eliot's view, lies in Shakespeare's failure to distinguish Hamlet from himself adequately. In contrast *Macbeth* succeeds: "The artistic 'inevitability' lies in [the] complete adequacy of the external to the emotion." By *external* Eliot means the enveloping world of the play advanced through an imagery ordinate to the actions to be imagined. Thus the actions are "inevitable." This essay is published in the same year that Eliot argues for the poet's mind as scientific, as desirably "depersonalized." What is not clear is the distinction between the poet's history as a danger to his art and the necessity of his *person*'s engagement in the act of making toward his own ultimate, collateral end: his own fullness as person. That collateral concern for person is not the same thing as psychological history, which comes to us as his literal history, for that literal history constitutes only the accidents of his essence. The psychological dimension of the maker, behind which he is sometimes tempted to retreat, is a manifestation of his being, but it is not his being, anymore than his body is his being.

It is our contention that it is the soul of the maker through which proportionality is understood. In that understanding, it becomes possible to the artist to imitate the action of primary making, primary creation, the significant action of the *person* as maker—as a being created in the image of God. (In speaking of *soul* we mean the substantial form of the body, inextricable in reality, though when conceptually taken that simple indivisible unity of *person* is spoken of as soul, intellect, and body.) From such a perspective, we may see an intimate relation of poet to his created agent, controlled and made proportionate by the poet's *reasoned making*. Wordsworth declares that the poet is a "man speaking to men" in his "Preface" to the 1802 edition of *Lyrical Ballads*. Wordsworth in his phrase has the poet as "man" speaking proportionately to the degree and limit of his personhood held in common by all "men." In this light, his proposition proves more than an empty, facile phrase, as it seemed to Eliot. It is this "Preface" which Eliot attacks in relation to his own characterization of the poet's mind in his "Tradition and the Individual Talent" (1919). But a decade later, Eliot will praise both Wordsworth as poet and this "Preface" in particular. By then, in his Harvard lectures in 1932–1933, Eliot has come to recognize, as Wordsworth had, that the underlying problem for the poet is the philosophical aspects of the poet's craft. Those aspects of craft—the problem of "point of view" in distinguishing the poet from his agent, for instance, or the necessity of suitable "objective correlatives"—are not reducible to merely aspects of craft. For craft is intimately anchored in the poet's nature as maker, and that nature is intimately involved in the larger realities of existence itself. The poet's concern for craft, then, is intimately related to his understanding or lack of understanding of existence itself, and most decisively to his understanding of the nature of his own existence as a maker defined by the limits of his finitudes as creator.

The relation of the artist as maker to the good of the thing he makes is determined in this sense by the limits of the thing the poet must address, directly or indirectly, by a metaphysics of being. Otherwise, the poet will very easily, and especially under the pressure of chaotic circumstances, mistake himself for priest or philosopher or legislator rather than as the maker of a poem. This is to say that a metaphysical understanding of his calling as poet, held either tacitly or explicitly, reveals to him the necessity of a metaphysical understanding, which alone is sufficiently inclusive of the specific sciences of intellect's discrete acts as a practical, rational nature. Those sciences appropriate to the peculiar gift of making are means to the necessary knowledge in the discrete person, whether he is called to make poems or discover structure through such sciences as geometry or physics. Such knowledge is not automatic consequence to vision. One hastens to add that to understand the necessity of a metaphysical vision is not the same thing as to be possessed of such a vision in any commanding way. It is only to say that Keats, in the moment of his intellectual anguish when he writes a friend for the titles of a few books from which he might derive a metaphysics, is right in recognizing the necessity, though naive in his facile expectations.

We are here, as in other points of our concern, to make distinctions between *knowledge*, *understanding*, and *wisdom*, and we depend on St. Thomas for our distinctions. In the *Summa* (II–II, Q8, Art 1) Thomas says that *understanding* "implies a certain intimate apprehension." The "sensitive apprehension," which responds to sensible qualities, leads to an understanding of that apprehension insofar as intellect "penetrates to the essence of the thing, for the object of intellect is 'what it is.' " It is important to observe that the understanding penetrates to "things that hide inwardly," for "the substantial nature of things lies hidden under accident." Thus "the meanings of words lie hidden under words; figured truth lies hidden under similitudes and figures." And because "the apprehension of man begins from sense, as if from the outward, it is manifest that as the light of intellect is stronger, so much more can it penetrate into inner things." It is here that one must, however, recognize a limit, since "the natural light of our intellect is of finite power." It can therefore attain only to "a determinate something." It is at this juncture that the "natural light of intellect" is supported by a "supernatural light given to man," a light which is called "the gift of understanding."

It is through the understanding that intellect approaches wisdom, as through knowledge it is prepared to receive the supernatural light of understanding, through the agency of the Holy Ghost, Thomas says. It is the apprehension of divine things that we call wisdom, whereas the "apprehension of human or created things is called knowledge" (II–II, Q9, Art. 2). Knowledge is "a common name . . . implying the certainty of judgment appropriate to a judgment made by second causes," and so knowledge is a possession at a level removed from the wisdom of divine things as apprehended by intellect. Concerning those "second causes," "the gift of knowledge is only about human things or created things." Such is the level of intellect's operation signified as the action of practical intellect through its rational (finite) "natural light." To know "what is to be believed," the certainty of judgment about human and created things through rational intellect, "belongs to the gift of knowledge." But to "know the believed things in themselves, by a kind of union with them, pertains to the gift of wisdom." It is when knowledge held by rational intellect becomes transformed by understanding that intellect itself is opened toward that larger wisdom, which is a visionary perspective upon creation, upon human and created things.

We might properly notice here that St. Thomas's description of knowledge so elevated, till it is the action of knowing "the believed things in themselves, by a kind of union with them," bears certain parallel to Keats's concern for "negative capability," a relation we explored in our first study, *Romantic Confusions of the Good.* It also is suggestive of that experience of Wordsworth's in which he remembers having seen "into the life of things." What we conclude from such observation is that these two Romantic poets, at least in the limited circumstances of their immediate concern for vision of "the life of things" and their sense of necessity for an openness to things in themselves through "negative capability," are at least intuitively pursuing that wisdom proper to the soul as St. Thomas defines it: a "knowledge" of "divine things." Important to that turning of intellect toward a perspective out of wisdom is an understanding beyond the limited knowledge of second causes, and so allows an apprehension of human or created things by rational intellect in relation to their divine cause.

What we are next led to say, in respect to the necessity of some degree of understanding whereby the poet orients his action by at least recognizing that his desire must be supportable through metaphysical vision, is that in that recognition the poet already understands himself to be larger as maker than merely a technician of language, of sign. And this is an indication of a maturity in him as he journeys toward wisdom. It is a recognition that affects his making, since he has reached a certain perfection to which craft alone will not speak. For craft, limited to reason in the making as exercised by the practical intellect, is rather restricted to the knowledge possible to rational intellect, a knowledge of human things or created things. We might speak figuratively of this distinction by considering the actual knowing craft of the making of a building as distinct from the craftsman's understanding brought to that making whereby the building becomes suitable to the housing of that complex spiritual creature, man. There is, we say, a distinction between a house and a home.

From that figurative suggestion, we might consider the poem in a distinction of its craft from the sense of the craftsman's understanding implicit in it. In that poem which we recognize as enlarged beyond the necessary support of craft, we might say of it that we respond to a resonant duration implicit in it as a made thing. It is this additional "presence" which justifies the maker of the thing, as the made thing is also justified beyond mere craft by the maker's understanding. It is an absence, or relative absence, of this presence that we associate with the mechanically produced or machine produced artifact. We say *relative absence*, in that there lies in the thing so made, if but remotely, the implications of its maker, which neither an artist's indifference to the good of the thing he makes nor even a machine programmed to make things can entirely remove. We are suggesting that wisdom is beyond and inclusive of understanding, as understanding is beyond the science peculiar to one's actions as maker, beyond craft, beyond mere knowledge. It is through understanding that the poet gives evidence, implicit in his well-crafted made thing (for one cannot set aside craft in the interest of understanding), of a sufficient duration of his own nature. That is, there is evidence of the maker's experience of things in themselves (human or created things in their actualities) which is possible only through an open enduring of life that will inevitably affect the thing he makes. This is to say that, though the poet may not be a *seer*, a wise man knowing "divine things," he must have advanced at least beyond mere knowledge as available through the practical intellect. He must have intimations of, intuitions of, complexities to that knowledge held by practical intellect.

It is through understanding, then, that the poem is marked by the authority of an intellectual existence, that of the maker. The understanding inheres in the made thing by virtue of its own nature as an imitation of intellectual action. That sense of similitude, though at a remove through art as suited to a made thing, nevertheless gives evidence of that actuality thus simulated, the intellectual action of making. For if art is an imitation of the action of nature, then it is most appropriately an imitation of the action of that creating intellect. The action at issue is that of the maker's intellect, which is thus in some degree a presence to the actuality of the poem as a made thing. Here lies the point of distinction between *art* and *reality* in relation to intellect as a maker. And in this point there is a more significant distinction than in Aristotle's distinction between *art* and *history*. For though the poet, through his imaginative supposition of the possible or probable, as governed by his knowledge of actualities, thereby removes his art from history in some degree, he cannot remove the immediate actuality of his intellectual making from the thing he makes. His "thumb print" is upon that made thing, we might say figuratively. That is why two poets possessed of the same resource of signs, a common language, though in the diction of their poems so restricted, or even a common prosody, reveal themselves uniquely in the use of a common language.

To approach the distinction from a slightly different direction, it is through the manner of the poet's deportment as maker that the effect of his presence affects the thing he makes. *Manner* here intends to signify that deportment of the maker toward the made thing which is larger than his deportment as simply knowing craftsman. And through this manner the thing is made proportionate to the reality of his understanding as maker, which is to say to the reality of his accomplishment of his potential as person. The maker is finite, being himself a made creature, in distinction from God as maker. But his poem will at last bear his presence insofar as it truely imitates the action of his nature as maker, in an analogy to that other "presence" of God as Creator in relation to human and created things, those "second causes" upon which depends the judgment of the practical intellect.

It is through the poet's manner in making that the poem is itself made to be, and so made proportionately anchored in creation as a *thing existing*. Its anchor in being is through that particular *ens*, the poet. In addition, it may be said that to make the good thing redounds to the good of the maker of the thing, which is a concern different from that for the good of the thing made in itself, a concern for the poem in its own "right" as a thing. But this point is important to the problem of proportionality at last, since the distinction is necessary between the poet as creator and God as creator. The poet is himself fulfilled through his making, as opposed to God, who is Perfection precedent to His making. God does not come to be through his making. Through the action of proportionate making—the poet's mannerly deportment in respect to the realities of his intellectual finitude—the maker by contrast realizes a potential as person, the potential signified when we say that he as a man, and like all men, is himself "made" in the image of God.

We marvel when such an authority of the maker allows the good of the thing made. For through the peculiar, particular gift to such a maker, as proportionately exercised, the thing made escapes a merely "autobiographical" entrapment. It becomes a thing enriched by its dependence in the *personal* which is common to the nature of man. That making we call art, we must remember, is peculiar to this nature among natures, man. As Gilson remarked in *Linguistics and Philosophy*, "except for man, we know of no dialectical, sophistic, rhetorical, oratorical animal who is concerned with judicial, political, or formal eloquence." Of the poem made by such a creature (or painting or piece of music for that matter) we are likely to say it is "universal." In recognizing this a marvel of the finite creation of the poet, we usually speak of it at the level of craft, but the mystery of art is ripe with both metaphysical necessities and metaphysical implications, all related to that larger mystery whereby we say man is created a creator, a maker—in the image of God.

And so we find Mark Twain's "point of view" more persuasive in his capturing the presence of a boy in the *Adventures of Huckleberry Finn* than in his other work. The recently recovered draft manuscript gives evidence of the labor Twain spent in achieving that simulation in language to reflect Huck's uneducated but perceptive youthfulness. We praise Eliot, himself still somewhat a "boy," who nevertheless catches a voice ripe with the durational authority of a middle-aged, failed intellect, J. Alfred Prufrock. Or we fault Wordsworth in his "Idiot Boy" for not exercising proportionately his own durational authority as an intellectual being in his attempt to imitate the action of a defective, retarded intellectual being from his own detached position. On the other hand, we are likely to praise Faulkner for his relative success in such an attempt, his echoing Benjy in *The Sound and the Fury*. For Faulkner, we might put it, through a "negative capability" superior to Wordsworth's in the "Idiot Boy," rationally manages sufficient "objective correlatives" to the purpose. And so through such considerations of art, we observe the necessity of an authority in the maker which cannot be accounted for merely by his craft. And in the relative success of such a maker, we encounter his sense of a proper proportionality in his manner which an understanding in him allows, an understanding whereby he is in some degree open to the possibilities of metaphysical vision, and so open in his actions of making. For what we recognize in that art is a gift of understanding that suggests that its maker has a sense of "a kind of union" with such possible creatures as a Benjy. Thus "negative capability" is an intellectual manner toward both reality itself and toward the thing being made. It is a manner of "both . . . and," not "either . . . or."

Such relative success in art (as opposed to the perfect success of God as creator) does not always signify in an actual relation of the craftsman's "lived years," nor should we think it necessary. For the "supernatural light" of understanding in support of the "natural light" of intellect is not a matter of the merely natural, world-held dimensions of the poet. One may understand the nature of an aging intellect without having to be an aged intellect. The poet's imagined state of being for his agent is not dependent upon the poet's age. May one successfully imitate in art the child only if one as maker is himself a child? Or only if older than a child? Or is Faulkner enabled to imitate an idiot only because he is himself possessed of his faculties? May the poet speak only for "man," meaning *mankind* as generalized? Or is he restricted to speaking for "man" if *man* is limited specifically to *male human*? Can he be persuasively artful in imitating the action of woman as well? We are in a period when much nonsense attaches to these questions in our criticism, and that nonsense escapes intellectual condemnation only because we lack the intellectual discipline and vision, the proportionate perspective upon such questions. Without disciplined vision we cannot discard pseudo-questions from those actual and appropriate questions that are to be asked of the nature of art.

Whether the poet's agent be boy or man, girl or woman, idiot or genius, we must come at last to the realization that where art is effective as art, there is that presence of the personal in a proportionate way deeper than the accidents of art or the accidents of nature itself. It is upon accidents that a negligent criticism tends to focus at the moment. For the *personal* ground to our making is deeper than superficially historical or biological accidents. It is only through such a personal presence of the maker, allowed through his understanding, that an imitation of the action of this discrete, peculiar creature, the human maker of this thing, that the work of art is possible. The artist through such understanding effects a relatively timeless, living thing, the poem—insofar as such person-made creatures may be spoken of as alive in a "timeless" way.

Insofar as such made things are in this sense alive, they are alive out of the life of their makers, lives which are not sufficiently accounted for by the "facts" of the history of those makers. It has been a popular clichè in recent years to speak of certain popular music as "soul" music, the term *soul* reduced to the level of nature from the proper supernatural implications of that term. Nevertheless, there is even in that use of the term still a residual recognition of its larger meaning. For the work of art, when it is good in itself according to the limits of its own nature, bears in it implications of the "soul" of its maker. Art itself is in this respect an evidence of the existence of the soul of a maker, just as creation is evidence of that Being we call God, who is that creation's cause. The modification in the analogy, lest it become facile equation as the artist would sometimes have it to be, is the principle of proper proportionality. That is why we are insistent that the finite maker in the act of his making realize in some degree his own potential as person. It is the principle of proper proportionality at issue in this respect when Gilson says that we must engage the problem of all problems most carefully lest we confuse our understanding of reality. "In Thomas' technical language," Gilson says, "actual existence, which we call *esse*, is that by virtue of which a thing, which he calls *res*, is a being, an *ens*. It is the being-hood or being-ness of being. It is *be* in being. It is *to be* that makes a certain thing to be a being. *Esse* is defined by its essence, namely that which the thing is" (*The Spirit of Thomism*).

It is in these terms that Thomas, in his *On Being and Essence*, argues the distinction of proportionality between God and his creations, whereby the created *ens* has *essence* by virtue of its being created, whereas God *is essence*, existence and essence identical in God as they are not in man. There is also that important distinction Thomas makes between man's practical and his speculative intellect, the union with the cause of his being made possible through the speculative intuition. In sorting out the proportionality between the soul as created being and God as uncreated being, Thomas considers intellect in its analogy to the Creator, God. His words bear repeating at this point. "The asserted likeness of the practical intellect to God is one of proportion; that is to say, by reason of its standing in relation to what it knows (and brings into existence) as God does to what He knows (creatively). But the likeness of the speculative intellect to God is one of union and information [the action of in-forming of the soul through grace, whereby it fulfills its potential being]; which is a much greater likeness" (*Summa Theologica*, I–II, Q3, Art. 5). It is a greater likeness in that, by its perfection its own doing and being are coincident and indivisible, in a likeness to the doing-being of God.

6

The Sins of the Fathers, the Virtues of Grandfathers

Sometimes the rational intellect, prematurely forced by the poet's will to a service of the intuitive intellect, may transgress the proper limits of intellectual sign by attributive action—by attributive metaphor. One may find such transgression of reality in that poet who, like Shelley or Pound, feels called to an activist, messianic office as if that were the office of the poet. His is a transgression shared with other intellects of various callings, of various scientific knowledges through which a temporal end is embraced as if a final end. This error is especially apparent in Utopian intellectuals, who would set aside the cumulative wisdom of human experience—"tradition"—in the interest of an immediate transformation of reality to some heart's desire. Such is always a tensional pole in community, though its fundamental ground is the specific intellect. The war of the younger generation against immediate fathers, which again and again ends in a recovery of certain elements of intellectual grandfathers, is a metaphorical way of speaking of that tensional friction in a present community. Just for some version of a "handful of silver," such is the tenor of complaint, one's fathers have abandoned principle, principle itself usually infirmly established by the protesting sons. In that war the young often (and sometimes justly) see the purported "wisdom" of their immediate elders as a timidity in the face of pressing necessity. That is a part of the youthfulness in Pound, revealed in his disappointment with Eliot by the mid 1920s. Similarly the old (and sometimes justly) see the purported vision of the young as arrogant transgression of reality. That was an experience Eliot endured in relation to his poetics, for both his poet peers and younger poets were uncomfortable with Eliot as poet in respect to his craftsmanship. Even some of his older traditionalist objectors recognized a traditionalist burden in Eliot's poetry, but were suspicious of his art.

What is at risk on either hand is the balance between that piety required of person in respect to finitude and his temptation to an action unrestrained by recognition of finitude. In the first instance, piety suborned by fear yields the refusal of action. In the second instance reality is violated by the excess of willful power. It is an understanding of this dilemma that Eliot comes to in "Ash-Wednesday." We see this recognition when we read this poem against "The Love Song of J. Alfred Prufrock." Prufrock refuses all action by tricking himself through a rhetorical shell-game with time, action being the shifted pea, hidden under the shells of time. Past is played against future to avoid the reality of intellectual action, which is never possible except in this present moment. By the time of "Ash-Wednesday," Eliot himself no longer resists the consequential present to intellectual action, surrendering the effect of present action to the province of grace but without abandoning the necessity to act in this present moment. There results a new state of the soul, in which creation itself appears restored through the senses, even though the senses are diminished by his actual years of living in nature. It is this recovered state of the soul that sets Eliot quite apart from Pound, who finds a timidity in Eliot from *The Waste Land* onward. "Ash-Wednesday's" prayer speaks to this recovered estate of intellect in service to the soul: "Teach us to care and not to care."

In our finding the balance Eliot prayed for between caring and not caring lies the orientation necessary to the journey in time and place which is made by intellectual action—action ordinate both to the limits of personhood and its discrete, specific gifts and to the inclusive finitudes of creation in which lie the circumstances of action. It is a balance which neither eschews the world nor submerges the soul in the world. One cares and acts in relation to the circumstances of one's existence, but recognizes that the effects of action in circumstantial existence are not to be made the final measure of intellect. It is here that one begins to discover the importance of an intellectual understanding of proportionality. One's proper making—the ordinate actions of intellect in relation to the circumstantial conditions of temporal, finite existence—are dependent in intellect's participation in being: first, as governed by its own proper proportionality in being whose measure is the finitude of the gift of particularity as an existing thing, a *person*; and second, following from that dependence, an engagement of the particularizations that one speaks of inclusively as *creation*. The *understanding* necessary to this action of making is the significant effect of *action*, possible through the exercise of that peculiar gift, intellect itself. For not the *effect* of intellectual action but *perfection* of intellect through action is decisive.

Concerning this proportionality, Thomas makes his argument in his treatise *On Being and Essence*, here abbreviated but (I trust) not thereby distorted. God's Being, says St. Thomas, is the perfection of perfections. That being as an absolute cannot be conceptualized, as can perfections—as can *esse* in particularized manifestations suited to intellect's encounter. Perfection is approached after acts of conceptualization when concept is anchored by *esse*. It is a proper anchor of concept in *esse* that governs the analogy of proportionality, by which anchor intellect avoids that entrapment in which it may mistake itself as the cause of *esse* by the very act of conceptualization. But by acting through concept as governed by *esse*, as opposed to an assumption by will that it confers *esse*, intellect moves on its journey. Its action is one of *judgment*, which must be understood as an active assent to existence. By such judgment one acknowledges a "thing" to be the thing it is. Hence the soul's journey through intellectual actions moves from an embrace of *esse* as mediate to the journey toward Being, toward that Perfection which is the cause of all perfections.

It is in this movement that intellect is returned from itself and toward that which is separate from itself, toward the complexity of existences constituting creation. We say *returned*, for such is an act of openness through which its own potency becomes actual. That is, such a movement recovers that ancient first movement of intellect, nostalgically associated with childhood by poets ranging from Wordsworth to Joyce: that openness to existence which is replaced by self-consciousness. Such is the *return* understood by Dame Julian or Eliot, the end of intellectual journey which brings us to the place from which we set out, enabled to *see* the place for the first time. The "place" is an orientation of intellect proper to its nature in respect to the reality at hand, as we say. Before that return became possible to Eliot, he regrets the arrest of his turning from "place" in this sense. In "The Hollow Men" he speaks of a shadow falling "Between the conception / And the creation," between "the potency and the existence," and finally "Between the essence / And the descent"—that is, the "descent" into the finitudes of particularity within which intellect must once more struggle to "see" things in themselves, through which struggle one may mount toward a visionary moment, a still point. The distinction at issue here is spoken to formally by St. Thomas, as opposed to the dramatic movement of a struggling voice in signs in Eliot's poems. Thomas's is a formulation: "God *is esse*; creatures *have esse* but *are not esse*." Being, Perfection (the *is esse*, the *I am that I am*) is that continuous uncaused action beyond conceptualization by intellect. Hence it is, as Thomas says, the Perfection of all perfections: the Perfection whereby beings (*ens*) are. St. Augustine acts out this movement of recovery dramatically for us, beyond the limits of sign, insofar as he may act it out through signs. In his *Confessions* he gives an account of a "Vision at Ostia." Following this Augustinian drama, Eliot himself acts out a more agonized version of the experience of the return, the attempt to ascend to the place from which he set out. Section III of "Ash-Wednesday" begins "At the first turning of the second stair," begins in a spiritual *medias res*, the voice in the poem remembering the struggle with "the devil of the stairs who wears / The deceitful face of hope and of despair." Issuing upon a balcony, in a setting reminiscent of that of St. Augustine's vision at Ostia, the voice finds "strength beyond hope and despair / Climbing the third stair."[8]

From St. Thomas's explication, through St. Augustine's and Eliot's re-enactments, we may arrive at a partial understanding: intellect "knows" this perfection possible to itself as a potency contained in this present moment of its action. In this sense, it is provided a foreknowing of a possible perfection suited to hope, through which intellect is *still* as it is still *moving*. It holds an expectation that the Perfection God will (in Eliot's words) "speak the word only" so that his "soul shall be healed." Now this foreknowing is through the *intellectus*, through intuitional recognitions of *esse* in created things that affirms that *Esse* of all *esse*, that Perfection of all perfections. Thus intellect knows its own possible perfection. And the ground to this knowledge it already possesses before any action of the *ratio*, whose significant operation is conceptualization. One might say, as I have suggested elsewhere, that we witness this knowledge as already operative in the infant's clasping its mother with an assurance beyond self-conscious love, an assurance beyond our later and easier rationalizations of its unself-reflecting love as merely physical hunger.

Further along in its journey, the infant, child, adult—ourselves—experience again such an openness from time to time, in what Eliot calls a "still point." It is a visionary moment in which are "con-fused" the intuitive and rational into a simple intellectual union with being. We might say of such moments that in them we have recovered known but forgotten things in their essences. Indeed, that was the initiating experience we explored in Keats, the moment adjacent to and precedent of the words of "Ode to a Nightingale." From that moment the poem's voice falls away by the very struggle to hold to it. It is his act of clinging to images through rationalization of them, which constitutes the poem's drama, that Keats at last concludes the cause of his falling away. The attempt by "thought" to hold a vision which is but "one moment past" so confounds the vision in the tangles of thought that, rationally, he cannot declare the moment visionary. And failing rational certainty, despair encourages his conclusion that the visionary moment was merely one of illusion. Such then is Keats's struggle with the devil of the stair with its "deceitful face of hope and despair" that Eliot, too, must escape. "Was it a vision or a waking dream?" That is the gnawing "thought" which Keats would escape.

In accord with the principle of proper proportionality, experienced intuitively as a reality by St. Thomas but rationalized as illusion by Keats (to put the philosopher and poet in each other's position), we must turn directly to that principle as rationalized out of speculative knowledge by Thomas. We begin with the poet's problem with indicative and figurative sign, the sign being both the poet's and the philosopher's projection of, or articulation of, understanding toward other intellects. For unless we can become comfortable with *some* dependence of sign in reality, we must continue in that awkward isolation which Eliot recognized in himself and effectively characterized at the outset of his career as poet. We shall find ourselves at best "moved by fancies that are curled / Around these images [floating in intellect], and cling" to them in desperation. That "notion" so clinging may be of some "infinitely gentle / Infinitely suffering thing," but in such Cartesian isolation we are most likely to conclude that the "suffering thing" is but our wishful desire, a waking dream imposed on images that are themselves disjoined from reality and floating free in intellect. We may wish that "suffering thing" were the Perfection of all perfections, but know that wishing is an inappropriate deportment of hope.

The poet makes his attempt to touch that reality which St. Thomas asserts as "the substantial nature of things" which lies hidden "under words," the "figured truth" that "lies hidden under similitudes and figures." He does so through a necessity intuitively recognized, prompting him to words and similitudes and figures: the necessity of a community with beings, a community only properly established when supportive of a final community with Being. It needs saying that such community support is that of a specific member as embodied in temporal circumstances. For what is at issue is the fullness of that member, his own wholeness and not his partial membership in a communal body. That is, what is central to the order and action of community is the Beatitude of the specific, discrete soul, for communal Beatification is not the issue, nor even a possibility. The specific soul, and not souls collectively, is rescued by grace. "It is the human *person*," Maritain reminds us, "who enters society." That person enters as a part of society, "as an individual," in which relationship to society his relationship as member is "inferior to the good of the whole." But as person, as a "spiritual totality referred to the transcendent whole," he is superior "to all temporal societies." That is why one must say that, "With respect to the eternal destiny of the soul, society exists for each person and is subordinate to it" (*The Person and the Common Good*).

It is a confusion of person with social group that results in a variety of "communal" sects in history, Utopian colonies such as those founded out of Puritanism's fractures. In such declensions from the soul's reference as person to the transcendent whole, secular, social ends become final ends. It is pertinent to observe that Eliot's first struggle with this problem involved his overcoming his own Unitarian inheritance. As for the particular soul, opening itself through its community with being toward its own perfection in relation to that ultimate Perfection, God, its resolution of journey in Beatitude: we must say that the journey it embarks upon to that end is a movement ordered by the tensional concern of caring and not caring. As we pursue this tensional paradox, it is well to recognize that to articulate a vision as vision is considerably more difficult in the limits of signs than to articulate a vision concluded an illusion, for reasons largely implicit, but made partly explicit, in St. Augustine's account of his vision at Ostia. Put in another illustration: Dante appears more persuasive in his *Hell* than in his *Paradise*.

7

The Violence and Violations
of Attribution

Our "Romantic" poet, in his growing concern for the relation of his sign to reality in the witness of his poem, may be sorely tempted to seize being by the violence of attribution, as opposed to summoning his soul in an openness to existing creatures. We saw the point dramatized in Keats's odes, especially in his "Ode to a Nightingale." And we found Wordsworth alternately turning to this summoning by intuition and by rational thought in "Tintern Abbey." The loss of his intuitive openness led him to speak of that poem as an elegy. In resisting that loss, he manipulates memory by thought, but it is a thought insufficiently governed by an understanding of the complexity of reality. Still, he exhibits in his made things a recognition of the mystery of intellect itself as the soul's means to an encounter of the existing world during its journey toward a proper end. Even so, that end seems always but vaguely recognized by Wordsworth. Thus he is tempted to simplifications of valid, though partial, perceptions of "nature," of creation. He declares the mind a mansion for all lovely form, leaving unaccounted for the unlovely shadows in nature's decay which so much troubled Keats but to which Hopkins was reconciled as "pied Beauty."

This concern, then, is a continuing motif in what we think of as Romantic poetry, but the same thread stitches the Romantic poet's prose as well, his letters and his criticism. And here we recall once more instances of this concern in Eliot's "dissociation of sensibility" and his insistence on the importance of proper "objective correlatives" to the control of a poem's effect upon a reader. These terms are initially for Eliot critical concepts explicit to poetry, seemingly specific to the technique of composition. They proved, however, to require a philosophical accounting deeper than either craft or an aesthetics unresolved by metaphysics could supply. The deeper cause of a necessity of unified sensibility or of controlled signs was at first obscure to Eliot as poet-critic, for he continued entrapped in history, particularly in the history of Romanticism in English poetry on the one hand and his own history out of Unitarianism on the other. He came to see idea itself as the problem, but beyond history's accounting for it as problem, since it was a problem immediate to his own intellectual actions independent of history. What he recognized at last was that concept, idea, must be proportionate in its significance in intellect to the reality of a proportionality in being itself—to the reality of the present created world, from which world intellect (his own) begins its pursuit of ideas. It is the same world to which it must return after that pursuit if it is not to be alienated unto itself by idea which is the mere shadow of reality falling between intellect and the existential world. He must return to the point of departure and see the world of reality "for the first time."

And so Eliot at first declares the "dissociation of sensibility," the "separation of thought and feeling," to have occurred at about the time of Milton and Dryden. It is with the shock of a recovery to reality that he realizes later that the disjunction is threatening the soul in every moment of the soul's journeying of the finite world—whatever the calendar or geographic coordinates that may locate a particularized, specific soul in the world. It was a recognition awaiting his understanding of the soul as the substantial form of the body, as constituting an essential unity which is indivisible save by our rational conceptualization practiced upon the simple existence of that created entity, the *person*. Such understanding hinges on a distinction which is possible to rational intellect when it yields at last to an understanding beyond knowledge, accepting that understanding as not full—as not comprehensive—of the truth understood, but as a movement toward wisdom. It is a position of the rational intellect whereby it is able, as Keats remarked, to live in uncertainties. Still, it would be as certain as it may, since it would be as perfect as its nature allows. And so it engages the concept *substance* as that concept may be reasonably understood as intrinsic to reality itself.

Substance, a necessary distinction holds, is that which *exists per se*, in one sense of the term *exists*. *Existence per se*, however, is spoken only of God. But there is substance which exists per se through *being*, differing thereby from the existence of God. In consequence of this special nature, this second substance is subject to accidents. That is, substance is a subject to which accidents accrue. This substance is a created being, known to finite intellect most certainly through those accruing accidents. The complicating difficulty to intellect, in its movement from *knowing* intuitively toward *understanding* what it knows, is that accident may be taken as substance by finite intellect through its sensual apprehensions. If its progress toward perfection may be said to move from an intuitive knowing to a rational knowing, the two knowings are to be reconciled by an understanding of the known. But a difficulty lies in the possibility that a progress may be halted by rational knowing. For understanding is, in a sense, knowledge embodied beyond either an initial intuitive or a subsequent discursive, rational knowing. What intellect requires to its health is an understanding of the "substantial unity" which is the nature of the singularly known thing in itself. That unity is seemingly divided into the thing's accidents and essence by the act of conceptualization. Thus by the conceptual action of intellect, the simple thing may seem to lose what is perceived intuitively by the preconceptual action of intellect, namely the thing's substantial unity. The scholastic formulation, in respect to the *essential* unity of an existing thing, is put: "The substantial form is not substance, with the one exception of the human soul. As separated from the body, that soul is an incomplete substance." And so the doctrine derived from this principle: the resurrection of the body is a perfection of the soul's simple being. That is the resolution for rational intellect of the conditions of existence constituting the nature of that creature in nature we speak of as *person* in person's substantial unity. And that is also the theological formulation whereby the distinct nature of man is argued as locating man in creation, from which location he must work out his relation to those created existences, both those like and those differing from his own nature, in relation to his mediate ends toward his final, transcendent end.

By presenting such an extended "scholastic" argument, we do not mean to argue that the given intellect only "finds" itself through exhaustive rational pursuits of the nature of existence. One finds St. Thomas's extended explication of the concept of the soul called *Quaestiones de Anima* of considerable help, of course. But his is not necessarily the only way of the intellect's recovery. Nevertheless, one recognizes the necessity of *some* resolution of such questions, since they trouble intellect as long as it is alive. If one is a poet rather than metaphysician, if one is a Keats or an Eliot rather than a Thomas Aquinas, he is no less haunted by these "questions of the soul" as formalized and explicated by Thomas. They leave him discontent at last with art as a sufficient rescue from the questions. For poetic monuments of unaging intellect leave the poet still disconsolate, since art answers not at all his desire, intuitively stirred in the soul, that the soul move beyond the oblivion which the rational intellect alone would force upon it, in which imposition death is understood as

the cessation of all being. Such a poet is little content with the promise
that his poem will survive in succeeding generations. And it seems little
consolation to end as a "sod" to any nightingale's "high requiem,"
whether that sweet bird be a succession of nature's generations or a
golden bird of art set upon a golden bough in a dream-held Byzantium.
Little wonder that a poet may be only "half in love with easeful death."

Eliot, old in thought, comes at last to his poetic version of St. Thomas's
Quaestiones de Anima, a version very directly and simply put out of his
own faith, and with a confident faith now freed at last from those modernist sophistications of intellect that so long governed his intellectual
actions. " 'Issues from the hand of God, the simple soul' " he begins his
own "Animula." The quoted words are Dante's, from the *Purgatorio*.
That soul, Eliot continues, issues

> To a flat world of changing lights and noise,
> To light, dark, dry or damp, chilly or warm;
> Moving between the legs of tables and of chairs,
> Rising and falling, grasping at kisses and toys.

And so proceeds Eliot's version of Shakespeare's stages of man between
birth and death, put in the context of the accidents of being and coming
in conclusion to a restatement that turns upon the essential, substantial
nature of the soul which lies deeper than the accidents through which it
journeys in order to fulfill the potency of its allotted substantial being:

> Issues from the hand of time the simple soul
> Irresolute and selfish, misshapen, lame,
> Unable to fare forward or retreat,
> Fearing the warm reality, the offered good,
> Denying the importunity of the blood,
> Shadow of its own shadows, spectre in its own gloom.

We said Shakespeare's stages of man, but we might append an anthology, from Oedipus's riddle-solving, to Wordsworth's meditations upon
immortality from recollections of the soul's early issue into nature trailing
"clouds of glory," to Joyce's ironic representation of the child Stephen
baffled by light-dark, dry-damp, chilly-warm. This catalogue is but to
emphasize the persistence of those questions of the soul as we encounter
them in our literary and philosophical history. But that history is no
longer Eliot's concern, except insofar as he must represent the simple soul
as it may suppose itself trapped by history. Even so, it is its own limited

history that constitutes the trap, the accidents inhering, the circumstances round about it. What Eliot is prepared to say now is that this simple soul must continue trapped in its own history so long as it denies the wise "importunity of the blood," that intuitive knowing of a "something" which is beyond its own shadowing by the accidents to its existence. We heard this note earlier in a first awakening in Eliot, in *The Waste Land*. The voice there turns inward in order to turn outward at last, though yet weak in hope. It is "My friend, blood shaking my heart" into an awakening to the necessary openness to existence characterized by *Da*, the necessity to "give" the self by openness. Such a turning is the key that opens time's, history's, dungeon which has long entrapped the soul by its unresolved denial, its "irresolute and selfish" intellectual isolation as described in the early lines of "Animula." This new recovery, celebrated in the "Ariel" poems and in "Ash-Wednesday, is a recovery beyond history, though history must yet be endured, leading to that moving prayer for intercession: "Pray for us now and at the hour of our birth." The hour, that is, of our recovery beyond the death of history's entrapment which the poet so often figures as three score and ten. It is from within that continuing entrapment, though now there are windows and an open door, that one begs, "Teach us to care and not to care / Teach us to sit still / Even among these rocks, / Our peace in His will."

By this point in his journey, Eliot has accepted as the condition to unified sensibilities of intellect the principle of the essential unity of the soul, a unity explicitly denied in "Tradition and the Individual Talent." A recognition of the reality behind that principle is realized fleetingly in "still points" of the turning world, through grace. Such are the recognitions necessary to a recovery of harmony to *person*, the harmony of that substantial unity of the soul from which follows an intellectual harmony proportionately responsive to that turning world. That is why we read "Ash-Wednesday" as Eliot's acting out of his own recovery of unified sensibilities. It has been a recovery made with considerable intellectual agony, within the accidents inhering in that substance: his own soul as issued from the hand of God within the turning world. (One avoids saying issues *into* the world, lest thereby acceding to a Platonic metaphor such as permeates Wordsworth's attempt to recover harmony through the action of poetry, his "Intimations Ode.") Through grace received by a right will, Eliot knows it possible that the soul may issue from history into the hand of God, despite that soul's inclination to fear that "warm reality, the offered good." To refuse grace's offered good leaves the soul a "shadow of its own shadow, spectre of its own gloom," an apt figuring of the soul as entrapped by Cartesian Idealism. This seemingly simple poem, "Animula," is taken as rather naive Eliot by some readers. But it is out of a duration of his own history through the labor of intellect, through which alone, in the light of his particular nature further enlightened by grace, Eliot could come at last to so "simple" a resolution of the questions intellect raises about itself. That his vision is not so simple as it may appear is suggested by its parallel argument which is advanced by Thomas Aquinas in *Quaestiones de Anima.*

In contrast, consider Ezra Pound's late insight into his own errors of attribution that seem even to him in the end possibly a violation of the nature of creation. The habit of attribution builds obstacles to the harmony of his own intellect with itself and with creation, to speak nothing of such intellectual obstructions as obstacles to grace. For attribution depends upon the accidents of being, not upon being itself. And, lest such a term as *grace* seem remote to Pound's own late concerns, let us pursue that concern somewhat as he speaks it. In the fragment called Canto CXVI, Pound laments that he has failed to make "it" cohere, the first point of reference of his "it" being the body of his great poem the *Cantos.* This is Pound speaking at the end of his life. Earlier, his rallying cry to poets has been to "make it new." In that slogan, the *making* and the *new* seem central, the *it* a vague presence, even though the slogan's axis. In the context of our argument, we might ourselves call that *it* rather *being.* Hopkins or David Jones or Eliot (after his *Waste Land*) celebrate this *it* by lifting up things through signs, themselves thereby lifted up. Now what Pound seems concerned with in the end is not so foreign to these poets as we might think, given Pound's early career as maker. He speaks a lamention, having lost an *it* which is more than poetry itself.

What Pound laments in the end is the failure of concept as sufficient to a coherent world. We saw an earlier attempt to make concept sufficient to creation by the poet in Joyce's sympathetic portrait of Stephen Dedalus as artist. Stephen is insistent upon making a world remote from existential reality, as remote as his imagination is capable of making it. In turn as creator of such a world, Stephen would practice a remoteness from it as well, thus escaping both the existential world and the imaginative world. His is a Nietzschean idea of God applied to the artist as god, an appropriation serving a most severe "Romantic" sacrifice. For in that sacrifice, Stephen as the God of his made world, his poem, would be himself "dead" through indifference. Such also is Eliot's "depersonalization" of the poet at its most extreme, though Eliot is somewhat late in realizing the point. By the power of concept, executed in making a "world" (the poem), Pound too would open intellect to a reality more significant than existential reality, that preexisting world as he encounters it through his senses. But art as he would practice it does not so much reject reality in a deliberate Cartesian, Manichean rejection such as Stephen seems intent upon. Though the principle is the same, the power of concept to execute being by autonomous intellect, Pound as maker differs from Stephen as maker in respect to the end he intends to his making. Pound's "made" reality would reconstitute humanity into a civilized body, the City of Dioce. (One cannot escape as significant accidents in those two souls, Pound and Joyce, that one is social, the other aloof and detached; the one gregarious among his fellows, the other jealous to the point of reclusiveness.)

What Pound has required in his early program for the reconstitution of being is, not the philosopher as king, but the poet as king, as does his most immediate Romantic father, Shelley. But now approaching his end, surveying his "it" made by his art, he concludes himself to have been no "demigod," for he had made a world which does not "cohere." At this point there comes to Pound a new intuitive moment in his dark still point of his closed turning world. Retracting the lament that he is no demigod, he looks beyond his made world. The labor of his made world, the *Cantos*, built on the authority of sign reflecting concept's power, he now calls a "great ball of crystal." Then he asks himself no less than his reader, "Can you enter the great acorn of light?" Or has its "light"—its beauty—been destroyed by a "madness" in its maker, Ezra Pound? Here follows the lament that his made world, his great poem, does not cohere, but that lament is followed at once by a resolute "it coheres all right / even if my notes do not cohere." *Notes* is perhaps to be taken in at least a double sense: as notes of music such as Orpheus sang into a world; and as "notes" signifying Pound's labor to rescue what he has believed viable from history, represented in the *Cantos'* aspect as anthology, whether reflecting Confucius or John Adams and a range of other intellectually made worlds between these two intelligences.

But we may observe in this late poetry that it is as if Pound's *it* is somewhat shifted at last beyond a mere reference to that "great ball of crystal" that is his poem, in which he had hoped to read the future. It is as if he has some intimation, out of the work itself, that insofar as he has been true to the good of the thing he made by being open to existence itself, something of value beyond his willed intention of transforming existence yet adheres in his made thing. In the fragment's conclusion he says, "To confess wrong without losing rightness: Charity I have had sometimes." If the *Cantos* do not in the end sustain him, do not justify him, still such a confession has prospect toward virtue in the confessing soul. And in the final lines of the fragment, recalling that virtue of all virtues proper to intellect, Charity, and admitting that he cannot "make it flow through," Pound implies acceptance of this *it* which insistence would have poets "make . . . new." There is a something, an *it*, justifying any making. Now the erratic love, the charity sometimes active in him, requires "A little light, like a rushlight / to lead back to splendour."

The light almost prayed for here is no longer the light of his own intellect. We remarked earlier that this note as struck by Pound is also struck by that poet Pound has roundly excoriated, "olde shepe Wordsworth." Wordsworth, too, had doggedly attempted to make that light of being flow through the signs with which he conjured that light in his "Intimations Ode." Wordsworth laments the loss of a "splendour in the grass," no less than the loss of intimations of something far more deeply interfused, perceived in the high and lofty cliffs along the banks of the Wye. What is lost is the perceived splendour of being, and the loss results in the loss of harmony in the soul so bereft. That is a harmony, so Eliot declared somewhat earlier than Pound's lament (and to Pound's earlier disdain), made possible through a Love at the ever-present center of things, the cause and end of things, the "Word within the word." For Eliot had come to recognize an infinitely gentle, infinitely suffering Thing, through whose offices of love all beings are. And he declares that one knows thereby, one understands thereby, that "all manner of thing shall be well."

In these fragmentary *Cantos* written at the end of his life, Pound at last invokes an aid beyond the limited power of his own intellect, that autonomous power upon which he has risked his all. It is as if he at last calls for a light of grace beyond the light of intellect, through which a "splendour" may be recovered. To put the desire in Thomistic terms, it is as if Pound at last recognizes the necessity to his "natural light" of intellect of that addition of "supernatural light," though he puts it in an understatement that speaks, not irony, but humility: "A little light, like a rushlight." It is a light, Thomas says of it, which "does not proceed from the natural light" of intellect, "but is superadded to it, as if completing it" (*Summa*, I-II, 2, Q8, 2, 2).

The old presumption of the autonomy of intellect supposes that to take intellect as gift is a denigration of the self. That prideful assumption governs Pound as maker almost to the end. In that presumption seems to lie his sense of power as poet, the power of attribution whereby being could be constituted by an imagination in service to autonomous reason. At his end, that confidence leaves him in disorder, incoherent as a person by his own acknowledgment, lost among the accidents of being upon which attribution depends. But there is that faint stirring, a faint recognition that accidents *depend*, not upon the transforming autonomous intellect, the poet's, but in a something that erratically comes to intellect through accident. Perhaps never so often as when one submits through charity, that love which by its nature is an openness toward being itself.

Our emphasis, in respect to man as artisan by his very nature, has emphasized the poet, the user of words. But the principles governing the relation of the maker to the thing he would make, actions dependent from the nature of existence itself, apply in both the liberal and fine arts and in servile arts as well. For in all, the issue is the prudential action of intellect in making, whatever the object as mediate end: the poem, the painting, the garden, the stone wall. In each of the arts, liberal or servile, a failure to govern the making by orienting the intellectual act of making to the reality of existence itself might be discovered, paralleling Pound's recognition at the end of his *Cantos*. For we have so generally lost the governance of action by prudence. An instance with a difference: Picasso on an occasion judges, not so much his art as art, but his cynically exploitative use of his gift as artist: "In art the mass of the people no longer seek consolation and exaltation, but those who are refined, rich, unoccupied, who are distillers of quintessences, seek [rather] what is new, strange, original, extravagant, scandalous. I myself, since Cubism and before, have satisfied these masters and critics with all the changing oddities which have passed through my head, and the less they understood me, the more they admired me. By amusing myself with all these games, with all these absurdities, puzzles, rebuses, arabesques, I became famous and that very quickly. And fame for a painter means sales, gains, fortune, riches. And today, as you know, I am celebrated, I am rich. But when I am alone with myself, I have not the courage to think of myself as an artist in the great and ancient sense of the term. Giotto, Titian, Rembrandt, were great painters. I am only a public entertainer who has understood his times and exploited as best he could the imbecility, the vanity, the cupidity of his contemporaries. Mine is a bitter confession, more painful than it may appear, but it has the merit of being sincere."

The editors of *Crisis* (December 1990) quote the passage in remarking the juror's comment in the Cincinnati trial over the Mapplethorpe exhibition charged as obscene: "It's like Picasso. Picasso from what everybody tells me was an artist. It's not my cup of tea. . . . But if people say it's art, then I have to go along with it." In doing so the exhibitors were exonerated of the charge of obscenity. That Picasso did indeed understand his times is thus underlined. Those "distillers of quintessences," out of a rage for the new, strange, extravagant, scandalous to fill their unoccupied emptiness of intellect and spirit subvert "the mass of people" from the intuitive desire for "consolation and exaltation." What is subverted is that innate, intuitive desire. And Bryan F. Griffin, in *Panic Among the Philistines* (1985), explores the exploitation of the mass of people by these distillers of quintessences who by that distillation make themselves vacuous. The difference between Picasso's confession and Pound's is Pound's realization that his "errors" are not out of a deliberate exploitation but out of failures of the "light of intellect." That is why one, going the long way with Pound to his late lines, has a sense of Pound as a tragic figure, in contrast to Picasso, who in his confession is merely pathetic. His claimed "merit of being sincere" rescues him to our affection not at all. For confession does not thereby obliterate offense or transgression from continuing effects in the complex community of mankind.

8

A "Something" Beyond
Subjective Attribution

St. Thomas's exploration of the principle of proper proportionality, establishing the nature of analogy as reflected in signs, is decisive to the
poet in his address to reality. Here we take a point of departure into
this aspect of the question from Gerald B. Phelan's distinctions between
analogy of attribution and analogy of proper proportionality, made in his
St. Thomas and Analogy. Our concern is a familiar one in modern literary
criticism, though seldom approached from this direction. It is familiar,
since the "Romantic" poet's pursuit of sign suited to the experience of
his existence in nature (which we contend initiated by the intuitional gift
in intellect) is again and again the crucial theme of Romantic art. However
much a poem may engage a narrative, sequential line, or concentrate upon
images out of an object, the thematic center turns again and again to the
validity of consciousness itself in certifying anything, either the intended
object or a sequence of events, or most crucially of all the very existence
of that awareness attempting to certify existence through the marvels of
image and concept. Far from proving reassuring, Descartes' confident assertion—*cogito ergo sum*—undermines whatever confidence residual in
the awareness of its own existence.

We pointed out that Wordsworth's "Tintern Abbey," for instance,
deals with an actual experience pregnant with allegorical suggestiveness.
The actual experience, however, serves only to turn the speaker back upon
his own speaking and thence to thought and the source or medium or
container of thought, his mysterious "mind" as haunted by memory. In
the middle of a journey at a point midway in a river's journey to the sea,
in the middle of the seasons, in (precisely) the middle of a day and at the
middle of an awareness's purported three score and ten: the coincidences

in the experience seem to cry out analogical messages to an awareness housed in a body which at that moment is at rest in the shade of a sycamore tree. All the world around it is bathed in light, wherever the eye turns. The buried question in the experience is whether metaphor is attributive and its origin only the finite intellect, or whether metaphor is fundamentally anchored in existence itself. If in existence, that speaks a unity in creation essential to the nature of existence itself, a "something" deeply interfused in nature as the poem has it. The speaker has intimation of

> A presence that disturbs me with the joy
> Of elevated thoughts; a sense sublime
> Of something far more deeply interfused,
> Whose dwelling is the light of setting suns,
> And the round ocean and the living air,
> And the blue sky, and in the mind of man;
> A motion and a spirit, that impels
> All thinking things, all objects of all thought,
> And rolls through all things.

One cannot, I think, escape in such a passage, first, the sense in this awareness of an encounter with a "presence" at a preconceptual level; and second, an attempt to articulate the experience of that encounter through signs which, though necessarily engaging the accidents of the existential world, struggle nevertheless to go beneath those accidents to a closer proximity of awareness to that "presence."

It is as if Wordsworth would find justified once more the connotations in *image*. Since the time of the Metaphysical poets, a playfulness with the sign as a pawn in wit's employ—for elaborating conceit—increasingly made metaphor a game seemingly divorced from reality. Furthermore, the emerging dominance of empiricism increasingly called in question the authority of sign as related to thing rather than assigned to thing by intellect. If one pretended that his signs were more than arbitrary counters in a reckoning of existence as sheared to merely material existence, he had not learned his Nominalism. Such a use of sign, indeed (inherited from Occam) prepared for the invasion of determinism in Western thought and the increasing panic to that thought which so much characterizes nineteenth century intellectuals as we move through that century. Sign is tolerable, in this inclination of intellect, only as formulaic description, as notation. Even so, there will become apparent in that development the necessity of some acknowledgment that sign reaches toward mystery. Or so the poet would have it. The C in our recent formula $E = MC^2$ will open determinism beyond the merely mechanistic as particle physics develops. And physics itself will presently feel an increasing desire for a metaphysics to make sense of sign as somehow touching upon more than a lifeless mechanics of existence, though intention would limit sign from that threat to intellectual authority.

What we here remember, in our concern for the relation of sign to concept and concept to reality, are confusions resulting from a Nominalistic restriction of sign. Sign was held suspect by the severe rationalist born of that empiricism developed by Enlightenment intellect. Intellect was held suspect if it pretended to any authority beyond the Nominalistic one, assigned by intellect itself—arbitrarily assigned insofar as sign might be attached to material existence. For the poet like Wordsworth to be *disturbed* by *elevated* thoughts which transcended formulaic sign is to experience existence as illusional in its implications, however much a poet might beg the possibility of paradox. Paradox suggests the unresolvable. Yes, says the Romantic poet, as when one attempts to explain the intellectual dilemma of experiencing light as a wave and experiencing it as a sequence of particles in motion. *Paradox*, from the position of the skeptical intellectual who would maintain the authority of intellect as autonomous, is a vague refusal by an uninitiated laity to delay an admission that one rather deals with a *seeming* contradiction, to be resolved in the subsequent discovery by intellect as it operates upon matter with the *ad hoc* instrument, the Nominalistic sign.

Such at least was Wordsworth's early sense of how his own intellectual community stood in its relation to existence, and he objected. As he puts it,

> Our meddling intellect
> Mis-shapes the beauteous forms of things—
> We murder to dissect.

And so to redress that collapse of language to denotative rock bottom so to speak, Wordsworth intends to disturb such presumption. It is here that he proves radically disturbing, not in his poetics as is the more usual approach to his poetry. Looking at Wordsworth as having revolutionized poetry and comparing his radical influence with that of, say, Eliot, a student specializing in literature is likely to wonder: what, in his prosody, justifies such a reputation? His insistence on using "common" language and traditional metrics hardly seems sufficient. Besides which, in poems like "Tintern Abbey" or the *Prelude*, he can hardly be said to use the

language of the street, whether one look to diction or grammar or rhetoric. Nor is his use of the pentameter line radically different.

The common use of language, let me suggest, lies less in the literal appropriation of the language of the street by Wordsworth than in his appropriation of a common address to the experience of reality, depending
upon reality to certify commonality. He depends more on common sense
than common language. It is significant to this point to remember that
such intellectual Thomists as Gilson and Maritain emphasize the point of
departure for rational intellect in its attempt to deal with complex reality:
"common sense." Through common sense, we observe, one deals with
immediate contingency, whether in relation to diplomacy among neigh-
bors or the setting of one's own literal or figurative house in order. To set
one's own house in order means, among other things, carrying away the
garbage, plowing and planting one's garden, repairing broken steps, and
so on. And lest we overlook the point, given our present high concern for
the importance of recovering metaphysical vision to accommodate intellect to reality, such actions are meant first of all as actual actions of a
householder.

We know from experience, our own and our fathers', that a whole complex of structures desirable to human deportment are spoken of analogically, in relation to the discrete person, to the family, and to the immediate community of families through a common language. Nor does
common language in this context have to do with ethnic or geographical
concerns, however much those concerns accrue ethnic or geographical
aspects of our actual experience. One need not live in the desert to respond to advice to build on rock and not in sand. This use of sign bears
a confidence in a common sense that common experiences of existence
justify metaphor beyond the accidents in metaphor that are so tempting
to attribution, attribution often justified in the name of ethnic or geographic or like considerations. The confidence rests fundamentally—
essentially—in the validity of experience as common, through which a
communal consent to sign as more than arbitrary is established in the
sign. It is of course evident that, given the anchor of sign in the accidents
of being, those accidents in time obscure the essence experienced, so that
a provinciality through sign begins to distort the common aspect. Still,
there is necessarily present in such use of sign, even if residual to the
discrete intellect, a knowledge that sign is not arbitrary.

Indeed, when the rational intellect has lost this recognition, the paro-
chial or provincial testimony to the commonality—to tribal possession of
truth—results in reactions. Tribal violence no less than tribal ceremony
has origin in this dimension of common experience, no doubt. Signs and

ceremony thus decay, and this inevitability leads Eliot to proclaim at a point of advance decay in the history of the West that it is his responsibility as poet to attempt to "purify the dialect of the tribe." He understands that to require the recovery of the sign in its relation to the reality of experience common to the tribe, the purification eschewing arbitrary manipulation of signs if one is to recover the common experience of reality through which community renews the intellectual and spiritual vitality in its discrete members. Such a restoration of dialect, it must be added, requires a recovery *through* the particulars of the local and the particulars of inherited experience, a recovery of what is too loosely spoken of as "tradition." For the *tradition* here at issue is freed of the restrictions of mere history or mere geography, without rejecting the immediacy of this time and this place as experienced by this discrete intellect. To reject the immediate in the interest of a generalized, universal community is to reject reality itself in that gnostic deportment whereby reality is distorted by intellectual presumption beyond intellectual finitude. Such is the difference one might make between that intellect typical of secular utopianism which is truly provincial and that intellect which is more accurately spoken of as "regional" or local in our defense of reality. And surely this is the recognition Eliot has come to when he affirms that our journey signifies a recovery of reality when we "arrive where we started / And know the place for the first time."

Ezra Pound might well have reflected further on this prospect upon reality, since in discovering the implications beyond pragmatic, literal acts of intellect he would exercise in establishing the order of community, he might have moved beyond the gnostic uses to which he turned Confucius. Perhaps here he made a fundamental error which comes back to haunt him. For, charged with lacking a "metaphysics," he responded that to the contrary such was explicit in arguments from *The Great Digest* in such passages as the following:

> The men of old wanting to clarify and diffuse throughout the empire that light which comes from looking straight into the heart and then acting, first set up good government in their own states; wanting good government in their own states, they first established order in their own families; wanting order in the home, they first disciplined themselves; desiring self-discipline, they rectified their own hearts; and wanting to rectify their hearts, they sought precise verbal definitions of their inarticulate thoughts; wishing to attain precise verbal definitions, they set to extend their knowledge to the utmost. This completion of knowledge is rooted in sorting things into organic categories. (Pound's translation)

Put in such a sophisticated structure, Pound may have overlooked our point: what he is describing is the first necessity in common sense itself, the sense of a necessity of order in response to experience. Even his final sentence here lies yet considerably short of metaphysics, such ambiguous words as "organic categories" requiring a considerable attention in relation to "precise verbal definition." His desire for precision toward certainty becomes increasingly problematic, given the complex relation of concept to thing that requires a metaphysical accounting.

One might, I believe, argue—given world enough and time—that Wordsworth's concern is closer to that expressed by Pound's Confucius than is at first apparent. The rectifying of heart in its relation to head, lest head be left free to murder for the sake of dissecting, is central to him. And so he must deal with an immediate experience not easily reconciled by thought through precise verbal definitions. He experiences himself as *disturbed* by *joy*, an effect seemingly contrary to our expectations of the effect sprung from *joy actual*. To be so disturbed is to be affected within intellect itself, and the effect has as cause an intellectual sense, "a sense sublime," of having actually experienced a "presence" in created things, a presence *deeper* than and *beyond* (for such are the weaknesses of precise verbal descriptions of experience which we must nevertheless use)— deeper and beyond rational formalisms directed by intellect toward things. Thus there emerges a sense of remoteness in the "quiet" of the skies. And recollection of bounding beside the "deep" rivers in Cumberland carries in *deep* more than a yardstick's measure. Wordsworth is castigated for bathos when he remarks a bit of water which is "six feet long and three feet wide," though he may make arresting use of banal detail on occasion. If not arresting as poetry, nevertheless touching upon the mystery he attempts by poetry. Consider his "We Are Seven." Talking with a "simple Child," he is unable to dislodge her from her account. Though two of her siblings lie in churchyard, the child still counts them present. Such is the inadequacy of merely verbal reckoning, in relation to our actual experience of existences. It is an inadequacy of word to thing which Wordsworth will capture more persuasively in "A Slumber Did My Spirit Seal" and in "Surprised by Joy." It is in this latter sonnet that *joy* becomes a disturbing joy to the poet, as the "simple Child" is not disturbed by her own continuing joy in being one of seven, the alive and the dead.

As for that "something deeply interfused" in creation, which impinges upon the attempt to witness that something through verbal signs: Wordsworth knows rationally that he has experienced a "something" through his sensual response to things. It is through the senses that image is acquired, wherefrom by conceptual action image must be ordered by sign, by word. Thus the mystery he must contend with: words struggle, in the grasp of thought, with an experience known anterior to both thought and words. And the words most amenable to a witness of that anterior experience are those with little of the denotative about them. It is this aspect of Wordsworth's language which led Aldous Huxley to write a devastating essay, "Wordsworth in the Tropics," whose burden is that Wordsworth's images have little of the force made popular in Huxley's day by the Imagist Movement. Huxley is right, but given our concern his point is rather beside the point at issue. His is a concern which only a vigorous, young, modernist intellect with an eye to Epicurean joy could conclude so dismissively. Wordsworth's concern seems rather to show that to limit sign to sensual literalness as the only purview of sign is to mistake a means as an end. It is a mistake which intellect itself feels uncomfortable with, as Aldous Huxley's own subsequent intellectual career will show.

The denotative literalness of image became an obsession among the lesser figures of the Imagistic Movement, to Ezra Pound's impatient disgust. It is an aspect of that movement which relates it more to a Nominalistic ancestry, mediated to it by eighteenth-century Enlightenment, than to the nineteenth-century resurgence of intuitive mysticism in the "Romantic" poet. Put another way, Eliot's concern for proper objective correlative is pushed to an extreme by the Imagist poet in an attempt at a precise verbal definition of his own impression of an object. Thus it ceases to be objective. It leaves that poet with the dubious accomplishment of a private poem, which to him may well be empirically precise through a restricted response of his feeling toward an object. It may well strike others, however, as merely subjective. There had already appeared in poetry an elevation of subjectivism, in a more sophisticated movement, that of the Symbolists, to whom Eliot is early inclined because intellectually superior to Imagism. Of course much later, in "From Poe to Valléry," he will argue a dead end inevitable to such a principle when exercised as a philosophical ground of a poetics. The variety of poetic movements from the mid-nineteenth century to our own day, represented here by Symbolism and Imagism, are responses to that entrapment of the poet by Cartesian Idealism: Symbolist, Imagist, Vorticist, Objectivist and other "movements" are attempts of intellect to "move" to a recovery of reality lost to intellect.

One thing these movements have in common: an attempt to reconcile intuitive desire to intellectual rationalism. They are highly sensitive to any suggestion of mystical implications that might require metaphysical perspective, depending instead on the authority of autonomous intellect. This dependence leads to the justification of subjectivism on scientific grounds, out of Cartesian Idealism. And that justification seems increasingly supported by the deterministic persuasiveness of physical and biological sciences as they emerge as authorative through Darwinian principles. They are further supported by the individualistic principle in egalitarian social and political institutions. And so in this respect these modernist poets prove prophetic of the dissolution of community that appears at our century's end to offer the "individual" only collapse into the chaos of a pluralism in respect to community. In that extreme pluralism, each individual is his own state and the king of that state. I mean *individual* here, of course, in counterpoint to our concept of *person* anchored metaphysically. Our contention is that only such an anchor promises a restoration of community beyond the Confucian ordering of "Organic categories" which may be established only through intellectual power divorced of metaphysical vision.

It is metaphysical vision, such is our contention, that makes possible an accommodation of intellect to mystery beyond finite and thus limited *comprehension*. It is mystery which intuitively the "Romantic" poet wishes rescued to an intellectual respect. Consider Wordsworth then as a resurgent mystic in "Tintern Abbey." *Light, setting, blue, motion, object, thought*: such words struggle in concert, as if to burst the arrested, denotative, formulaic restrictions upon sign imposed by rationalism. In those words a struggle goes on, in respect to the reality of experience, against a merely "subjective," and so "fanciful" intrusion of intellect upon the experience. For subjective fancy brings an attributive confusion to sign which is as destructive of reality as is the Nominalistic stringency on sign. *Elevated, sublime, dwelling, setting*: such signs seem to take advantage of the experience, as if to "half create" what has been only "half perceived" by intellect through the senses. For there continues a conviction to intellect that it has experienced in the past, and is even now experiencing, a "motion and a spirit, that impells," that "rolls through all things."

In these words from "Tintern Abbey" we find anticipated subsequent echoes, specifically those in that "Lucy" poem that follows the intrusion of death. It is a death more immediate to Wordsworth's experience than that encountered in "We Are Seven." The death close at hand will call in question the visionary witness of "Tintern Abbey," and the consciously repeated words are self-accusing by a shocked intellect for whom those words bear only a denotative meaning, edged with shocked bitterness. "Tintern Abbey's" visionary dimension is thereby declared to have been illusional. The dead child becomes a dead object, a "thing" with no "motion." She is "rolled round" indifferently in a mechanistic universe with "rocks and stones and trees." The earlier sense of a deeply infused presence comes to be seen now as caused by a "slumber" of the poet's "spirit," self-sealed from stark reality. From his later perspective, the speaker of "Tintern Abbey" seems to Wordsworth to have deluded himself by subjective attribution. Any "presence" in existence separate from that of his own intellect seems now at best a projected chimera. And this is the state of that little world of lone awareness which Eliot presents in his "Preludes," whose title by allusion touches upon Wordsworth's great attempt at a metaphysical poem, his *Prelude* to *The Excursion*, the attempt at an epic account of the poet's mind. In his "finger exercises" with images, Eliot suggests it impossible to relate the presence of images in an awareness to the actual existence of things as distinct from those images disjoined from whatever things there *may* be. The reading of the poet's mind in Eliot's "Preludes" and in Wordsworth's "A Slumber Did My Spirit Seal" are depressingly similar.

9

The Habit of Heresy

Neither Wordsworth nor Eliot welcome the conclusion seemingly forced upon them—that sign is attributive, applied to existence by the paint brush of concept whose source is awareness: an awareness which can find no convincing faith in its relation to existence separate from itself, being therefore a closed monad. Our perspective, from the position taken by Thomistic realism, yields a more satisfactory solution to this dilemma experienced by awareness when we speak of a relation of intellectual action to the spiritual dimension of the *person*, a context which modernism would disallow. But modernism disallows the position less on the ground that the Thomistic position is unreasonable, one suspects, than because it recognizes that the Thomistic position threatens the comfort of intellectual autonomy. This is but to say that modernism is Pelagianism secularized, a position which when called to account requires of the Pelagian— the "modern gnostic" in Eric Voegelin's term—that he restructure his thought from a new grounding in the preconceptual experience of truth which he must confess as actual. Such a new position makes intellect dependent in a manner which autonomous pride finds difficult to accept.

Now we both hear and say much of the necessity of virtue as a habit, even among Pelagians, who are likely to be activists in the social and political arenas. But we would do well to hear more of the habit of heresy, a violation of the truth of experience itself as a defensive protection by Pelagian intellect in its strategic defense against realism. One might multiply instances of this judgment, but we need only remark a present disarray among those intellectuals in the West who have been long committed to Marxism, following the collapse of Eastern Europe and the accelerating chaos in the Soviet Union. For the principles supporting social and political Pelagianism in the West are more derivative of Marxist ideology than of Christian charity. Sin against social order is deplored by the Pelagian—or drug abuse or even gluttony if it can be related to wasting natural resources rather than wasting the soul.

What is missing in our concern is a critique of the established heretical habit in intellect itself, a steady violation of reality. The violations are reflected in disturbing ways, as for instance in the shibboleth used to defend abortion, "the right of choice," which so clearly underlines the operative principle of Pelagianism: self autonomy. That principle can in the end be defended only on the ground of the self's intellect as autonomous, such a radical pluralism that community is possible only through a strict, literal contract. In the end this means an isolation of that self except insofar as it is convenient to acknowledge other autonomous selves. Of course some are more autonomous than others, depending upon the power commanded.

The Pelagian habit of heresy against reality is the most formidable obstacle to the recovery of intellect to reality, and never more clearly evident than in our attempts to overcome social problems such as drug abuse or abortion. For any suggestion that solutions are to be found in a recovery of the reality of the intellect's spiritual responsibility to creation will seem partly conceded by the strategy of obfuscating that suggestion. What results, however, is a dislocation of the implications of sinfulness as specific to the soul. *Sin*, taken as a metaphorical term only, is then rested in another metaphorically taken "thing": the social "body." But the *social body* is accepted as if a term descriptive of an empirically established entity. Thus the manipulators of being take advantage of whatever residual sense of sin remains in us, a sense out of actual experience by the discrete person. The spiritual context of *sin* is thus shifted to temporal context, as the *social body* becomes preeminent over communal spirit. That such is our present state of intellect might be summed by analogy. I write these lines in Lent, during which the discipline of fasting is important to the reordering of the soul. That is the orthodox position, still granted a certain "tradition" in our habits spiritual, though more in the interest of Mardi Gras than the forty-days sojourn in any wilderness. Mardi Gras is not followed by the season of fasting except by a few. Yet the *many* are much exercised by the necessity of fasting, a disquieting concern for that necessity bombarding us at every hand. Not a fasting toward reconciliation with the God of all existences, however, but toward reconciliation with a new, ambiguous god discovered by us through science's knowledge. We must fast to placate that new dark god in the blood of our body, cholesterol. Thus what is left of our spiritual concern is focused on our material nature; as our social concern is focused upon the structure of that intellectually established entity, the state, the *body* commanding each person's ultimate obeisance.

Our spiritual dimension is touched only indirectly as a sociological consideration. The secular Pelagian thus makes use of a residual, vestigial spiritual concern in persons now dislocated to a temporal focus by treating the concern collectively, focusing the concern upon "society," as opposed to the real center to that concern, the spiritual state of the discrete soul. Thus essential concerns are transformed in their accidents and imposed on a false being, the body social. And the argument is concluded at last by the reduction of our concern to signs, to words, habitually responded to in a response to social disorders. Television advertisements announce the millions of days lost to grammar school children because of the common cold, and sell a variety of cold formulas. The number of work days lost through drug abuse; the number of lives lost through accidents caused by drunk drivers; the number of "lives" lost if teenage pregnancy isn't solved through sympathetic consent to abortion on demand— one could extend the list of "factual" evidences to support Pelagian heresy, but what is most usual as the final and presumed most persuasive fact is the actual monetary cost to the body social, the cost in tax monies.

Or consider another aspect of our manipulation by Pelagian secularism. The latest discoveries about the effects of animal fat or cholesterol is reported in the prestigious *New England Journal of Medicine*, leading to dietary alarms to the general public. Whereupon, the latest scientifically justified solution: solid or liquid substitutes, dressed as only the camera is capable of dressing them, in a celebration of the body's salvation through what seems a perpetual Mardi Gras. The ads for such products are produced more elaborately than most of the program fare they pay for on your favorite TV channel. A sexy performer performs sexily because she drinks Brand X. Or an aging athlete has recovered his body's prowess by drinking or eating magic potions. Such is the new "Mass" celebrating the human body, its litany most various.

Not the expense of spirit is at issue, but the expense of body, body elevated to the metaphorical as in *social body*. But the concept derives in actuality from the individual's fear for his actual body, whether in respect to crime in the streets or the devastation of body by cancer or AIDS. One does, of course, care about such concerns as they affect the body social. But one may not, as a realist, consent to a Manicheanism secularized on the authority of autonomous intellect in its late Pelagian stage of development, because that position dislocates the soul from reality. Its ultimate reduction is that of the much lamented and little understood "materialism" that characterizes Western society. It is a condition symptomatic, this materialism, and what it is symptomatic of is the dislocation of intellect from reality whereby accident is taken as substance. If the spiritual dimension of existence is to be recovered to our intellectual seeing, we must reform intellect so that substance is not dismissed as accident (as in the argument that spiritual concerns are remnants of antiquated superstition) or accident affirmed as substance (as when the question of abortion depends on a woman's "right" to her own body).

This is seemingly an aside from our concern for the poet's intuition in pursuit of that philosopher's principle of proper proportionality which is revealed by the structure of reality perceived by the unified intellect, by sensibilities reassociated. But we need only be reminded that such concerns, though not in our specific terms as here advanced, were very much a part of Wordsworth's and Eliot's concerns as poets. It is a concern to the poet which he must deal with in relation to the question of whether, as poet, his office is vatic or prophetic, and if so in what manner that office is to be properly ordered so that he not violate the nature of art itself. It is no accident that for Eliot, Dante is the great poet; nor that for Dante, Virgil is so. But from Virgil to Eliot the position of the poet in relation to the "social body" is recognized by poets as increasingly complex. A Virgil would justify Caesar to Rome; a Dante would justify the poet himself to office of leading the wandering soul back to the true way. Milton would justify God's ways to man. Eliot, in that tradition, discovers his most effective role as poet to be that of bearing witness to himself, to his own intellectual and spiritual journey through nature, burdened by history. And it is in this that he shares an understanding of the poet's calling with Wordsworth.

Not that Eliot isn't often direct, assuming a conspicuously vatic stance through poetry, but that is a characteristic of his less successful poetry *as* poetry. This is to remark a difference between, say, his "Choruses" from *The Rock*, or "Coriolan" or the fragments of *Sweeney Agonistes* and the remaining poetry from *Prufrock* through *Four Quartets*. Similarly with Wordsworth: he is more effective as poet, and so as vatic poet, in his *Prelude* and "Tintern Abbey" and some of that earlier work, as well as in that great, sad poem, the "Intimations Ode," than in some of his deliberately vatic poetry. Still, we must recognize that at the center of his best poetry, as in Eliot's, is his concern for the spiritual nature of existence, his own and the world's. That he becomes distressed when his contemporaries refuse that center needs only our recalling those few lines from one of his lesser poems, already introduced, his sonnet addressed to Milton lamenting England "a fen / Of stagnant waters" where "altar, sword, and pen, / Fireside, the heroic wealth of hall and bower / Have forfeited. . . inward happiness," having abandoned a "cheerful godliness." Still, he bears surer witness to the loss in "It Is a Beauteous Evening" than in his address to Milton or in "The World Is too Much with Us." It will be Eliot who gives fuller witness to our stagnant waters in *The Waste Land*, as it will be Eliot who stirs those stagnant waters of the spirit in his "Ash-Wednesday," both poems very English in respect to place, even explicitly situated in London. But place has come to be understood beyond the accidents of place to the discrete soul. At his best, Wordsworth plumbs accidents for substance, which is why Eliot, when he turns himself from accident to substance, will declare Wordsworth "more deeply Aristotelian" than Coleridge. Wordsworth is the most "philosophical" of English poets, concerned (along with Coleridge) with poetry as the mode in sign whereby intellect may best express "a totality of unified interests." For, Eliot says in a note appended to this lecture in which he praises Wordsworth, the "history of English poetry" reveals "the splitting up of personality." Wordsworth, in opposing that splitting, is concerned for a reassociation of sensibilities such as would effect an integration of *person*. Indeed, one might suggest (as we have been doing) that Wordsworth at his most perceptive is more Thomistic than Aristotelian. He is, in intuitive moments, on the borders of that country in which proper proportionality reflects the order of creation in relation to its creator.

For the poet as for any intellect, the basis of true analogy must be located in the proportion existing between essence and existence as encountered in things taken singularly. Such an approach is crucial to his figurative use of sign if he would anchor sign in reality through his conceptual actions. First one must see the thing itself as intellect may do in accord with its nature as intellect. In thinking about what is seen, in that action of conceptualization, one must seek a measure of proportionate being first within the thing itself—the primary level from which intellectual action proceeds—and not merely attempt a measure of one thing against another, lest the accidents of existence to any two separate things bound in metaphor confuse one's penetration to being which is necessary to understanding. For the relating of one thing to another as the initiating move in analogy becomes so entangled by the accidents of being in disparate things that attribution becomes the nature of the analogy so attempted.

The recognition of likeness in unlike things, the basis of analogy, if approached at the immediate level of accident may have a limited convenience to intellect as it traverses the world of accidents. But that use is an arbitrary one, not fundamental. We agree that *red* means *stop*, *green* means *go* in our managing of traffic. One might even, with ingenuity, argue for some fundamental grounding relating the specific color to specific action. But common sense at least suggests the convention an arbitrary one, like that of driving on one side of the road in one country, the other in another. The continuous necessity of the movement of city traffic justifies such arbitrary convention, which depends on common consent whereby the arbitrary becomes conventional. But, to put the matter at an extreme, the use of sign to direct traffic flow and the use of sign sacramentally, as in the Mass or—more appropriate to our distinction—the sacrament of marriage are self-evidently different in the grounding of sign. This distinction is self-evident even to one who rejects any use of sign as sacramental. But in a general rejection of sign as sacramental, there will emerge as necessary at least an arbitrary use of sign. Such is required for a modicum of social order. At least civil marriage as governed by common consent to arbitrary signs is necessary in directing the traffic of lives in the polis.

We are suggesting, in such observations, that there is a necessary relation of sign to reality, understood fundamentally by intellect in its discovery of its own ordering as affected by the order of reality. This is to say, then, that in this recognition lies a possible discovery that the use of sign to whatever end requires a sacramental orientation of intellect: there is a piety required of one in his intellectual response to existence, a piety developed in a hierarchy of attention to reality, culminating properly in the formal sacraments. There is a recognition of this necessity, whether or not oriented formally through sacramental observances, in many poets, even those not ordinarily thought of as "religious" poets.

One might well look, from this perspective upon sign in service to ordering person, at the recent poetic address to existences subsumed under the rubric of *environmentalism*, in which movement there is a stirring of that recognition which usually lacks the support of a metaphysics that might orient it sacramentally. The movement is heavy with poets in its membership. But the environmentalist might discover his best poet to be David Jones, rather than some of the radical rhyming activists associated with the movement. Jones, in his introduction to that great but neglected poem *Anathemata*, expresses the point of and the importance of sacramental piety toward existing things. That piety rises to the sacrament of ordinate consummation of desire in the Mass, wherein meet things with that Thing of all things. Jones says, in explaining the title of his great poem, taking his term from St. Luke to express the soul's full deportment to all that is not itself by a "lifting up":

> I mean by my title as much as it can be made to mean, or can evoke or suggest, however obliquely: the blessed things that have taken on what is cursed and the profane things that somehow are redeemed: the delights and

also the 'ornaments', both in the primary sense of gear and paraphernalia and in the sense of what simply adorns; the donated and votive things, the things dedicated after whatever fashion, the things in some sense made separate, being 'laid up from other things'; things, or some aspect of them, that partake of the extra-utile and of the gratuitous; things that are the signs of something other, together with those signs that not only have the nature of a sign, but are themselves, under some mode, what they signify. Things set up, lifted up, or in whatever manner made over to the gods. ("Preface," July 1951, *Anathemata*)

In this impassioned definition, David Jones characterizes the deportment required of this rational creature man toward existence, including his own. Intellect is that special gift toward ordering such a deportment to being, first his own and then, communally, an address as a body whose head, as Jones affirmed, is Christ. We are saying that this deportment of address to being is sacramental in its nature, through which ordering alone is it possible to follow that first and great commandment that we love God properly, thereby properly loving all his creation, with all our heart and all our soul and all our mind.

The alternative as we find it widely evident in our age is but the studied reduction of this commandment so that autonomous intellect may supplant God as authority justifying that commandment. In our deportment as persons and as collections of persons, we still echo the openness required of our finitude as creatures to the cause of our existence as creatures, even as we deny the proper end of that deportment. With all our heart and soul and mind we incline to a habit of obeisance to Pelagian manipulations of the principle of intellectual order toward perfections. We reduce heart to instinct, mind to computer function, soul to the psychological matrix of the instinctive (biological), formulaic (deterministic abstractionism). Such mystical account of being by autonomous intellect allows our replacing God as the end of our becoming with our own arbitrary power. The habits of virtue proper to an existence as person are supplanted by habits of consent to arbitrary authority, insofar as that authority possesses a sufficient power to dictate habit. What we only begin to recognize slowly, out of intuitive desire, is that the arbitrary power based in a faith in mechanistic determinism and operating by sign arbitrarily used, replaces that Cause of being in whom "arbitrariness" is more properly called "Love." Nominalism as a principle, desired by arbitrary intellect in its gnostic inclinations, is itself still a faint echo of that true principle to which one comes at last by understanding the structure of reality. By contemplation one moves beyond that understanding:

Nominalism as an arbitrary principle in respect to signs is a true principle
to signs only as attributable to God as arbitrator. To recognize the point
is to approach that mystery whereby man is said created in the image of
God. It will be also to see that Nominalism is an attempted usurpation of
God's perogative as Perfect Being.

Meanwhile, the presumption of a "Nominalist authority" which is
proper only to God—the presumption of arbitrary authority in the making of things through arbitrary management of the names of things—
fosters dictatorships, large and small. The smallest, let us say, is that dicta-
tion of the discrete person through its own willful intellect whereby the
magnitude of person is self-reduced. We have suggested Eliot's Prufrock
as representative of such a dictatorship, his intellect willfully defensive
against any action other than a falling away from being into strange
"chambers of the sea" drowning awareness itself. Larger dictatorships en-
large therefrom, our own century overflowing with such, whether established by the single intellect or a committee of intellects capable of exercising a sufficient power over those whose habits of submission to
authority have been relocated from a proper object. By habit as mere
mechanism, the soul loses the proper object in whom authority rests,
God. The relation between the manipulator and the manipulated, we must
say, constitutes a co-conspiracy, whereby the possessor of arbitrary authority through power and the losers of personal power through intellectual consent to arbitrary authority together establish those false versions
of community that have plagued the body spiritual increasingly since the
Renaissance. Once more, it is through his recognition of this condition to
our modernist civilization that Eliot speaks in declaring that the poet's
task in our time has been to "purify the dialect of the tribe," restoring
community to health by the restoration of sign itself to a proportionate
authority in respect to being. Such is his opposition to the modernist
determination of sign by arbitrary intellect itself. The restoration of sign
is through a recovery of a vision of the structure of reality understood in
proper proportionality.

10

Dilemma in Likeness and Unlikeness

We have depended often on Eliot as a figure representing the modernist intellect as it gradually finds itself beyond gnostic, Pelagianist reductions of its person. It is a recovery Eliot acts out in his poetry. Not that he set out with such an intention, but one need only observe the changing use he makes of the "mask," of personae as voice, in that poetry to discover his growing discovery. The speaking voice of "The Hollow Men" does not dissociate the poet in his actual person, as the irony of "Prufrock" attempts to do. And by "Ash-Wednesday" we may put it that Eliot speaks as spiritual citizen of our age. He speaks to us, but also *for* us to that Cause of being in whom he rests his faith, as he has guarded against doing up to that time.[9] By the time of the *Quartets*, finding the "whole earth . . . our hospital / Endowed by the ruined millionaire," he is prepared to say as well that now he knows that the "poetry does not matter / It was not . . . what one had expected." What "one" had expected, if that one were the Eliot of earlier years, was a rescue of intellect through its manipulation of sign. But what is being said in these words from *East Coker* is not that poetry no longer matters, but that it matters in a different way from what Eliot "had expected." For it is clear, if one study the craftsmanship evident in the *Four Quartets*, that Eliot is still concerned, as he had been earlier, with the good of the thing he would make through reason in the action of his making. What is changed is that he now sees a quite different end implied for the maker in respect to his action. For his making now is in response to a Calling larger than his art. This was a lesson Eliot did not learn easily, causing him such spiritual turmoil as to leave him almost a victim to despair. If art is not sufficient to rescue the artist, still art is the responsibility of his calling. He must learn to care for his art, but also not to care for it; he must reconcile himself to this paradoxical circumstance of the soul in its accidental condition of being proved agonizing to the poet's intellect. For it is not easy to re-orient intellectual habits long practiced by the authority of intellectual autonomy, even when one is prepared to admit a necessity to do so. That is why Eliot says, in "Second Thoughts about Humanism" (1928), "Rational assent [to orthodox dogma] may arrive late, intellectual conviction may come slowly, but they come inevitably without violence to honesty and nature. To put the sentiments in order is a later and an immensely difficult task: intellectual freedom is earlier and easier than complete spiritual freedom."

As Eliot discovered, if one insist that only through a metaphysical grounding in the practical intellect may the accidents of existence be dealt with in both an orderly and proportionate way in worldly activity, then that insistence at once encounters the entrenched Pelagian habits of our secular gnostic intellects. (In Eliot's experience, the encounter was first with the humanism grown out of Babbitt's and Santayana's persuasive arguments. Eliot's two essays on humanism are helpful to our understanding both the nature of that humanistic authority and Eliot's struggle to extricate his own thought from it. See both the essay quoted above and "The Humanism of Irving Babbitt," 1927.) To grant as a given to intellect a visionary, an intuitive, recognition of being out of which that intellect develops conceptual analogy suited to the writing of a poem (or even the direction of city traffic for that matter) is to endanger the established attributive authority available to "intellectual freedom." That established authority is most reluctant to give its rational assent. For, as Fr. Phelan says in *St. Thomas and Analogy*, the true analogy consequent in conception when intellect is properly ordered to the structure of reality—properly ordered to the proportionality *in* things themselves—is insistent in its requirements, being independent of intellect. Intellect must recognize that "the analogated perfection be not univocal either in its *being* or in the *concept* of it, but . . . that it both exist intrinsically in all of the analogies and in each according to a different mode."

In such a proposition lies the argument for a community of intellect in which poet and politician alike participate, according to the peculiar gifts definitive of person. It is a proposition requiring consent to an intellectual vision of the nature of reality, not by an arbitrary imposition of dogma, as if the opening to such a vision by the rational explorations of a St. Thomas were instead merely attributive authority decreed by the Pope. Eliot chastises this very superficial caricature of his own intellectual estate in 1928 when he says in "Second Thoughts about Humanism": "Most people suppose that some people, because they enjoy the luxury of Christian sentiments and the excitement of Christian ritual, swallow or pretend to swallow incredible dogma." His point is that such dogma is not incredible when understood as also testified to by the structure of reality itself, available to free intellect, but only through an intellectual conviction that comes slowly by an intellectual labor which does not commit "violence to honesty and nature." We should remark here incidentally that this point is one Eliot will have encountered in the works of Cardinal Newman, and we recall Eliot's saying that the philosophical and theological issue of Wordsworth's thought comes to fruition in Newman's writings.

Fr. Phelan's remark emphasizes an important point: the necessity that intellect recognize that concept—that is, awareness formalized in relation to thing—is anchored in reality independent of any intellectual act through concept. This recognition is crucial to the poet, governing as it does his analogy when rightly taken. But the concept of likeness in unlikeness is not the poet's peculiar responsibility. It is also the scientist's concern, whether social, political, or physical scientist. It is the responsible concern of any intellect to value an essential unity as primarily in the existent thing, to be reflected by any analogy, whether the thing which intellect focuses upon is the atom or the state.

It follows from this recognition that the proper unity in any instance of a "scientific" making, whether of a poem or of a city government, must be in accord with the diversity incorporated by the principle of proper proportionality, if analogy is not to violate reality. The proportionate accord in analogy must reflect the nature of diverse entities taken each in itself. The specific natures of entities—discretely existing things—are determined by the relation of the specifically actual to the potential within the specific nature of the discrete thing. That is the ground in which the order of making is to be discovered by intellect, without which initiating ground the order made is in some degree attributive and so arbitrary. The structure of concept is more or less in accord with the structure of reality, depending upon whether the making more or less derives from the reality of proportionate being in things as things rather than from attributive action of intellect. A concert of things directed by intellect through concept is authoritative only insofar as that concern for a music of order to intellect originates in reality and not in an intellect which imposes order arbitrarily upon the reality which it engages through concept.

Likeness in unlike things, then, in respect to conceptual analogy, depends properly upon that *essential* unity in the thing which intellect is never content to ignore, even though it may not recognize its intuitive awareness of that unity as necessary to analogy. Analogy is a structuring of signs in correspondence to a vision of the structure of reality itself and not a structuring of that reality. Under the pressure of its desire for a rest in perception of unity, intellect may very well be inordinately inclined to half construct what it only half perceives. For under that pressure, born of intuitive hope, intellect is easily tempted to an authority of concept as governing actuality. Such is its hunger for understanding, a proper hunger but one which must be satisfied without intellectual violence to the "food" it requires, the structure of reality *seen* but not *made* by intellect. By concept, intellect may attribute likeness in unlike things and assume thereby a structuring of being by the intellectual act of conceptualization. What may well result therefrom is a conceptual structure through analogy understood (explicitly or implied) by the coloring of "fancy," to echo Coleridge on the problem. What intellect is left with in that event is not a vision but a waking dream. From our late intellectual confidence in such matters, our modernist position, we are likely to look at Aristotle and his concerns as at least primitive, if not outmoded. But it is in recognition of this intellectual danger through fancy that he would have one always test concept by the experience of reality, a timeless wisdom to intellectual operations. One moving from a definition of *cow*, arrived at after repeated experiences of particular creatures sharing likeness in their unlikenesses, nevertheless is understood as required to continue a testing of the concept *cow* empirically, even as one uses that concept. That is perhaps the most fundamental legacy of Aristotle to Thomas. For both understand that what is important is not what a concept says of reality, but what the truth of things, the actuality of reality, is.

What we are insisting upon, along with Aristotle and St. Thomas, is actuality, the way things are. And then we affirm that this reality governs analogy. It does so through intellect's *insight*, its *seeing into* the particular actuality. Seeing the thing itself, Thomas says, is to perceive the essence of the thing. And by that insight, by the seeing into the thing—or in Hopkins's term by encounter with the *instress* of the thing—one is thereby intellectually prepared to embrace the accidents adhering to the thing because of its nature and not mistake them as inhering in the apprehending senses of the responding intellect. That is, intellect may avoid confusion of accident radically taken by intellect as the essence of the thing, rather than those accidents accrued by virtue of its essence. Such seems a most elementary requirement, easily consented to upon reflection, yet it is a consent so variously denied with the rise of modernist thought that we feel compelled to restate it as fundamental to intellectual action. We might be minded, given its elementary, "primitive" (as opposed to "sophisticated") nature, of that child's game once popular. The director of the game, who is also the object toward whom the players move, gives directions: take two giant steps, three frog-hops, and so on. What is necessary, if the player is not to be required to go all the way back to the starting point, is his preamble to the action granted: "Mother, may I?" What we are attempting to recover is a deportment by intellect which asks by its piety, "Reality, may I take a giant step or frog-hop by means of my concept?" In the question, intellect is deferentially oriented to reality through acknowledgment of the authority of reality as making such movement legitimate because reality makes concept itself legitimate.

The principle here to be recovered, we need to say, is suited to the possible range of intellectual disciplines in their games of "science" as governed by reality. To return to the poet and his poem, this is the principle understood among some of the so-called New Critics who influenced our reading of poetry most decisively in this century. Theirs was a concern for the nature of the particular poem, its nature to be discovered as it is borne by the poem itself, independent (in this initial approach to the poem as thing) of the maker of the poem. It is a movement whose analogy one finds in the assertion by St. Thomas that one moves toward the nature of the cause of this mysterious "poem" called creation through the elementary movement of intellect effected through the senses. By the recognition of this necessity, the body is also recognized in its importance and to a degree which the gnostic or Manichean is incapable of acknowledging. It is through the thing that one may move toward encounter with the Thing which is the thing's cause. And it is through the senses that intellect must approach that thing. It is through the poem that one moves toward encounter with the Poet. Here, then, we may further understand the analogy of poet as creator to God as Creator. That is an indication that we are approaching a wisdom necessary to intellect beyond "knowledge" of likenesses in unlike things. And so for some of literature's New Critics, a critical departure through the text proves most just to the critic's judgment of whether the maker of the poem has been attentive to the good of the thing he makes. It is thus that the critic may justify the ways of the poet to the reader, to echo John Milton's epic theme. It follows from this assertion that a "New Critical" approach to the poem is the beginning of the critic's intellectual concern, not the end, as some among those critics misunderstood.[10] As a beginning, it is paralleled in the work of St. Thomas and St. Augustine. I have intended to be more than playful, then, when I suggest that St. Augustine is not only the author of our first significant modern novel (*The Confessions*) but is also our first New Critic in *The City of God*.

What we are declaring is that the principle affirmed as governing intellect's relation to reality is common with and necessary to the attention of any intellect in its concern for the truth of things, whether for the botanist or zoologist no less than for the literary critic or poet. For the nature of intellectual attention at the practical level of that attention is to discover what may be said of a particular creature that does not violate the nature of that creature. It is from such an address to the thing itself—the flower, the bug, the rat, the poem; or the state, the academy, the intellect itself— that the thing may be seen as truly itself and seen as also truly "like" things not itself. The *truly like*, under our principle, is only a true likeness if monitored by that proper proportionality which exists in the thing it- self in its relation as created essence, as distinguished from the uncreated essence of its Cause. There follows a relation between its actuality and its potentiality. There follows also a relation between its nature and the accidents adhering in it because of its nature.

Such may seem a subtle approach to distinctions, given the long absence of good habits of intellectual action as justified through metaphysical vi- sion. Western thought has long since rejected metaphysical vision in order to embrace pseudo-metaphysical visions of varying kinds. It had seemed necessary to the modernist intellect, in its rising to autonomous authority out of the late middle ages, to reject metaphysical vision. If a Pelagian or gnostic dominance over being were to be effected, through which that dominance could expand to empire empirically, then metaphysical vision as the common ground to intellectual community must be rejected. Otherwise, the dominant intellect which is now pervasive in consequence of the rejection of metaphysics must acknowledge a gift of grace to intel- lect, a gift whereby intellect thus gifted is enabled to see truly into the life of things. That *seeing* requires always a "Mother, may I?" to creation itself, which is a request following from a recovery of a "Father, may I?" Such an address to intellect's own existence by intellect itself orients that intellect so that it may return to the place from which it set out and see that place for the first time. It will thereby understand its dual necessity: to care and not to care. What arrests in that vision is the understanding that *life*, existence, *depends in* its existence by means of the discrete es- sence of the depending thing. In such a recognition it becomes impossible to intellect to establish itself as transcendent of being, the presumption necessary to intellect if it is to presume to manipulate being.[11] When we say *life* as inclusive of all existing things, we mean the term analogically and not actually. This is to be reminded that even with such a metaphysi- cal vision as Thomas's, as it is dependent on Aristotle, by its rational extension it may confuse the actual with the analogical. Gilson points out this difficulty in Thomism in relation to the realities which dictate the varieties of science. Gilson remarks, in *Methodical Realism*, a certain "the- oretical sterility" of peripatetic philosophy which prevented its giving "birth to modern science." It is a weakness, not in Thomas's vision of truth but in his explication of that vision, a weakness which has been used ever since as if that aspect of medieval thought vitiated the whole of that thought. Renaissance literature is founded on that thought, the poet's metaphor justified by it, and when that thought is at last rejected by Western philosophy the poet found himself in exile, with his first necessity a recovered justification of analogy. We have seen Wordsworth attempting that recovery.

It is this aspect of medieval thought that Shakespeare also depends upon in speaking of "tongues in trees" or "sermons in stone," on which dependence see both Tillyard's *Elizabethan World Picture*, but especially C. S. Lewis's *The Discarded Image*. From Lewis's study, one begins to realize that, if the medieval "chain of being" upon which Renaissance poetry depends is in some respects flawed, it nevertheless speaks more nearly to the complexity of reality than our modern version of that chain of being. The modern version is the medieval image of the structure of reality from which the angelic link has been removed, along with the removal of the Anchor of that Chain that steadies the tossing individual self, namely the Anchor God. But the Darwinian chain of being, we discover more and more, is the medieval one secularized, through which additional confusions are added to those already in that old world picture. As for the poet, he may well have come to recognize that the sermon in stone is less the fossil deposit of Darwinian fame than a witness to being itself. Gilson, in speaking of the "scientific sterility of the Middle-Ages" as an effect of Aristotle's error of "biologizing inorganic nature," adds than the error was nevertheless "philosophically less dangerous" than modernist reductionism "because it was an error of fact and left the rights of philosophy intact." It is the "rites" of philosophy through which intellect recovers itself to a realism about existence from which modernist thought excludes it on the inadequate ground to that exclusion whereby errors of fact in the old vision of reality are taken as philosophical errors. Such is the deportment of modernist thought, as Gilson might well agree, which has made modern philosophy so largely a game played by sophists.

11

Intellect's First Act:
In the Beginning Was Love

A thing may be seen as truly like another, but truly so only within the limits of its *given* proportionality, its own essence in relation to being, whereby it is the thing it is. In that recognition lies the intellect's guidance in acknowledging *unlikeness* as well as the wonder of *likeness*, thus avoiding a reductionism of things to identities of each other. For if the gift of seeing likeness in unlike things is crucial to the maker as poet, as Aristotle says, it is a gift subject to abuse when the limit of likeness is ignored. It is in respect to *unlikeness* that intellect establishes and values the particularity of each thing in itself, avoiding the illusion that there is an *essential* unity in creation which the accidents of particular existences may tempt intellect to conclude an illusion through which particularity is obscured. That was the destructive element in Averroes' theory of intellect, for instance. Indeed, it is the recognition of the "life"—the existential being of the discrete thing itself, the substantial *unity* inclusive of the thing's actuality and potentiality—which effects the intellect's intuitive seeing of *essence*, the seeing of that which makes the thing the very thing it is. This is the preconceptual seeing discovery through intellectual openness to being which initiates concept in intellect. And so, this is the point of encounter with reality in which Thomas's "supernatural light" affects the "natural light" of intellect.

Concept, then, is by its nature only properly, only truly, anchored in reality through such recognition, through such preconceptual knowledge. And intellect is thus anchored despite its subsequent temptation by the will to propose *concept* as an action of intellect independent of reality. That is an action whereby there is but a slight step further to the conclusion, directly or implicitly, that intellect in and of itself is the cause of

103

being. And that is the step almost inevitable out of the Cartesian state which mistakes intellect as the point from which its own existence may be justified. The intellect, moving to take advantage of its Cartesian isolation, becomes victim to the illusion that its action infuses substantial nature *upon* a thing which it has encountered at the level of the thing's accidental aspects which adhere to its *essential* being. It is by this erroneous movement of intellect, presumptuous even when not aware of its presumptuousness, whereby it would seize being through its limited power to gain a dominance—to gain a transcendence—over being. Through this separation of intellect from being in the interest of dominance over being it appears possible to manipulate being.

But for intellect to assume, or to act as if, its own being were the first cause of concept is to defy the mystery of being which is beyond *comprehension* by finite intellect. It is to reject that question first necessary to intellectual movement through concept, *what is being*? It can only make that rejection by declaring of its own volition that *being is*, as if creating thereby an actuality by the power of its own will. What is most conspicuously ignored in this operation of intellect is the inescapable reality: the precedent givenness of intellect's own nature, an error of cataclysmic consequence to intellect, leading it to the edge of the abyss. For such is to lose sight of its own perversion of its own nature which effects its isolation from reality, leaving it not only alienated from the largesse of reality constituting the whole of creation but diminished dangerously in its own reality.

As for this presumption by intellect which is a perversion of its own nature, it is well to recapitulate the Thomistic position concerning the giveness of intellectual nature, in which givenness its operations are made possible. Thomas Gilby in his *Poetic Experience: An Introduction to Thomist Aesthetics* (1934) reminds us that Thomas's central definition of Beauty, *that which when seen pleases*, has as its "precise point . . . that a thing satisfies the innate desire of mind" through beauty, but that this beauty when seen does not hold the affections after it is seen. For it to do so would mean an intellect mesmerized by beauty, the first step toward an idolatry of the thing seen. What beauty rather effects is a "quieting of the primitive craving of mind for the whole of the real." Fr. Gilby's point leads us to that intellectual action we have already spoken of, that engagement of the "whole of the real" thing which we said was a preconceptual engagement by intellect of thing, whereby the thing in itself comes to be part of intellect's knowing. Thomas says, in words immediately relevant to this concern, that "Loving draws us to things more than knowing does." Knowing the thing through reason differs then from loving through encounter with the loved thing. Thomas develops the distiction: "The reason distinguishes what are really united, and associates in some sense what are really diverse, and its perfection lies in knowing separately whatever is in the thing, as its parts and powers and properties." But love is quite other than reason. "Love is the desire which regards a thing as it is in itself."

From such a distinction, then, we may conclude that the first action of intellect is an action of love, whereby intellect moves to the thing in itself, to the knowledge of essence. The intellect discovers itself already possessed of a knowledge of essence before its conceptual action. It is through reason that intellect comes to know the loved thing's "parts and powers and properties." The precedent knowledge through love is granted through the intellect's initial action of love toward the thing itself. It is the action of love that accomplishes the knowledge of essence. I think we need only recall our observations of the small child's fascination with things, an instance we used on another occasion being that of a small child's first encounter with a litter of young rabbits. The experience to intellect in this event is beyond self-awareness, and in this event the love of God and the love possible through intellect are coincident before any rational pursuit of a recovery of love. Fr. Gilby speaks of this love of created things in another context: "His will makes them exist; our will makes us know them. They are established by love; they are experienced by love."

The child's experience well represents a mystical knowledge such as rational intellect must labor toward. That is a knowledge which St. Thomas says is an "unteachable and mystical union," of which we are able to speak only through "symbols." And that mystical knowledge, he says, "consists rather in tasting than in knowing, rather in love and sweetness than in thinking." But thinking will follow upon such knowledge. We found our "Romantic" poet lamenting that it does. The desire of intellect to dwell in beauty becomes frustrated in that impossibility of holding steady in a mystical knowing. But reason must order that "mystical knowledge" to its growth toward a much fuller mystical knowledge beyond the grace of this initiating moment, a sustaining of intellect through its intuitive and rational faculties brought into concert in pursuit of a love of existences.

That complexity of this intellectual desire requires a considerable labor of intellect toward an openness to being through love, once it has experienced a falling away from that initiating mystical knowledge whereby it finds itself on reflection possessed of a knowledge of essences, possessed of a union with the nature of things in themselves which is the effect of love. On the point, Fr. Gilby once more: "Attachment, not detachment, is the law of the life of the mind." And to that end it is "joined to a body, not that it may be clogged up [as Plato might have it], but precisely for its perfection, that it may be rescued from generalities and by entering the particularised experience of the senses reach somehow to the real concrete things in the world around it." It is through the senses that an openness toward being is effected by rational intellect, unless there occurs a perversion of that intuitive love. That perversion is effected when the will turns love back upon the self, back upon the intellect as if it were the beloved. But innate desire is to be satisfied only through an outward inclination, for intellect desires properly not being but "more being," Gilly observes. That desire if rightly followed makes it impossible that love be reduced to self-love, the reduction which is a perversion of love by the will. Neither can intellect explain its "need for another by the sufficiency" of itself.

And so desire (Eliot's old nemesis) is at last to be related to memory. For in memory, what intellect is most delighted by are those moments in which there was an openness, such moments as Wordsworth recalls in which he saw "into the life of things." These are moments the "memory returns to," says Gilby (though he is not remarking our instance). It is the "mysterious appreciation of a single situation, the sense of being on the point of beholding a thing just as it is, of being on the edge of discovery." And these are the sort of moments which no doubt leads St. Thomas to say of memory itself that in these moments one recognizes God's presence in the soul, a present "memory of Him." In Thomas's words, that presence is "the mind's memory of God." We should here remember, of course, St. Augustine's discourse on memory in his *Confessions*. But such a memory is not that of our ordinary understanding of memory, as when we say we have a memory of a merely temporal event out of our past. It is a present recovery to the reality of God as transcendent of event, and in that recovery lies the recovered recognition of the soul's proper end.

On this point, then, it is well to recall St. Augustine's extended discourse on memory in Book 10 of his *Confessions*. The important recovery is not the revisiting of an event as a part of the history of that intellect which remembers, but the recovery of a known but forgotten Thing: an encounter through intellectual event with the Cause of intellect and the Cause of the thing encountered, the coincidence which characterizes event. In that event, as Thomas says, "Knower and known become one." They are joined "to become a common principle of the act of knowing." It is an event in which "Grace builds on nature, and its activities imitate and complete natural process," as Gilly remarks.

What Thomas concludes of the effect of such event upon the soul is important to the Romantic poets' difficulty with image, for by event the soul is changed in relation to its openness to event. There is, Thomas says, a "something . . . within the soul by its natural being and not by a likeness." And when this something "is known, then the natural being [*essence*] of the thing takes the place of a representation." If that "something" (*essence*) is not known in its presence in intellect by intellect itself, then intellect is left to deal with its "representation," its image. Through the image—through the concept—which is unsupported by the actuality of the thing itself as known, the intellect will be denied its own knowledge. Image intercedes between the action of intellect and the thing toward which it would act. It is therefore inclined to suppose image substantial, leading to such assertions as Wordworth's that the "mind is a mansion for all lovely form," in which words it is evident that *form* is supposed substantial.

Eliot will react, as we have seen, to such an assertion, but he does not react radically. That is, he does not descend beneath the "representation" to the thing itself. Instead he substitutes *unlovely* form in an ironic refutation. In other words, he leaves the problem at the level of image, which when denied the substantial thing as its support is merely another species of representation, sordid image instead of lovely image. In either event consciousness, intellect, is thus left with floating "representations," the shadows of things. And shadow without substantiation by substantive thing allows no opening of intellect to the thing itself, neither to an awareness of that substantial thing, that essence already resident as truth in intellect, nor to an encounter through the senses of substantial things in the existential world. Eliot in his "Preludes" sees the difficulty but not a solution. He is left with "a thousand sordid images" which the "street" (the existented world independent of intellect) cannot "recognize" as representations of itself. But whether lovely or sordid representations, isolated as shadowy images in intellect, that intellect becomes unable to riddle either the beautiful or the ugly. It is captive of image on either hand, a victim of shadows, and its desire for substantial unity in being frustrated. It is "hollow" because that "shadow" falls between desire and potency.

If the soul is put off from its recognition of this proper end, as it sometimes is in the Romantic poet through his approach to art, there will follow a confused understanding of the experience of beauty in things. Art, St. Thomas reminds us is "a local end." But it is through prudence that we come to an accommodation with the local, and "prudence concerns the whole of human life and its last end." "Beauty is difficult," Ezra Pound repeatedly insists in his *Pisan Cantos*, but so Thomas insisted, though on different grounds. We have suggested that Pound comes somewhat closer to Thomas at the end of his life, and he does so through his concern for beauty, so that we might recall Pound's own insistence that "art is local." (Pound adds that "stupidity is national.") Now we have considered that art bears an immediacy to intellect when it is good art. Gilby remarks a parallel of art to play, based in what Thomas says of *play* and what we experience on reading a good poem. Play, says St. Thomas, is not ordered "to an extrinsic end but to the good of the player in so far as it gives delight and content." And, "In a game nothing is desired outside the game." Such, we might say, is an aesthetics proper to play, in which the player responds to the good of the thing itself, without requiring of it any extrinsic end. In this light, it is art as a sort of play that tempts the poet to art as its own end, as a good to the player to purchase his content. And that temptation seems encouraged as conclusion from our own experience of the good poem. As Gilby observes, "Where most of our thought is concerned with means, the poetic experience comes with a sense of finality." We enjoy the experience, as we enjoy play. As for what it means *to enjoy*, Thomas says it is "to cleave by love to something for its own sake." But to cling to art as an end, even through love, may limit that responding soul from its proper end. The love of things is a mediate love, whose end is the fullness of our love for the Cause of all things. A love improperly exercised, in which means are taken as end, is idolatry.

We have already remarked the danger of idolatry born of desire misunderstood, as when the soul is mesmerised by the beauty of a thing as beheld in itself, a moment's satisfaction of intellect's desire. But satisfaction in a means as end is destructive to soul. That satisfaction may not properly be reduced to a *continuing* affection for the thing. We would judge the child arrested who, taken by the squirming rabbit litter, never is able to move beyond the arrest of that moment of love. Reason will not allow that arrest, an arrest which would be a lesser, a worldly substitute for beatitude, when the larger fuller Beatitude is the proper end to be come to through those mediate ends which arouse but cannot satisfy our capacity for love. And so mediate objects when loved must not be inordinately loved. They must not arrest our inclinations to the fullness of our capacity to love that is granted us through the grace of our nature as creatures created in the image of God. One grows in a capacity for love, and one grows through the reason's increasing recognition of the complexity of beauty as responded to by intellect. Again, Fr. Gilby is very helpful to our advancing this point. There is, he says, "a mysterious unity in diversity of beauty which must be taken in its uniqueness and entirety as beyond analysis. Not without cause did the Romantics see a strangeness, a sort of deviation from accustomed proportions, in the manifestations of beauty." Our argument has been with the failure in some Romantics to acquit those deviations through the uses of reason which would lead to a larger vision of what beauty signifies. For it signifies at last beyond the local, even as Keats hoped it might, though he took poetry as an instrument sufficient to his reaching beyond that local beauty that seemed capable only of leaving him high sorrowful. Unless there is that larger vision, then art will fail in its supportive rescue of the soul from the encroachments of nature and history, as proved true for Keats. And that brings us to Fr. Gilby's pregnant conclusion to his *Poetic Experience*: "The aesthetic experience is a discovery, not an escape. . . . Thus at the end the mind rejoins the senses, and the activity of all joins in the human experience of the beautiful. The immediacy of mere sense has been purified by the application of reason which prepares for, though it does not elicit, the experience. Poets, lovers, and saints must pass through this stage of detachment, must in this way become other in order to become one, in order to know a thing for itself and not for themselves; the poet through appreciation of form, the lover by the restraint of temperance, the saint through the definitions of faith."

In the light of Gilby's words consider Keats's Odes in relation to Eliot's "Ash-Wednesday." Keats's imaginative detachment, which should indeed prepare him for a return in the end, a return in which "the mind joins the senses" in the activity called the continuing experience of the beauty of existential things, does not return him to that condition. He is left with his "soul self" instead. Both art and nature seem to exclude him from satisfying his desire to love. Eliot's "Ash-Wednesday" in contrast seems to begin where Keats ends, in a moment of seeming exile in the world such as that Wordsworth addresses in his "Intimations Ode." But Eliot's exile turns out to be rather a homecoming within the local, though that "home" is not local. There emerges a new understanding in Eliot of that "mysterious unity in diversity of beauty," which he takes both in its uniqueness (for it is experience peculiar to him) and in its entirety (for it speaks beyond the uniqueness of beauty's envelopment of his being, speaking of the Beauty of that Perfect Being). It is a moment advanced to that discrete, unique soul as it sees at last an accord between the figure of Priapus in the green garden and the Lady at the garden's edge who goes in St. Mary's colors. As Thomas says, it is "of the essence of beauty that with the knowledge of it desire is at rest." And insofar as desire comes to a moment's rest in that desiring soul T. S. Eliot, it is a rest that is also a movement whereby it approaches its perfection as soul, a perfection beyond the temporal entrapments of *history* as memory or *nature* as decay. What is being rescued, in such an opening of the soul to being through beauty, is what St. Thomas calls the "most perfect reality in nature . . . a person." That is the being Eliot celebrates in the opening lines of his poem: "Because I do not hope to turn again . . . I rejoice that things are as they are. . . ."

12

Intellectual Error: Sin Secularized

It is from suffering his intellect's isolation from reality that the "Romantic" poet *thinks* himself into a conclusion that he is entrapped within the self with no exit possible, leading either to a despair of spirit or to the machinations of *acedia*. And so it follows that avoiding this error is crucial to spiritual health. It means, for instance, that the poet must find a way to truly see, before any possibility of partially saying, his vision. And what he sees as poet is that there is no mingling of likeness and unlikeness *within* the circumstantial accidents of existing things. Merely because intellect itself desires that all existence constitute an essential unity, the desire cannot by will effect that unity. The poet can only by such an error project his desire upon existential reality and thus reflect only his own false hope. The error in this attempted prescription upon existence of an essential unity under the auspices of intellectual action, we might recall, is our modernist inheritance of that Averroist heresy which St. Thomas refutes in his treatise *On Unity of the Intellect against the Averroists*. But despite Thomas's refutation, the Averroist heresy is propelled into modernist thought by way of Siger of Brabant, aided by Occam's Nominalism. These late scholastics mediate the heresy to its presence in the modernist intellectual climate. There has disappeared in this modernist mind even a nominal regard for intellect's relation to God. Thus in the modernist world, only error can be admitted, error being sin secularized.

In a secularized account of sin as merely intellectual error, that error must be accounted for as comparable to the eye's failure to distinguish red from green. Error is made resident in defective bodily organ, the brain. By such a shifting of the account, one moves beyond the organic sensual errors as in color blindness to the intellectual realm as anchored in the organic, and consequent to its organic nature intellect is decreed "prone to error," as opposed to being touched by original sin. When intellect

111

fails in its control of concept, it is a failure of a defective intellect, but the role of willfulness in the failure has been circumvented as a possible or probable cause. To admit as possible, let alone probable, such a failure as caused by defective will is to open the question of error toward the question of sinfulness in the will itself. But the abuse of being, through concept willfully employed, is for St. Thomas a species of dire sin. From a Thomistic perspective, then, to use false metaphor, either willfully or careless of the possible perception of the true through the given nature of intellect itself, is of serious import to the soul.

In this context, one might conclude that more is at risk than economics in advertising as it is practiced in our world. One may so conclude if granted such a position as Thomas's on the willful distortion of likeness in unlike things, as when sexual innuendo is used to sell the latest model automobile. And in that light, we might be given pause, recalling a heroic moment in one poet's life. Ezra Pound was insistent that "to use the wrong word is to bear false witness." When he was arrested in Italy at the end of World War II as a traitor, his immediate response was, "If a man will not stand by his word, either he is no good or his word is no good." From that principle he expected to be examined as to whether or not he was, in fact, a traitor. Our summary point, from a Thomistic position, is that intellectual error in relation to reality which results in false signs manipulative of being, whether willfully or ignorantly practiced, is culpable. Still, one is moved by a pathos in Pound as opposed to anger under the bombardment of advertising which is slyly traitorous to the soul. One believes from Thomas's position however, that the particular soul is given an intellectual nature sufficient to its discovery of its proper relation to the truth of things, and so may not blame either Pound or advertising for its own failures. Which is not to say, of course, that the discrete gift of intellect is therefore necessarily sufficient to its own *understanding* of the truth of things. And we note as of particular significance in the gift of intellect that the intuitive knowledge, however limited, is sufficient to stir a desire for a proper end.

Fr. Phelan in his explication of Thomas's understanding of analogy as based in proportionality cautions against a conclusion that likeness among things "is based upon a formal identity and difference is based upon a formal diversity." Such a conclusion confuses the truth which intellect perceives in its conceptual response to encounter with things in themselves. For the likeness is not in a formal identity, whereby the assumption becomes that essence in the like things is common and not particular to the thing. Such a response is, again, a species of that Averroist error which holds that separate intellects are intellects by participation in a common essence, and so not particular, as if diverse bodies had but one head. What is to be recovered here is the position that concepts of identity and of diversity, of likeness and unlikeness in respect to discrete things seen in conjunction, are true to the reality of the disparate things only when anchored in and derived from the perceived reality of things, each thing seen in itself. Conceptions built upon perception of essence are advanced by the *ratio*, but the perception is through the intuitive mode of knowing. In this conjunction of active intellectual unity in the discrete intellect, between speculative and rational operations, intellect is oriented to truth by understanding, not by the more limited (though necessary) formalizing action of intellect in its rational deportment. Formal identity is an operation of intellect reductive of reality. As Thomas says, "properly speaking it is not the form that exists but the composite, which is determined by the form as a certain kind of thing." When intellect entertains the concept of form, it is "knowing separately whatever is in the thing, as its parts and powers and properties." By such an operation of knowing, intellect may at last recover its wonder in the presence of the thing itself which it has disassembled into concepts, though that operation does not affect the thing as "really united." It is an operation supportive of intellect's higher response to the thing, love's "desire which regards a thing as it is in itself."

The response of intellect to an encounter with reality, we are saying, continues incomplete if it is only formal—if the encounter is arrested conceptually. What is necessary to understanding is that sort of *seeing* which Thomas speaks of, whereby "To see truth is to have it." That is to have that thing that hides "inwardly," so that "the apprehension of man must penetrate as if intrinsically." Thus Thomas himself puts formally what is in its actuality an experience mystical in nature and so in a degree intransient through any formal articulation. It can be spoken of only by "symbol" he says, being that "mystical knowledge" of an "unteachable and mystical union." What he is confident of, however, is the actuality of that experience of things. It is an experience of the thing "as if intrinsically" penetrated by intellect. We remarked earlier Keats in his pursuit of this experience as if it could be commanded rather than as if it were an action natural to intellect (though easily distorted by the activist rational intellect). Keats calls this experience that of "negative capability."

Understandably, one may become somewhat nervous at the prospect of St. Thomas as mystic, given his formal reputation, and never more so than when one is rigidly Thomistic. That is why we have remarked elsewhere the insistence of Thomas himself that the end of philosophy is not what men have thought about reality but the truth of reality itself. He recognized an inescapable truth which does not yield easily to rational discourse, the truth that intellect, as soon as it begins to address the very first question put to itself, finds itself already possessed of some knowledge. It knows in a preconceptual state of its being. That is a mystery upon which the rational intellect may turn its "natural light." But that light is limited in its sufficiency to the mystery, to which it must in the end defer as in some respects beyond rational comprehension. To do so does not require a repudiation of the truth held by intellect, though intellect may not completely explain how it holds such truth, save through such proposals as the relation of intuition to rational actions of intellect, the complementary offices of *intellectus* and *ratio*, or the support of intellect's "natural light" by a "supernatural light." It should be noted that the same limits to understanding among modernists obtains, mystery not so acknowledged but called *the not yet known*, lest intellect be admitted finite. One might, for instance, consider that truculent gnostic agnostic, Sir Peter Medawar, in his treatment of our point here, in his *Induction and Intuition in Scientific Thought* (1969). In doing so one may see how awkward this mystery of intuitive knowledge becomes to the fundamentalist gnostic such as Medawar.

We must note Thomas's figurative way of putting the experience. For *apprehension* "begins from the sense" and is by the senses transmitted to intellect. Failing through apprehension to penetrate beyond the accidents which are apprehended sensually, intellect may come to some knowledge but not to an understanding. For to know the things that "hide inwardly" in things is necessary to an understanding. Thus "substantial nature of things lies hidden under accident; the meanings of words lie hidden under similitudes and figures. And intelligible things are in a certain way inward with respect to sensible things that are sensed outwardly, and effects are hidden in causes and conversely" (*Summa* II-II, Q8, 1). Such is Thomas's preparation to the introduction of his terms "natural light" and "supernatural light." The supernatural understood makes possible an intellectual penetration of the thing to its substantial, essential nature which natural light is insufficient to effect. It is through this experience of penetrating to the very nature of the thing itself, wherefrom one "has" its truth, that one is empowered to bear witness, as it were, to the true nature of likeness in unlike things.

To assume, Fr. Phelan says, that intellect is itself the ground of "a difference in the very likeness and a likeness in the very difference" is merely to mingle concepts in an intellect which has already abandoned reality by that assumption. The recognition of likeness in unlike things, the special gift that makes one a poet according to Aristotle, must be understood by the poet as rested, not *in* concepts, but in the particularity of the like-unlikes, the things in themselves. The thing, then, must be first taken separately, in relation to its *dependence* as an existential *res*, in being by virtue of its particularizing essence. By that virtue its unlikeness to all other things is fundamental. Only by an intellectual game played with form disjoined from actuality is "identity" possible as a play of fancy. A thing's dependence in being is therefore independent of both any *likeness* to any other thing and of any *intellect* which may perceive it. It is here that a proper relation of intellect to thing is anchored and finds guidance to an analogy which does not violate reality, as attributive analogy is inclined to do. We have, let us recall, seen Wordsworth struggling to recover this guidance in his "Tintern Abbey," in his concern for accepting through thought what he has intuitively recognized, a "something" deeply interfused and holding all creation in creation's existential particularities, creation's diversity of things.

In true analogy "it is *in being* (*essendo*) that all beings are one yet the *very being* (*esse*) by which they are one is diverse in each, though proportionate to the essence of each." Here Fr. Phelan's emphatic *very* carries an insistence upon the particularity *inhering* by virtue of *esse*. It is in this respect that one has the scholastic emphasis upon *substance*. *Substance* terms the existent, an *ens*, in which the accidents appropriate to its particularity adhere. For we speak here as always of *accidents* in a manner that carries no implication of *randomness* as the term does in popular use of that term. The limits of particularity, governed by the substantial being of the thing, also governs the adhering accidents. This is to say that the range of accidents adhering in a particular thing is determined by substance. Thus some accidents, but not all possible accidents (for there is that aspect of *randomness* as possible) adhere in discrete substance. Both substance and the adhering accidents constitute a complex: this particularized *being*, this particular *res*. Nor should one confuse *accident* in this scholastic sense as bearing any suggestion of a *distortion* of the particular being, for not only are those contributive accidents to being governed by the substantial being itself but are as well elements to the actuality of whatever *thing* is in existence, in being. One might say, then, that accidents are the manifestations of the actualization of the thing that *is*, that is *actual*, substantively and essentially actual.

There is nevertheless a community of things *in being*, made a community by virtue of *being*, each certified by distinction as a discrete thing through its particularity. What is common is being. What grounds a thing at once as both its particular self and member in the *community* of being is its particularity. Such is the truth to which true analogy testifies. If one does not recognize this truth, he is very likely to be precipitous in attributing likeness to unlike things on the mere, the mediate, evidence of accidents of particular things as apprehended by the senses. But to "feel" toward one thing as one "feels" toward another on the evidence of sensual apprehension does not mean a likeness between the two things. Intellect may easily suppose a substantial likeness to have been engineered by intellect through the authority of concept over accident on the uncertain evidence of "feeling." The undermining of reality by Cartesian Idealism makes such error not only possible but probable, the more so when the idealism is dominant in the whole of an intellectual community.

Through inherited strains of idealism out of such miss-taking of essence, descended from Pelagius and Averroes no less than from Descartes, the "Romantic" poet is affected toward attributive metaphor. His inclination is in part in concert with those ideas, but in part also as an action more or less in opposition to them. For such a poet is intuitively disquieted by the implications of a tacitly recognized attributive nature in his own figurative language. Not recognizing recourse other than to act intellectually as if autonomous, disturbed by an inadequacy sensed in such action, he finds allegory and metaphor problematic. That is why since the eighteenth century the poet has felt it increasingly necessary to justify figurative correspondence of sign to perceived thing, through image reduced as much as he may from any ambiguous connotation. The rise of the literary school of "Realism" in opposition to "Romanticism," from which there follows a further movement called "Naturalism," signifies the difficulty as permeating the literary mind in the late nineteenth and early twentieth centuries.

As these new literary schools evolve, we discover that the poet's intuitive intellect recognizes that he somehow has lost the true ground of community in being. His attributive sign, taken as strict image or advanced to metaphorical implication, proves inadequate. The sign of his recognition of that inadequacy is the manner of the poet's deportment, in which there is likely to be an assertive arbitrariness, as if to insist on intellect as sufficient authority. Or there may be a nostalgic pathos in response to a faint memory of reality as once upon a time more adequately accommodated by intellect and its sign. Or there may be the response of an ironic dissociation, a rejection of the problem itself, in which response the sardonic increasingly overwhelms the poet. What this means, from our Thomistic position, is that the poet's intuitive nature recognizes its loss of the ground of community in being, has mistaken or refused the *essential* nature of beings as grounded in common existence itself.

He will have recognized an inadequacy in his signs, since they refuse to hide their attributive nature as sign and so point accusingly to their origin in intellect acting as if autonomous. In this sense, these signs bear a true witness. For they witness the truth that the assumed intellectual position is false to reality. Attribution, being merely conceptual in its nature, is inescapably subversive of the visionary, the intuitive response to being. Attributive metaphor is not properly anchored in reality through the intellect's gift of "seeing" into the nature of things as aided by "supernatural light." Nor does the poet require the scholastic philosopher to make him aware of the disparity, though the scholastic may indeed provide a rational perspective toward his understanding that disparity. The poet will have recognized it whenever he becomes aware of finding himself lost in a dark wood, whatever recourse he may then take toward finding the true way.

13

Image's Struggle with the Real Thing

From our speculative reflections on the problem which makes of the poet a "Romantic," we may better understand his growing discomfort with metaphor, a discomfort which grows in English poetry from a delighed abandon in the "metaphysical" poets such as John Donne down to Eliot and beyond. Donne still held a sufficient confidence in a commonly held vision of creation, bequeathed him by Medieval scholasticism. It is from this confidence that he can afford fancy's participation in the making of conceits. For he is confident still of fancy's anchor, the rational intellect's confidence in reality itself. Confident of substantial nature hidden under accidents, of meanings hidden under words, of truth lying beneath similitudes and figures (to echo St. Thomas), he assumes a freedom which will become but license when that confidence is lost. By the time Wordsworth came to consider metaphor and the proximate relation of sign to thing in his concept, the old confidence that the poet's intellect is sufficiently anchored by reality had been disturbingly called in question. The prospect of metaphor as dependably related to reality by a dependable signification of sign (word) appears overthrown. Analogy, once accepted as supporting the intellect's encounter with reality and thereby justifying intellect's desire to understand an essential unity in particular things, revealing a community among things called creation, seems irretrievably lost. Lost unless the imagination purge itself of attributive fancy toward its recovery of reality.

Here we recall that Coleridge will find Donne a poet worth rescue, though it is rather Eliot who succeeds in making Donne once more generally acceptable as a poet. Coleridge's and Eliot's interests in Donne, however, differ. For Coleridge, it is Donne whose poetry seems to promise a welcomed recovery of a largeness of vision to the poet. But it is Eliot's interest in Donne's manner that makes him attractive to Eliot before *The*

Waste Land. If, however, one read the sophistications of wit in Donne in relation to the sophistications of wit in Eliot, what emerges is a significant difference between them. For Donne we have already characterized a playfulness of wit through fanciful delights, made acceptable by Donne's own confidence in reality as not violated by his wit. But wit in Eliot is deadly serious. His "metaphysical" devices in the employ of his irony are a defense against intellect's dislocation from reality. It is a manner evident in his poetry, even (or perhaps particularly) evident in his titles. There is his first collection, *Prufrock and Other Observations*, in which title the poet dissociates himself, as Stephen Dedalus might do, from his persona. Later the representation of "Sweeney Among the Nightingales" has through the detached wry irony of *among* the effect of reducing all the creatures to such a level that no order of being seems evident. Sweeney's relation to prostitute or to an actual bird is equally reductive of all. The irony is an effect of attribution, but not like that of Donne, in whom fancy has yet a stay in a reality not available to Eliot's wit.

We reflect that, with the appearance of Bishop Berkeley and the Cambridge Platonists, between the time of Donne and the time of Wordsworth, intellect's confidence in metaphor comes to be suspect. Sign itself is problematic, so that the intellect using sign toward that which is not itself operates awkwardly, as the lab technician using levers and small cranes and pulleys to manipulate fascinating but perhaps dangerous elements on the other side of protective glass plates, under fluorescent, abstract light. Such seems the state of intellect from the Platonist position as observed by such a vigorous person as Samuel Johnson. Dr. Johnson, for one, objects to absurd detachment. He protests against both the Metaphysical Poets and the Cambridge Platonists, no doubt intuitively recognizing these somehow related as causes of the growing dislocation of intellect from reality. Dr. Johnson's London made omnipresent to him the rough, smelly, loud, decaying fecundity of reality in which he lived and breathed and had his being.

Dr. Johnson anticipates some of the philosophical difficulty that will engage the "Romantic" mind at the close of the eighteenth century. With the emergence of the Romantic poet upon the intellectual scene, Coleridge makes a cautionary distinction of fancy from imagination, as if to heal the rupture between a Donne and a Johnson. Where the "secondary" imagination, "co-existing with the conscious will," exercises itself in dissolving, diffusing, dissipating "in order to recreate," it continues anchored by that Primary Imagination, "the infinite I AM," and so is "essentially *vital*," though Coleridge concludes that all its "objects (*as* objects) are essentially fixed and dead." But fancy on the contrary "has no other counters to play with but fixities and definites. The fancy is indeed no other than a mode of memory emancipated from the order of time and space." Thus liberated it becomes manipulative in its play, irreverently disposed to reality. (I have considered at some length Coleridge's famous definition of the imagination in chapter 13 of his *Biographia Literaria* in my essay, "Around the Prickly Pearl: Eliot on Coleridge on Sir John Davies," *The Reflective Journey toward Order.*)

While Coleridge's position may not adequately serve the necessity of intellect's recovery of reality, he nevertheless recognizes that such a recovery is the problem. He attempts to anchor the poet's secondary imagination in the cause of things, the "infinite I AM," and govern the liberty which fancy would transmute to license. What is of interest here is the relegation of a state of intellect, in which it finds itself in a Wordsworthian "spot of time" or an Eliotic "still point," to the province of fancy when liberated through a "memory emancipated from the order of time and space." One supposes Coleridge would maintain that Donne recognized the mischief of fancy in relation to reality, but thought it sufficiently controlled by a common intellectual consent to reality in the seventeenth century, which consent rapidly decayed in the eighteenth century. It is relevant to our consideration of *fancy* that T. E. Hulme, the father of Imagism, is quite explicit in declaring the fancy superior to the imagination. Following Bergson, Hulme argues that it is through the fancy that the poet discovers a viable immanence in things. The five short poems by Hulme, which Pound includes in his own *Personae* under the title "The Complete Poetical Works of T. E. Hulme," show Hulme busy illustrating fancy's authority by means of attributive metaphor. There is, for instance, that "ruddy moon" that leans over a hedge like a "red-faced farmer." Amy Lowell would love the figure, as Pound himself would not—had it been perpetrated by Amy Lowell rather than by Hulme.

Hulme's is a position advocating fancy which Eliot will refute, but only later in his career as poet and critic, in his "Second Thoughts About Humanism." By that point, Eliot is discomforted by Hulme and by Hulme's immediate successors who posited Humanism as a philosophical justification of attributive analogy, since in that philosophy the intellect must be held on faith as autonomous. He becomes explicitly precise in his rejection, from what we have suggested as his increasingly Thomistic position. The influence of Jacques Maritain on Eliot's thought, and especially through Maritain's *Art and Scholasticism*, is of importance to his emerging Thomism. (We should remember that Eliot translates some of Maritain and publishes the translation in his *Criterion.*)

Wordsworth, in contrast to Coleridge, finds the excess of metaphysical poetry through fancy's liberation unacceptable, as had Dr. Johnson, though Wordsworth's response is at the level of testimony to his own immediate encounter with existing things in nature. He depends on the intuitive mode rather than the rational mode of Johnson's critical response to metaphorical abuses of reality through the fancy. And so Wordsworth's exploration of this mystery of metaphor, such as we consider in "Tintern Abbey," is instructive, especially because his exploration constitutes a natural concern, as opposed to formal scholastic concern, for an epistemology. That is, he would recover a confidence in metaphor and metaphor's sign through a close response to immediate experiences of existence as mediated through the senses. Event experienced by intellect, here and now, and measured against event remembered through summoned images, becomes his concern in his early engagement of the problem.

There is nevertheless a scholastic dimension in Wordsworth, if only as that natural as opposed to formal scholastic engagement. He speaks confidently of *form* as possesed by mind out of the apprehensive encounter of things, and he has an initial confidence in the continuing sustenance of intellect through experience. He remembers having known, and knowing still, "sensations sweet" stirred by images summoned from memory. Even later, after having such experiences called in question by the event of death, there remain aftereffects, with the added mystery that those effects occur while he is in a vacant mood as well as when in a pensive mood ("I Wandered Lonely as a Cloud"). What engages his reflection is the present effect of such image remembered from past experience. For the image recalled can restore *sensations* that are actual to the senses in the moment of remembrance as if immediate apprehension. There is a re-uniting of thought and feeling, overcoming in the poet's person what Eliot will call the "dissociation of sensibilities."

If we suggest a certain scholastic dimension to Wordsworth's concern, we must nevertheless see it as an inclination not actively pursued by the rational intellect. We note once more, for instance, a certain innocence in Wordsworth's concept of *form* if we consider it from a scholastic position. St. Thomas insists that "Intelligible forms are accepted by abstraction from things, wherefore they lead to a knowledge of the thing, not regarded as that thing from which the abstraction is made, but under that aspect which is isolated." For, "properly speaking it is not the form that exists but the composite, which is determined by the form as a certain kind of thing." Wordsworth, we would say from Thomas's perspective, confuses *form* as an abstraction from the thing with the *essence* of the thing. Our point is, however, that there is in Wordsworth a desire to accomplish what Thomas says is necessary to understanding beyond the initiating knowledge effected by an experience of the thing, an experience which (says Thomas) is always of the thing in its singularity. In that experience, Thomas says, "Knower and known become one. . . . Knower and known join to become a single principle of the act of knowing." Wordsworth's failure to make such distinction in relation to "form" in the "mind" prepares a way for the confusion in his thought that follows when he must deal with the question of death in relation to the soul, following the death of "Lucy" and of his brother John. That confusion, we have seen, leads him into the Platonism of his "Intimations Ode."

Nevertheless, in "Tintern Abbey" Wordsworth recognizes a dissociation of sensibility in himself, though he concludes it to have been occasioned by his sojourn in the city of man, by the "din / Of towns and cities" or by one's being isolated "in lonely rooms." The restorative effect of image remembered is

> Felt in the blood, and felt along the heart;
> And passing even into my purer mind,
> With tranquil restoration.

One observes in these words at least a faint echo of the Medieval understanding of the harmony of soul in nature through the body, a recovered sense of an *essential unity* of the soul from which there results a comfortable relation to created things. Wordsworth declares, at this point of his mid-life journey (1798), that such a community with the existential world continues effective beyond a present event. It does so through intellect in its reflective mood, in which mood it summons remembrance of things past or is visited by such remembrance even if not actively summoned by the will. The key seats of response that are typically Medieval are the *heart*, which governs passions, and the *head* ("the purer mind"), which governs thought in relation to passions. Together these constitute the soul, a term Wordsworth's poem arrives at as the poem ("Tintern Abbey") progresses.

The terms and their relationship are more in accord with Medieval concepts attempting to describe the essential unity of the soul (lacking only the office of the "liver" which was thought to anchor the discrete person in the natural world) than Wordsworth himself may have known. Wordsworth's lines prescribe the circumstance to consciousness which Eliot will treat with such bitter irony in section III of his "Preludes": Eliot's dramatization of awareness in a lonely room of a tenement of a city whose "din" is just beginning as that awareness comes to self-consciousness. The

difference, of course, is that in Eliot's poem image seems capable of per-
forming no such annealing unity of sensibilities, being removed from reality and at best projected against the ceiling by the awareness, those "thousand sordid images" dislocated from any existence, which may have
occasioned their presence in the mind. Eliot's version of the circumstances, as we have seen, leaves the sensibilities quite disjointed to the
awareness. The images projected are foreign to the sensations of the body
at this moment of its encounter, defying any possibility of an essential
unification of the awareness and so denying any possibility of touching
anything or any other person beyond the closed world of the awareness.

If, then, we consider as historical sequence these responses to sign, and
through sign to reality, by the poet from Donne to Wordsworth to Eliot,
we may observe that Donne manipulates the dissociation of sensibilities
in an audacious game which fancy plays with imagination, forcing the
reassociation by an audacity, as it appeared to Dr. Johnson. Such is that
"yoking of disparates by violence together" in making the body of an
elaborate conceit. The relation of disparates from this view seems less to
engage our response as if a revelation of the inevitable, a vision of the
structure of reality through analogy, than to engage us by a delight in the
forcing of conceit which often comes perilously near to absurdity.
Thought manipulates feeling in such a game, the delight of which is the
marvel of a structure in the poet's made thing, his elaborate conceit. In
such conceit, likeness in unlike things is extended by a proliferation of
correspondences among terms, in which our expectation of having
reached the conceit's limits is rebuffed by additional proposals of correspondence by the poet. There is such delight in a poem like Donne's "The
Flea," or in the more elaborate representation, his "Canonization" or
"Ecstasy." There is always, however, an implicit expectation by the poet
that we remember it is but intellectual play, though the play turns serious
for Donne himself in his "Holy Sonnets." In this respect, Donne's metaphor is a sort of parlor game for the entertainment of nimble wit.

The more disturbingly uncertain becomes our common understanding
of the relation of intellect to reality, of intellect to image, the less tolerant
we may in turn become with such play. We need but recall the impatience
that certain readers exhibit to our best modern practitioner of poetry as
parlor game, of conceit as the instrument of wit: the poet Wallace Stevens.
And a response to Stevens's virtues as poet is made the more difficult
because he, unlike Donne, does not hold a confidence of mind's relation
to reality like that which was supported for Donne out of scholastic metaphysics. Instead, Stevens makes his own metaphysics as he goes, the imagination declared the "angel" of his creations, necessary to those supreme

fictions, his poems. And so between the time of Donne and the time of Wallace Stevens, a considerable rupture of intellect and reality has occurred. The Cartesian tide had risen high by Dr. Johnson's day, especially as forced by Bishop Berkeley, who called in question the existence of the created world as aught but the shadow of *idea* projected by intellect itself.

Nor should we fail to note that Eliot, for all his championing of Donne as poet in his early criticism and poetic practice, comes to a very Johnsonian judgment of Donne by the time of his homage to Lancelot Andrewes in 1926. Before that time the instrument of his wit, learned of such poets as Donne and turned to a sharp edge by irony, seems the only means of survival of his awareness in its "lonely rooms," whether in a run down tenement occupied by Sweeneys and their mates or in that other room in which the women come and go talking of Michelangelo. It is also in this early period that Eliot is critically severe with the Romantic poets of the nineteenth century, and especially with Wordsworth. In "Tradition and the Individual Talent" (1919), having already appropriated the Wordsworthian circumstances of the awareness in his early poetry, Eliot attacks Wordsworth's formula of poetry as "emotion recollected in tranquility" as inadequate, indeed superficial. The phrase is from Wordsworth's "Preface" to the second edition of *Lyrical Ballads*, a passage apt to our reading of "Tintern Abbey." But Eliot is so disdainful of the argument that he does not even name either Wordsworth or his "Preface" in attacking the formulation.

At first Eliot seems Wordsworthian in his essay's argument: emotions are not suitably "personal emotions" in poetry, though they are required to be complex. The complexity is not that of emotions "with the complexity of the emotions of people who have very complex or unusual emotions in life," but rather must be "the ordinary ones," which "in working them up into poetry, . . . express feelings which are not in actual emotions at all." Emotions which the poet "has never experienced at all will serve his turn as well as those familiar to him." And so "we must believe that 'emotion recollected in tranquility' is an inexact formula." What is evident is the sense of necessity to Eliot to remain aloof in his own making, indifferent to reality lest he be too much drawn into the action of making if he is unprotected by a "formula" for poetry. (We have already recalled Eliot's later rejection of his own argument, his fulsome praise of Wordsworth's "Preface" after his own experience of reality as memorialized in "Ash-Wednesday.")

Wordsworth, midway Donne's playful irreverence of analogy and Eliot's despair, is confident of the validity of his own experience of reality, though not confident that he understands the meaning of that experience.

We have suggested that Donne is sufficiently confident of both the reality of his experience and of its meaning to his personal journey of soul to allow him to play high and wide with sign. Eliot at first finds the implicit abuse of sign as deployed by wit in Donne's poetry the only promise of an authority to his own awareness in its condition of entrapment. And so he adapts that address of intellect to image as held by memory as the possible means of intellect's survival of its isolation, a position which makes him scathing in his attitude toward Wordsworth, though he avoids the bar-room brawling of Pound's attack on "olde shepe Wordsworth." Wordsworth, contrary to both Donne and Eliot, procedes methodically ("maundering on" as Eliot and Pound see him) in an attempt to recover from his own seeming isolation from reality which settles upon him in proportion as he must increasingly reason his way through the world. His *Preface* and the unfinished *Excursion* are over-ripe in the attempt. Those works, incidentally, may well have contributed more than even Pound recognized, through the accidents of prosody, to Pound's remark that when he and Eliot appeared on stage as poets, they found the first thing necessary was the complete overthrow of the iambic pentameter line.

It is Wordsworth's dogged faith in the reality of experience no doubt that at last recovers Eliot's respect, though he recognizes how detrimental that faith is to Wordsworth's sense of prosody, Wordsworth's reluctance to abandon traditional metrics. That respect restored, Eliot turns from Donne as dangerous because of the very sophistication of his poetics, and especially his sophistications of prosody. Such lack of piety is detrimental to intellect's recovery to reality. His "Lancelot Andrewes" (1926) is a farewell to Donne. And we may note that the virtues he sees in Andrewes are similar to those in Wordsworth which Eliot will praise a decade later. Eliot says that "Andrewes's emotion is purely contemplative . . . wholly contained in and explained by its object." Donne, on the other hand, "is constantly finding an object which shall be adequate to his feelings," in contrast to Andrewes, who "is wholly absorbed in the object and there-fore responds with the adequate emotion." One recognizes here a modi-fication of Eliot's early address to the problem of the objective correlative, along with a changing attitude toward emotion as legitimate, a legitimacy disallowed in his early rejection of Wordsworth. Andrewes "is the more medieval," while Donne by contrast "is the more modern" and "much less traditional." If Donne has "a cunning knowledge of the weaknesses of the human heart," he appeals in the end "to those capable of a certain wantonness of the spirit." The essay is focused upon Donne and An-drewes as divines, but one recognizes that what is said of Donne as preacher extends to Donne as poet for Eliot, as it had not a few years earlier.

As for Wordsworth's concern for what the philosopher would call epistemology, that concern rises out of the question most haunting to Eliot himself: the nature of and the uses of memory. In a present event (such as that recorded in "Tintern Abbey") and in response to present perceptions of existences distinct from intellect itself, Wordsworth summons images from memory, images residual in some mysterious way out of past experiences. Those experiences he supposes to be more or less objectively certified as real, both those of this present moment and those from the past. He accepts event confidently as historical. That is, he has (in 1798 at least) a confidence in them as actual, feeling no frustrated necessity to refute a Bishop Berkeley by kicking a stone as did Dr. Johnson. We have already remarked, of course, that this confidence is called in question, subsequent to "Tintern Abbey" and the *Prelude*, by the shocking intrusion of death close at hand, though it does not follow that in his abandoning what we have called his initial Thomistic approach to the problem of the nature of existence that his approach was wrong as he himself came to fear. It was at that point in Wordsworth's life as if contemplation such as Eliot credits to Andrewes was natural to Wordsworth, from which he fell away to disoriented reflection following the shock of death's intrusion. He could no longer, as Eliot says Andrewes did, be "wholly absorbed in the object [of contemplation] and therefore respond with the adequate emotion."

What we might say, in the light of our earlier reflections, is that Wordsworth in the event could not respond to event at the deepest necessity to his *person*. He was overcome by circumstances which forced intellect back into the limits of the temporal and spatial as it were—back from visionary states within "spots of time" to a reflective state buffeted by the insistent conditions to the worldly existence of the soul. Under that pressure upon intellect, he tends to the conclusion (though he resists that conclusion) that his visionary moment, his "spot of time," was rather an illusional moment in which he was removed from reality. In that state of mind, circumstances, through the manifestation of the accidents of being, will most likely seem the reality, confounding intellect's natural light in such a way as to rebuff the supernatural light. Such is that state of mind reflected in "A Slumber Did My Spirit Seal" which gives that poem its poignancy. We must not leave this concern before remarking that Wordsworth, in his struggle to recover epistemological certainty through experience rationally accommodated (as opposed to an attempt at that recovery through studying what men have said of epistemology, which is more nearly Coleridge's approach) is dealing with his personal *history*, rather than with his *person* in its timeless nature.

We raise this last point to observe that Eliot's late respect for Wordsworth rests in Wordsworth's address of intellect to the personal, which
Eliot in his earlier Donnesque deportment as poet and critic had repudiated out of hand in requiring the "depersonalization" of the poet. We see
Eliot modifying that early position in his homage to Andrewes, though
without the precision of terms one might wish. (Maritain rebukes Eliot's
carelessness with terms like *depersonalization* in *Creative Intuition and
Poetry*.) Andrewes's emotion, Eliot says, is "purely contemplative; it is
not personal. . . ." But he rather certainly means here to characterize a
state of openness of the *person* to the object, finding Andrewes's person
rescued by such an address to the object, to the things of creation. It is a
deportment of intellect to things quite distinct from Donne's (in Eliot's
appraisal of the difference), since Donne's attitude is to "find an object"
which suits his feeling, which is a manipulation of objects not unlike those
by that intellect Eliot long ago characterized as J. Alfred Prufrock. Donne's weakness, he says, is that he is "fascinated by 'personality' in the
romantic sense of the word," or at least he indulges those readers so inclined. That is precisely why Eliot calls Donne as Divine "dangerous,"
since by his deportment toward the object he encourages "a certain wantonness of spirit." It is the same wantonness which Dr. Johnson found
encouraged in Donne's poetry, though given Eliot's distance from his
own early fascination he might better understand its appeal to the poet as
dandy or fop or (perhaps a more acceptable term) as *poèt maudite*.

Eliot in his early stage as poet-critic had known, as he says of Donne,
"the weaknesses of the human heart," without which knowledge he could
not have so well presented that convincing representation of the social
lounge-lizard, Prufrock. What he is not better able than Donne to understand at that point, or so I believe, is Prufrock's misery as person, a misery
nevertheless reflected truly in Eliot's made thing, his "Love Song," because he has been true to the necessity of the thing, to the nature of the
thing itself, the poem in his making of it. In this sense the poem is a
naturalistic one, reflecting the action of his agent's psychological nature.
Which is to say that Eliot's own poem is fuller of reality than his understanding might accommodate in the making. The naturalistic writer, if he
be true to existence even at the naturalistic level—even at the level of the
accidents of things—will (given a gift as poet) write more largely than he
may understand. It must be possible if reality is independent of that intellect, even if it suppose itself the cause of reality.

It is in this sense that we may find Wordsworth himself a "naturalistic"
writer, not in respect to sheer imagism but in respect to his response to
his actual experiences of "nature," his own encounter with the created

world. It is a "psychological" naturalism that holds him in "Tintern Abbey" to the necessity of a viable epistemology, no less than Eliot is held in his early poetry by that same necessity, though neither in that stage of his journey quite answers the necessity. And despite the deliberateness of Eliot's masks, the studied attempt to separate his own voice from the voice in the poem, it is the personal "nature" of this discrete soul we know as T. S. Eliot that informs, that makes the poems, in an attempt to discover its orientation in the dark woods that close upon it.

Five years ago, in this place, Wordsworth enjoined intellect in an experience of the world separate from intellect, through an intellectual action then less given to the necessity of thought than now necessary. There was then a natural openness of intellectual action. By this contrast, Wordsworth begins to constitute a sort of metaphor by juxtaposing the remembered event and a present event to intellect, considering the likenesses and unlikenesses of the intellect's response to those separate events, whose circumstances nevertheless appear to be more or less the same. It was *himself* remembered as in this place and in like season five years ago, summoned to this present self. His intellectual state on these disparate occasions is the poem's center. Here and now the likeness and unlikeness appear anchored, not in the accidents of the two events, but in the very nature of intellect itself. And it now appears that intellect, observed to be reflective in its present response to external circumstance, is problematic in both its past and its present estates in nature.

Up to this present moment, intellect had apparently been accepted tacitly, unselfconsciously, as a constant, but this present state is one of reflective thought in which are perceived changes in this particular intellect itself. Now existences other than this particular intellect are tacitly accepted as unchanging, as intellect assumed itself to be of yore. But now occurs this new fascinating discovery of intellect itself as the arena of change. (Such an either/or as a tacit assumption will lead, we know, to that shocked awakening by intrusive death which makes Wordsworth subsequently declare the condition of intellect in "Tintern Abbey" a "slumber" of "spirit.") It is within this arena of intellect, newly lighted by intellect's "natural light," that a present consciousness is so intensely conscious of itself. It is that self-consciousness that Wordsworth must certify as valid, as real, in which respect the realities beyond consciousness itself are neglected by intellect.

Thus there occurs his attempt to certify as valid his present consciousness by empirical evidence, though that existing thing which he would certify is now seen as a changing thing. We recall with what relief the speaker of the poem turns to his companion, Dorothy, for proof. What we may note as well is that, to a degree that her own *person* as distinct is ignored, she is reduced to an object, albeit an object presumed capable of response to his excited words. The movement by this speaker is as if intellect, through the body, reaches out to grasp the real, sensual world. There is a sort of reductionism practiced on Dorothy at this point, in that the speaker is insistent that the evidence in her eyes speaks the remembered state of intellect five years ago as hers now. There is an inclination to identity, whereby person (Dorothy) is reduced from particularity. Nevertheless, that turning seems conclusive to this reflecting intellect of the validity of what thought has yielded to that intellect through such reflective metaphors of itself. What this intellect is now confident of is its own existent though changing nature.

Dorothy, being five years younger in this present moment, seems to evidence a response in the present circumstances which his own senses perceive, but hers is in the manner of his own response five years ago. Thus it seems justified to conclude that the remembered event is valid as remembered and suitably juxtaposed to his own present experience in justifying thought itself. The justification depends not only upon likeness but upon unlikeness, for though she is now as he was then, she is not now as he is now, in respect to intellectual response to common circumstances. But more is accepted as certified by this self metaphor than can be sustained by such deliberate, analytical thought, if that thought becomes dislocated by an entrapment in the accidents of circumstantial existence. Wordsworth is dangerously near to such dislocation at this point. There is nevertheless a truth seen by this vision into the mind's reality, if only seen as through a glass darkly. It is this truth which we must value.

If there seems to Wordsworth in this present state of thought a constancy *in* existence independent of intellect, it is a constancy seen intuitively as *in*, as underneath, circumstantial accidents. Most specifically the constancy is of an actuality, a "something" deeply interfused in nature, akin to, but not simply a projection by this present intuitive intellect. Eliot will suggest in his "Preludes" that this is but a *notion* of a something, not a perception of an actual "something": some "infinitely gentle / Infinitely suffering thing." *Notions* and *fancies* are *curled* and *clinging* about images in the intellect which find no anchor beyond conceptual images floating in an awareness isolated to itself. But for Wordsworth the images in memory are not fancy's foils, and the sense of a *something* sustaining existence is not taken as a desperate notion but as an insight, however difficult to articulate. There was a time when articulation was not important, a time before this new necessity of thought that follows the loss of a spontaneous openness to existence, characterized as his roe-like state in nature.

Now, as if to certify a discovery about the relation of perception to reality, of concept to perception, of sign to concept, Wordsworth gives his poem a title which emphasizes, if subtlely, his growing confidence that metaphor has firm ground in existence itself and need not be merely the toy of fanciful intellect. The title concentrates on metaphorical implications of perception, available to reflective thought and so appropriately pointed to by signs that invite reflection. The central metaphorical emphasis is upon the middleness of his own journey. The details are actual, the signs denotative. The metaphorical implication in such "empirical" notation is not attributive, but analogical in relation to the reality experienced. The literalness seems certified objectively, but without an intentionality in the signing poet, the recorder of his experience.

There seem embedded in the experience itself metaphorical implications not unlike those which Dante with deliberate intent (as opposed to Wordsworth's attempt to record "factual" encounter) begins his great journey poem, *The Divine Comedy*. Wordsworth's signs of the experience occur as he stands in the shade of a tree. The world at large is bathed in noon sunlight. (He tells us that he composed the poem in his mind as he and Dorothy walked away from their noon rest and that he set the composed poem down on paper that evening.) This poem records an encounter with his own intellect that occurred in the middle of a particular day in the middle of a particular season in the middle of his particular life (as measured by three score and ten) in the middle of an actual walking journey, mid-way a river rising in the hills and emptying into the sea. The actualities are most real, the implied metaphorical coincidences arresting to his reflection. His is an "elegy" he says to life past. He sets it down as precisely as he can, against which we may suppose that this present experience so registered in its historical particulars may serve as a certain measure of anticipated experiences further along the journey. He calls it "Lines, Composed a Few Miles above Tintern Abbey on Revisiting the Banks of the Wye During a Tour. July 13, 1798." What is not engaged by the poem we already know: the question of death in relation to the whole of the intellect's journey in the world. If one discovers himself in the middle of his journey and recovers the memory of that journey to this middle, one has begun to discover the nature of the journey. One has recovered a beginning and a middle. The end lies yet ahead, but that prospect is not engaged by Wordsworth as it might well have been, given the extrinsic world's metaphorical message to him.

14

The Image as Node,
The Poet as Conjurer

Wordsworth's concern for whether metaphor is anchored beyond mere attribution comes to a crucial focus in our century, for both poet and philosopher. It is in Pound's active rejection of metaphor, concomitant with his initial embrace of Imagism. For image must, as a sign in poetry, be more firmly anchored in reality than it seems to have been for the "Romantic" poet against whom Pound is scathing in his rebuke of nineteenth century makers, Wordsworth in particular. But Pound finds himself increasingly estranged from the Imagists, in whom there is a naive submission to emotion, to feeling, unjustified by image. Hence his founding of Vorticism, in opposition to what he spoke of derisively as "Amygism," since Amy Lowell had preempted his leadership of the movement. In Vorticism there is the Bergsonian sense of image as a focus of immanence, so that one intending a management of the "life force" must be in control of image. "The image," Pound says in *Gaudier-Brzeska*, "is not an idea. It is a radiant node or cluster; it is what I can, and must perforce, call a VORTEX, from which and through which, and into which, ideas are constantly rushing." Image then is the arena in which his own intellect encounters and commands being in order to structure the world. These words Pound wrote as World War I was coming to a close.

At the end of World War II, the psychiatrists declaring Pound incompetent to stand trial for treason argued his mental incapacity on the evidence of his speaking in "clusters" of images. Meanwhile, for like reasons William Carlos Williams parted with Imagism, on the grounds that as practiced image was so far removed from the immediacy of reality as to become sterile justification of feeling. He helped found a movement himself, Objectivism, whose principle is the necessity of intellect's getting back to the thing itself, though Williams is most wary of intellect in its rational mode. The return to the thing is, in our terms, a return conducted by the intuitive mode. It is revealing to juxtapose to Pound's and Williams's rejection of Imagism the response to that movement by another modern Romantic poet, who had been drawn into the movement on the evidence of his poetry but against his will. Wallace Stevens insists that, while the "imagination is the romantic," the poet's "word must be the thing it represents; otherwise it is a symbol. It is a question of identity." It is a question of identity of the sign to the thing signified, this is to say. That is the question Pound answers in seizing upon the Chinese written character as most immediately the means of incorporating sign with thing.

But there is a considerable difference between the uses of the sign as Pound and Stevens would use it. While both consider the poet the supreme arbiter of an acceptable reality by virtue of intellect's power over being through the sign, Pound is intent on constituting thereby an ideal which is also an actual world, not one he conjured up for the entertainment of his own intellect as does Stevens. It is a world others will be forced into, willy-nilly. The direction Pound takes through image as a "node" under the command of the poet leads him to St. Elizabeth's Hospital to wait the outcome of the formal charge of treason. If we say Pound intends an imposition of order upon society, he does not suppose himself the dictator of that order, though we are very likely to conclude that he is. For he is religiously persuaded that any intellect when it truly sees sign ("node") as it is (that is, as Pound sees it) must consent to an order which the sign itself dictates.

Stevens on the other hand holds only that the use of sign is simply a delight of intellect, the poet's own. "One writes for one," he says. And that writing, that making, is the imagination's projection of a "supreme fiction," the poem. While Pound fervently holds that the making of his good poem is related in its end to a reconstitution of society, Stevens holds it merely an entertainment suited to the whim of the intellect which is staging an entertainment. The implication of Stevens's position is an extreme solipsism of intellect as the only arena of art. His "Idea of Order at Key West" makes this clear to us. As to whether we should accept such a position, Stevens if pressed would declare himself indifferent. But Pound, if we resist his fervent intention to transform the social body through his poetry, becomes violently angry in his rhetorical deportment to our opposition.

It is worth some further reflection on Stevens's attitude toward sign, especially in relation to what we have said earlier of him in relation to John Donne. Both are playful manipulators of the accidents of being through the agency of fancy, though Donne's is from a confidence in creation as creation, seen with an inherited metaphysics. Stevens is fancifully playful in a similar way, but he is so because he rejects all metaphysics, except as any imagined principle may serve imagination in a moment. Such a principle itself is an accident of intellect, as color is an accident of an object. One might with such a proposed likeness in unlike poets read Donne's "Ectasy" or "Canonization" in relation to Stevens's "Sunday Morning" or "Idea of Order at Key West" to discover fancy in the employ of two imaginations unlike in their commitment to reality. As for *metaphysics* as that term might be taken by the schoolman, as ideas of what men have thought whatever that thought, Stevens can be as scathing as Eliot ever was. Consider for a moment his "Cuisine Bourgeoise" (1942).

The poem is a concerted attack on intellectuals and intellectualism. The intellectual's words "are written, though not yet said." But so intent have we been on these "written" words that we find ourselves in this present an "outpost" of modernism. The world so held is "this douce, this dead, in which / We feast on human heads," having lost "the ancient cake of seed, / The almond and deep fruit" upon which the pagan feasted. The old pagan feasted on the world's body rather than on men's heads, on words written. Now we are reduced to "This bitter meat" of words, though it "sustains us" only palely where the world has been made a table, "a mirror in which [we] sit and look." This speaker summoned to the banquet will not sit down, asking "Who, then are they seated here?" Which question reminds us of another, namely Keats's "Who are these coming to the sacrifice?" Keats asked it of those pagan figures on the urn. Stevens asks it of the intellectual, his answer: they are "men eating reflections of themselves."

Now St. Thomas would be most sympathetic to Stevens's argument here, but only up to a point. He would certainly understand Stevens's bitter rejection of such bitter food as provided by modernist cuisine, by words written but not yet spoken as an actual reality of words in relation to a speaker. Such is food sterilized of being. That is the effect on sign when intellect becomes obsessed with what men have said rather than with the truth of how things stand. For a moment, St. Thomas would stand with Stevens, refusing the empty feast. But then he would find Stevens's solution toward a tolerable content no less tolerable than the empty intellectual fare removed of all reality. In this relatively late poem (1942), Stevens has not abandoned the position reflected in the other poems of his we have cited, a position made quite explicit in "Table Talk." There the premise is that "we die for good," not for *a* good through sacrifice, but that when we die, we cease to exist. From that it follows that "life . . . is largely a thing / Of happens to like, not should." And that being so, the speaker affirms his happens-to-likes are as valid as anyone's. He happens to like "red bush / Gray grass and gray-green sky." Such likings signify nothing beyond the accident of liking accidents. That is "one / Of the ways things happen to fall." It is significant to his point that what he happens to like are what are traditionally, since Aristotle, spoken of as the accidents of things such as color. It is the "red . . . / Gray, gray-green" of things that delights, the things themselves (bush, grass, sky) he lets "fall" indifferently.

Stevens is the end to which fancy may lead us out of Donne, and so justifies further searching, lest the argument be made infirmly. Consider Stephens's "Anecdote of The Jar" (1919) his version of Keats's "Ode on a Grecian Urn." It is as if Stevens points to Keats's failure of faith, in which he turns in his desire for vision at the expense of imaginative fiction. In the end the expense of that failed faith is that the poet is left in despair. In an imaginative act, not a literal one, the Stevens speaker creates a memory. "I placed a jar in Tennessee." No visiting of art's residue of history in a museum is at hand as with Keats, but a making of an imagined history. A clear-glass fruit jar on a remote (and from New Haven and its environs) backwoods hill in that strange foreign land, Tennessee. The jar *jars* mere reality, even a mere reality imagined. And so that "wilderness" rising up to the jar in submission is "no longer wild," though sprawling. The jar is "tall and of a port in air," perhaps most of all a "port" in the refined air of an imagined fiction in which to cast a steadying anchor. The jar, "gray and bare," does not "give of bird or bush / Like nothing else in Tennessee."

That is, unlike Keats's urn, Stevens's bare jar is one in which one might see the reflected accidents of the slovenly wilderness mirrored. It is not inscribed by art reflecting anything. By such artful images as those on Keats's urn there might be a signifying relation to actual reality deeper than the accidents of life. For surely such are those figures on Keats's urn, through which he enters the lives of "maidens loth," stirred in a "mad pursuit" of a breathing world beyond nature's decay, beyond his own "burning forehead" and "parching tongue." But image so approached returns Keats to his desolation. He has been only for a moment "teased out of thought" by art's images—teased as "eternity" teases one out of thought. But then comes the shock. He has been seduced into an illusion of reality by his wishful thinking.

Art as wishful thinking is sufficient to Stevens; such is his point, requiring of the poet only that he continue firm in his recognition that he is engaged in wishful thinking and not to be transported to a reality beyond nature's decay by the sorcery of his images. Better an imagined plain bare jar in a wilderness, sufficient to any fiction as a port in the rarefied air of the imagination's fictional world a-making, than a storied urn that steals imagination into history out of its present burning nature. For nature as the waster of each generation is not to be itself overcome through sorcery. The pretense of rescuing nature and history by art, in a moment's escape of the present, can but result in being returned like a burning comet into the actual air of nature. One will be burned up intellectually by the attempt, however slow the burning. The urn maker, so Keats knows by implication, is dead long ago, as are fair Madeline, her lover, the old nurse, and the Beadsman of "St. Agnes Eve." This is to say that for Keats, any moment of thought summons the terror of death, the oblivion of consciousness.

If life is dependable only in relation to accident, in relation to what one happens to like, the poet may be fortunate if he happens to like the accidents of those things which seem to yield readily to the game of making supreme fictions. Only, ye makers of such metaphors (says Stevens), forget not that what is thus made is fiction. Such then is Stevens's "message," his argument. And one of the amusing ironies of his poetry is that, committed to poetry as a making done for oneself alone and indifferent to other imaginations, Stevens's poetry turns out to be largely an argumentative justification of a principle which, did he fully accept it, would obviate any necessity of argument from him. Indeed, accepting the principle it must appear to him not only unnecessary, but rather foolish to argue his point, since argument is as futile as supposing that art could transport one through imaginative engagement beyond nature itself.

The objection to the usual Imagist poet—who tends to lack either Stevens's audacity or Pound's and Williams's social consciousness or Eliot's gradually emerging religious concern for the sign—lies in that Imagist's submission to mere feeling unordered by any intellectual authority governing his use of image in the thing made. Though dependent on a cultural sophistication, indeed upon a residue of "high culture," the Imagist movement tended to fondle its inheritance as if old mementos stored in attic trunks. Nature, too, tended to be fondled by feeling as if it were a pet, rather than engaged in its various creatureliness. Nor was there an active attempt to recover cultural history to a present vitality, as Pound would do. Nor appropriations in the lively making of outrageous history as Stevens would. Nor is there the empathetic, Keatsian action of negative capability to touch other lives through things as Williams would have poetry do. (Williams, we remember, in his beginnings as poet imitated

Keats, using a nineteenth century prosody. He came to discover for himself, through abandoning that borrowed prosody, just what it was in Keats's poetry that so affected him, Keats's gift of negative capability.)

To see what these principal poets of our century reacted against in their several ways and from their severally-taken understandings of the uses of poetry, consider in contrast Amy Lowell's "Lady" (1914). "You are beautiful and faded / Like and old opera tune / Played upon a harpsichord," while "My vigor is a new-minted penny, / Which I cast at your feet." Images here well enough, and in profusion. But none of them carry a conviction of immediacy to reality encountered by intellect, even at the level of the accidents of things that might enlighten imagistic sign. A faint hint of oriental delicacy, but one need only juxtapose Pound at this imagistic game to see difference at once. His faces in the metro are apparitions, petals "on a wet, black bough." Or his own "Portrait D'une Femme," a poem whose audacity of metaphor might delight Stevens but seems almost an intentional rebuke to an Amy Lowell. Pound's lady is as both body and mind "our Sargasso Sea," since "London has swept about you this score years." She is a vortex, out of which and into which Pound's satiric ideas and images continually rush. Pound extends his metaphor at some length, as if to show not only how one properly addresses image if one is to be an Imagist, but that neither Donne nor Stevens holds patent to conceit.

Pound's conclusion about what happens to Imagism seems inevitable. Out of a weak or failed making by the lesser poets of the Imagist Movement, there follows the decay of Imagism into "Amygism," as Pound has it. That T. E. Hulme, basing his poetics in Bergson, had already endangered poetry by insisting that the *fancy*, not the *imagination*, was the proper faculty of intellect to the making of poetry seems not to have disturbed Pound. Hulme is arguing a deliberate refutation of Coleridge, and his argument appeals to Pound in that it justifies his own inclinations to attribution. Conceptual attribution is an instrument suited to Pound's attempt to remake the social world on the authority of autonomous intellect. When he publishes "Complete Poetical Works of T. E. Hulme" in *Personae*, he writes a "Prefatory Note" setting them in the context of his own thought in abbreviated manifesto. The "School of Images" he says "may or may not have existed," though for all its faults it was at the outset (1909) "sounder than those such as the Impressionists or Post-Impressionists" or of "a certain French school which attempted to dispense with verbs altogether." But what is more important to Pound now is the "principles . . . of the 'inherent dynamists' " who published two issues of *Blast*, namely Pound and Wyndham Lewis, who in that little magazine announced Vorticism. Hulme contributed his "ruddy moon" leaning over a hedge, but also another moon poem in which his moon is hanging tangled in a ship's "tall mast's corded height" so that, though it seemed far away, is only "a child's balloon, forgotten after play." Fancy playing the game of attribution, hardly a poetry persuasive enough to warrant anthologizing in this anthologizing age. Such is the practice of a principle that will reveal itself inadequate to Eliot, but also to Pound. Following his release from Saint Elizabeth's Hospital for the insane after World War II, Pound in exile in Italy confronts that inadequacy in those fragmentary *Cantos* that conclude his poetic journey. Pound's entrapment in Vorticist principles at the beginning of World War I is such that we might remark it a bit further.

Pound's "inherent dynamists" have only a brief showing in the two issues of *Blast* in 1914, Eliot contributing his "Preludes" and "Rhapsody on a Windy Night" to the second and final issue (July 1915). What Pound means by *inherent* is important to our concern. Hugh Kenner in his *Pound Era* (1971) finds the origin of meaning to the term *Vorticism* orginating in Pound's thought in a 1912 article. There Pound speaks of words "as electrified cones, charged with 'the power of tradition, of centuries of race consciousness, of agreement, of association.' " Words, then, insofar as they bear anything independent of the poet's own inventions in them, do so as a sort of container of cultural-intellectual history, accorded an agreement by the poet or critic whereby the contained tradition is made viable, presumably through associating present contingencies in the act of making the words "new" as it were. Wyndham Lewis supplies an emblem as *Blast's* motif, a cone pierced by a wire. Words as cones strung by a continuity of agreement through time (the wire) is in the keeping of the poet, and to this position Pound would convert the King of England himself to Vorticism if possible. Says Pound, electrifying his words through upper-case type, "A VORTICIST KING! WHY NOT?"

Not long after, Pound's and Lewis's version of the word as cone will be adapted by Eliot as his version of the poet's mind, "a receptacle for seizing and storing up numberless feelings, phrases, images" out of tradition to serve the poet's individual talent. For Pound, what is *inherent* in the word is not essence of things as witnessed by concept, but the residue of intellectual history. Mind itself serves that office for Eliot at that point, from which the poet must extricate himself by a "depersonalization" in order to deploy mind's residue in the service of his individual talent. Unlike Pound, he is not concerned to convert the King, to transmogrify the residual presence of the past in the language of the tribe, purifying it for the sake of the tribe's social order of lamentable refuse, most of which to

Pound is of recent origin. (See *Hugh Selwyn Mauberley* to the point.)
Later, changed as he becomes, Eliot is still unlike Pound, in that he understands the poet's service to the tribe, his purifying the tribe's dialect, as
directed to an end beyond social or political or cultural ends, though not
indifferent to those ends. What he denies is that they are final ends to
intellect's journey, as Pound is so heavily inclined to conclude.

One might maintain convincingly, I believe, that it was Stevens among
these principal poets who saw most clearly, and early on, the implications
of, and the end of, an assumption of authority to the principle of attribution, though Pound and Williams later came to that dead end of intellect
which attribution determines. We have shown that recognition in Pound.
We may see that recognition rising in Williams as well, becoming increasingly evident in the development of his prosody from his abandoning the
Keatsian stanzas he set out with to his final content with the triadic stanza
and the variable foot. Indeed, the recognition becomes increasingly the
burden of his song. It is revealing to read Williams's *Paterson* in relation
to Eliot's *Waste Land* to see that in Williams's late epic there are some
echoes of Eliot's address to London and the Thames in Williams's address
to Paterson, New Jersey, and its Passaic. Williams's growing concern to
know the place beyond its natural and historical limits does not mean, of
course, that he is "influenced" by Eliot. Indeed, Williams is, from the
time of *The Waste Land*, severe in his rejection of Eliot, holding that Eliot's poem returned poetry to the academy after all the labor of rescuing
it from academic control. He sees Eliot as an intellectualist, then, unlike
Pound's view of Eliot. Pound goes to the heart of Williams's disturbance
with Eliot, as when Pound refers to "Parson Eliot."

In *Paterson* Williams is shoring fragments against his ruin, and in doing
so is recovering a depth to his intuitive discomfort with an old attributive
inclination. His late poem "The Sparrow," reveals a growing Hopkins-
like recognition of something in things very like that *instress* of being in
the thing itself which Hopkins would lift up through the *inscape* possible
to signs. This new recognition is more evident in Williams's late work
than in the pagan content of his earlier attentions to the thing itself, from
which he moves to his declaration of himself as Objectivist. Randall Jarrell
in his "Introduction" to Williams's *Selected Poems* says most perceptively, "He is as Pelagian as an obstetrician should be." But Williams is
considerably less Pelagian in his later life as he encounters and addresses
the limits to making, whether in the delivery of poems or babies. The
recognition of those limits, the recognition that the making of a poem
involves a mediating office as "creator," provides him at least a partial
understanding of the nature of the thing he makes: he assists its becoming,

as it were, and is not absolute in its cause as a made thing, since it depends, though through him, upon his own dependence in existential reality. That is an office a general practitioner of medicine can hardly avoid seeing. With this suggestion in mind, we may read his "Sparrow," dedicated to his father, considering it in relation to Keats's early and Eliot's late concern for negative capability, the nature of which refutes Pelagianism. For one can hardly surrender the self in an openess to the being of other existing creatures through "negative capability" and continue a Pelagian. The frustrations of Keats's and Eliot's attempts at the intellectual action of negative capability raises despair in both poets, though Eliot is at last able to move beyond despair to a hope sprung of faith in existence itself as created. Having said these things, we add finally that Williams's "Sparrow" is perhaps most interestingly read in relation to Eliot's "Ash-Wednesday."

As for that firm Pelagian, Wallace Stevens, his response to the vagaries of Imagism is to insist upon the power of his imagination as exercised by the authority of his will. Thereby he makes his "supreme fiction." Stevens does grant a level to existences independent of intellect, whereby he prepares for the contradictions he must eventually face, but by that admission he delays that necessity. The level of existence which he grants, in relation to the intellect's imaginative exercise, takes things as a sort of prime matter available to and even suited to imagination's requirements, though how or why available and especially why suited to intellect is a question not to be asked too searchingly. To pursue that question is to clip imagination's wings, that necessary angel no longer able to rise into the purer air of supreme fictions. Thus for Stevens, intellect dominates the used (and abused) realities by willing metaphorical structures as fictions. In rare, or rarefied, metaphor, Stephens does not suppose any essential alteration of reality, as do some other species of Pelagian gnosticism which intend as primary a reconstitution of reality, hardly interested in fictions, though in actuality capable only of *fictions*, a term suited to such remakings of being. There is for Stevens a more limited transubstantiation by intellect, his own fiction occurring at the level of intellectual play only, and intended only for the delight of intellect itself. Thus Stevens finds as the danger in attributive metaphor as the poet uses it the poet's possible confusion in which he mistakes his own fiction for reality or as an instrument through which reality reveals itself in a visionary way. If one fail to know his attributive actions are merely attributive, and as such suited only to fictions, he may even mistake through his fiction illusion as a vision of a transcendent reality. Keats deliberately makes such an attempt through his imagination. Fiction mistaken as a vision of essential nature or vision of transcendent cause of nature can but end in de-spair. To suppose that one may by willed fictions perform actual transub-stantiations of reality, as Pound believed possible, must end at last in the bitter defeat waiting any naive Utopian. That is the danger Stevens would avoid, and his poetry as argument insists on the point again and again.

From Stevens's view of the problem, in forgetting that intellect moves through fictions one may even come to believe a "something" deeply interfused in nature as well, as Eliot comes to do. Accused of having been influenced by Eliot, Stevens replies to William Van O'Connor (he is re-sponding to O'Connor's book on Stevens, *The Shaping Spirit*) "I don't know him at all. . . . After all, Eliot and I are dead opposites and I have been doing about everything that he would not be likely to do" (*Letters*, Apr 25, 1950). To see what Stevens is talking about, another comparative reading: Stevens's "A High-Toned Old Christian Woman" and, once more, "Ash-Wednesday." Though the actual history of Stevens's poem does not allow us to conclude it a direct response to this particular poem by Eliot, such a reading nevertheless shows clearly why Stephens was shocked to find O'Connor quoting him as saying "I knew Eliot . . . prin-cipally through correspondence." For Stevens at this stage of his life, nei-ther is there a "something" deeply interfused in nature as believed by Wordsworth, Hopkins, Eliot, nor may intellect itself infuse nature with substance, as Pound acts as if he believes.

Nevertheless, for Stevens "Poetry is a means of redemption" of intellect in its moments of fictional delight. Again, "After one has abandoned a belief in God, poetry is that essence which takes its place as life's redemp-tion." Poetry is salvific in that through it intellect forgets itself in de-lighted makings, so long as intellect does *not* forget it is delighted by fictions. The danger for Stevens is of quite another sort of "fancy," that of imagined essences taken as real. Imagism failed to see this possible Stevensonian escape of intellectual isolation in the use of image. "The vice of imagism," says Stevens, "was that it did not recognize" that "not all objects are equal." And failing to do so, we might add, Imagism can but practice a species of identity, not one in which all objects are reduced from their particularities (Stevens's objection), though that reductionism is evident. But more destructive of the poet's intellect, there develops an identity of response, arresting intellect. In this limited sameness of re-sponse all "feelings" become the same feeling, all emotions the same emo-tion. They become the same not only in their nature but in degree. There follows an endless sameness in the poetry, affecting subsequent poets to such an extent that it is difficult very often to distinguish as different poets speaking the poems in an issue of a periodical, except for the name attached and information in the "Contributors' Notes."

In one sense, however, objects are equal for Stevens also. They are equally available to imagination as contributors of accidents to the ingenuity of that necessary angel's making its fictions. It is only in the confusions of the relation of *accident* as image and of *image* as speaking the *thing* that Imagism comes afoul of reality. For it becomes victim of its sentimental illusion that a desire for an egalitarian brotherhood of all existing things is sufficient to accomplish that effect upon things. One of the vices of Imagism, sufficient to set Pound's teeth on edge, beholds what it takes to be an *essential* unity of creation on the evidence of the accidents of existing things. Thus there occurs that deportment of sentimentality through which intellect presumes a universal "likeness" that reduces all things to a fake unity, making (in Stevens's phrase) "all objects equal." Reality itself rebels against such disjunction of intellect by an illusion believed to be a vision of reality. To put the point another way, in respect to Stevens's objection, a sentimentality so deferential to the accidents of being prevents the appropriation of accidents to audacious uses in metaphors of a supreme fiction. Such a sophisticated intellectual as Stevens could not abide such sentimentality. But neither could Williams or Pound—or Eliot. Each rejects Imagism, though on different grounds, from different understandings of intellect's relation to reality and of image's role in this relation.

Stevens's position is of considerable interest in the light of his own late commitment to a belief shared by Eliot. For in the end he and Eliot are no longer such "dead opposites" as Stevens believes in 1950. At the level of reality which Stevens accepts as suitable to poetry, all objects are in a sense equal. For objects are sorts of rocks so to speak, though differing in being large, small, oddly shaped, differently colored, to be used by imagination in building its fictions. Objects as source of accidents commanded to fictional pleasures are themselves let "fall" as things, the imagination indifferent to things in themselves, to essences. For essences would interfere with the imaginative play of reconstituting accidents as fiction suited to the intellect's appetite. Intellect is fed most variously, but one may not read Stevens's poetry without concluding that his own intellect is that of a sophisticated gourmet. It is in Stevens's intellect a refusal to address things in themselves, and thus he justifies raiding reality in order to commandeer the booty of being, the accidents. He can do so for a long while, so long as he can deliberately ignore the problem of the essence of things—what things are in themselves—which problem always survives because independent of the raiding intellect. Meanwhile, things are let "fall" most deliberately, and it is that attitude toward creation that leads to the charge some critics have made against Stevens while others praise him for it. He is first and last a hedonist.

From the Pelagian position Stevens would maintain by such arbitrariness, he must let things fall. To consider things beneath their accidents: St.
Thomas insists this is not only proper but inescapable. Eliot found
Thomas right. He could not avoid the encounter since that *beneathness*
proved already a knowledge in intellect despite its attempted rejection. To
consider *things* in the Thomistic perspective is to call into question the
presumptuous authority of intellectual Pelagianism, whether that of the
hedonist or the would-be reformer of the universe. Whether intellect
would raid reality for the booty of accidents suited to its fictional appetite
or would invade reality and settle down to reconstitute it, accident and
not the thing in itself must be made the focus of intellectual action. It is
only thus that the *word* of an intellectual action (concept) may be declared
identical to the thing, by which declaration it is presumed that the thing
is transmogrified by the word. For the *thing* is for the Pelagian, at least
from the Thomistic view of that error, not really a thing at all. It is only
unwanted accident preventing a wanted thing, namely a pseudo-reality
transformed to Intellect's "real" reality. Thus is that *thingness* which is
independent of finite intellect denied by rejection, lest the whole entertainment of intellect collapse, whether only that making of fictions or that
remaking of creation to fit desire. For unless *thingness* is rejected, all is
lost to the Pelagian intellect.

The denial of essence in things makes possible an exploitation of things
at many levels, from the fictions of attributive metaphor to the abuses of
the body of creation against which environmentalists protest in confused
ways at this moment of out collective abuse. The protest is confused, I
would contend, precisely because it is not effectively anchored in a metaphysics of being. Because it is not, whether we speak of fictional or actual
abuses of being, of essences, what proves at risk in the end is not the body
of creation but the soul of the abuser. We might see in that soul, if we
could see it in its own essential nature, a growing discomfort, a growing
restiveness. It is a spiritual discomfort over intellectual willfulness, the
transgression of the reality of the soul itself, that brings Stevens in his last
days to his conversion to Christianity, and it is toward our understanding
that discomfort that we have pursued Stevens as one sort of "Romantic"
poet, one who solves his initial intuitive unrest by an intellectual strategy
differing from the one Eliot at first attempted. For Stevens does not take
recourse to severe irony as did Eliot, though he is given to playful irony.

That attempt through irony, we might suspect, is likely to serve a more
rapid descent to despair, resulting in either a spiritual collapse or a new
movement of intellect out of irony. That was the contingency to Eliot's
soul whose manifestation, we suggested, is his *Waste Land*. But Stevens

chooses rather the delights of fancy, a rescue of the soul from its discomfort through a delaying tactic, the play of metaphor. His irony lies in his
insistence that the play he makes—his "fiction,"—depends on its deliberate disparity from any "reality" as solemly pursued by such poets as
Keats or Eliot. Such play may distract intellect from its recognition of
soul's uneasiness. All things are not the same, Stevens says, but that is a
principle accepted without metaphysical pursuit of the recognition. Instead his is a rapid turning from things by the strategy of commanding
accidents, which are themselves the same in respect to their forced service
to the imaginative willfulness of attributive metaphor. Thus a moment's
breathing room for intellect, but the dungeoned soul is let fall as well as
the things in themselves.

Stevens is right in declaring that all things are not the same, an objection
one might well make on reading several poems by the same Imagist poet.
In reading H. D., one is hard pressed to distinguish "Heat" from "Pear
Tree" from "Sea Rose" through attention to the poems themselves
without a steady reference to elemental accidents. But that inequality
of things, if addressed beyond the level of accidents as convenient to
such poetry, must at last call imagination itself—Stevens's "necessary
angel"—into question. What one begins to realize is that the imagination
so understood or so used requires that it assume the offices of the "Lord
and Giver of Life." That means that the imagination must be continu-
ously active if intellect itself is not to fall into the dark tangles of reality
through the inevitable questions that rise to haunt it at the moment an
entertainment, a poem, ceases to be *being made*.

The difficulty here is not only that of intellectual finitude but the finitude of that thing housing intellect as well, the body. One must rise and
go, not to Innisfree or Byzantium, but to food and drink and rest. And
intellect thus recalled from its making of fictions turns to elemental practical attentions. And therein it encounters, willy-nilly, things in themselves, though they be so simple as a piece of bread and a glass of wine.
Intellect cannot be maintained uninterrupted in its actions of making fictions, though Stevens recognizes such as his desire. At least we might
suppose so from his suggested title for the whole of his poetry. His title
for the *Collected Poems*, he suggested, might well be "The Whole of Harmonium." (Pound alludes to his *Cantos*, as we noticed, as a great "crystal
ball.") His title for the collected poems is implicitly a recognition by Stevens of the difficulty of his poetic principle. What cannot be accommodated, as he knows well, are the interstices, those portions of the life of
his intellect dated 1879–1955 when he is not writing or reading fiction. It
is this whole measure of Stevens which requires a harmony through a

wholeness which imagination cannot itself supply and toward which he reaches in the end. His position is untenable, then, at both the practical and the philosophical level.[12]

In retrospect it seems naive of so sophisticated an intellectual as Stevens to suppose otherwise, even when we acknowledge other ways in which he filled those interstices: his service to his firm or his working the rose garden in his yard. Not that he was unaware that the problem was festering in him. He responds ambiguously to questions put to the content of his professed faith in the imagination and its poetry as savior once "one abandons a belief in God." He recognizes as well the "hedonistic" aspect of that adopted faith, whereby imagination transforms accidents of things into a delicate cuisine to delight intellect, an elevated, pseudo-pagan deportment of intellect to reality. *Pseudo*, in that the pagan believes actual gods in actual things. A moment of insight, confessional to Stevens, is his comment on "Sunday Morning," the one of his poems most generally known. It is "not essentially a woman's meditation on religion and the meaning of life. It is anybody's meditation. . . . The poem is simply an expression of paganism, although, of course, I did not think that I was expressing paganism when I wrote it." The disturbing nature of this confession he may well not have recognized at all, or only recognized at his end. For the paganism expressed is that of, and suited to (in Eliot's words on Donne), those intellects who are "fascinated by 'personality' in the romantic sense of the word," for whom personality is an ultimate value, thus forgetting "that in the spiritual hierarchy there are places higher than that of a Donne," or Stevens. It is in this respect that Stevens is, as Eliot says of Donne, "dangerous" since tempted to a "certain wantonness of spirit" at the expense of the soul.

15

The Shock of Sepulchral Verse in the Cauldron of Chaos

Until late in life, not Pound nor Williams nor Stevens would, or did, engage the problem of the relation of intellect to certain givens involved in our intellectual response to present reality, givens not accounted for by social and cultural accretions in language. As for those presences in language, Pound (and Eliot for awhile) attached the term *tradition* to them. When Pound, in praise of Vorticism and in celebration of Hulme's "Collected Poems," speaks of the deportment of Vorticist intellectuals as a school of "inherent dynamists," he means those intellects for whom a dynamic energy, cumulative in language, is possesed through the exercise of signs. The sign becomes the focal point of that energy. In image, then, one has a point in time, controlled by intellect, "from which and through which, and into which, ideas are constantly rushing," as Pound puts it on another occasion. What is lost is an echo in sign, out of concept, of the intellect's own intuitive, preconceptual recognition of being, its knowing things in themselves, without which inherent knowledge (as when intellect ignores or defies that knowledge) intellect is reduced to associationism, to attribution. It is thus in its contentions with reality reduced to the accidents of being.

In sum, intellect when committed to Pound's understanding of a dynamism "inherent" in sign is thereby trapped in history. It becomes noticeable, then, that in the light of these poets' response to existence which requires their attributive address, Pound and Williams are most cautious about metaphor, recognizing it as seductive of intellect's control of sign. They either avoid metaphor or exert firm control upon it lest through metaphor intellect succumb to fancy. Stevens, to the contrary, welcomes such seduction, as if thereby he might seduce the seducer, fancy. But Ste-

147

vens always maintains, in theory at least, a firm reason in regard to metaphor's fictions: that is, he is always insistent that intellect be aware that it is fiction and not an independent reality which its play makes. We have seen Stevens at this play. Consider in contrast Williams.

Williams's speaker in one poem sees a paper bag rolling along a street. It is "about the length / and apparent bulk / of a man." A car runs over it, a moment's shock to that perceiving intellect who is tempted by metaphor out of reality. It is a stance in the voice speaking the words which pays insufficient attention to its own *apparent*. For "Unlike / a man it rose / again rolling." The poem is called "Term," a cautionary commentary on the *terms* of metaphor. The actuality restores intellect from metaphor's penchant for identity in the "unlike." Williams would avoid violating the thing itself through fancy's metaphor, for to do so is to disorient intellect. The unlikeness, the thing in itself as perceived, is fundamental to an intellectual orientation to a world which proves itself independent of sign. Sign must be more carefully controlled by intellect. We have, by such observation of Williams, discovered that though his stance tends to be Pelagian, as Randall Jarrell says, there is nevertheless a hesitation in him to violate the thing in itself. There is a sort of mysticism short of understanding as yet, but it will grow in Williams toward those final recognitions we have spoken of, signified in such poems as his "Sparrow." He is most wary of engaging the question of being as implying a transcendent cause of being, but he responds again and again to the thing in itself. His own insistent putting of this position is in his "Sort of Song": One must get "back to the thing itself" he says, and that is to come very near to seeing the *thing in itself*, the essence borne in a sensual encounter of the accidents of that thing. That is why Williams's poetry is engaging to a degree that the Imagist poetry of H. D. is not.

Without the deliberate recognition of being as possessed in preconceptual knowledge, intellect will fail to realize its own nature as vortex, as the center in which essence encounters soul. It may easily, through metaphor, find itself caught up by metaphor into an illusional state far removed from any reality possible to the desire when fed only by the illusion. Consider, for instance here, that Williams is, on the basis of metaphor as mis-taken by intellect, calling the Christian idea of resurrection itself into question, which is not the same thing as to find the metaphor inadequate to the reality which has tempted to fancifulness. For the bag rises only as a man might after lying in the street if not run over. It is through such self-deceptions through metaphor (Williams might put it) that one may find himself pursuing ancient rumor at Bethlehem on a Sunday morning. And so it is in a defense against such deception through metaphor as made by fancy, through attribution, that Williams is agnostic, falling back (as Jarrell sees) into a secular Pelagianism. Here Williams no doubt agrees with Stevens's position, seeing John Keats endangered by the delusion that imagination can lift the soul beyond the empirical level of things as they entrap the soul through the senses. To become so entrapped, is to become victim to a "thought" capable of focusing only on a burning forehead and parching tongue.

That is not a mistake Williams is prepared to make in his own adaptation of the Keatsian negative capability. For if Pound insists that his mentor Kung (Confucius) was very careful to say "nothing of 'the life after death'" (Canto XIII), neither will Williams. It is as if both these poets, Pound and Williams, fear that attributive action by its very nature not only allows the imaginative freedom desired but at the same time conditions intellect to take refuge in its invention itself. But to be thus removed, to thus escape into his poem, is to forfeit intellect's empowerment over its relation to the context of reality, within which alone it may effect its desired ends. Thus the ends intended through their poetry as instrument would be endangered: for Williams, a recovery of community between people and things, between people and the very "stones"; and for Pound, a recovery of order among people and things whereby words order the ideal state. What both recognize intuitively is that when metaphor is fundamentally attributive, not anchored in the structure of reality, it cuts intellect free of reality's requirements that are additional to the poet's desire to make imaginatively. Stevens insists on such freedom. In this respect he reverses Williams's insistence that there are "No ideas but in things." For Stevens, it is rather that there are no things but in ideas so far as the art of poetry is concerned. It is only through this principle that reality may be seduced of its accidents, necessary to metaphor as Stevens would have metaphor be.

If Williams resists being made captive to fancy through a metaphor that makes illusion attractive to desire, neither will he remove himself by an aloofness such as Stevens's, whereby intellect feeds knowingly on illusion, upon its own "supreme fictions." Stevens chooses not to risk even his own poems to the possibility of their becoming a "bounty to the dead" poet, that is, the poet as he is once his poem is shed from his active making. Poetry is salvific for Stevens, but not as a monument to the poet. He would be delighted by Donne's imaginative conceit in "The Canonization" of the sonnet as first "a pretty room," then as "well-wrought urn" as Donne's speaker intends in his seduction. But Donne's speaker is intent upon seducing, not intellect through metaphor, but a woman by her lover—through the fiction that is the poem. Donne's speaker attempts to deceive the intellect of his mistress by an illusion made persuasively, as if it were rather a vision of the full reality of physical love.

It is Keats dying who turns to the poem as such an urn, though in the end he finds no comfort to his particular person by so turning. Between Donne at his urn-making and Keats at his, we discern how the person of the poet becomes drawn to an immediacy, a presence in the act of making of the maker to himself, though that welcomed beginning can be seen only as an end by Keats. Stevens will take his direction from Donne's playfulness, avoiding Keats's high seriousness that leaves him "forlorne," reduced to his "sole self." As Stevens sees it, art may be mistakenly supposed as providing such sepulchers of intellect out of forlorn wishfulness, but that makes of the poem only another sort of tomb like the "tomb in Palestine." That imaginative gathering image, the tomb in Palestine, supplies only an untenable myth against the "old chaos of the sun." It is untenable because its myth is believed by the simple in their waking dreams. The chaos of the sun is constant impingement upon intellect up to the point of death. And for Stevens, to deny this is but to prepare intellect for crashing descent into the cauldron of chaos when fancy fails to maintain an ascent of faith in support of myth as reality.

Stevens would take lesson on this point from Keats's lines in his "Ode to a Nightingale," lines artfully apt to the unity of that "Ode" precisely because they are poor poetry, as Keats himself knew but as sentimental readers of him do not. "Already with thee!" the speaker cries in delight, having escaped thoughts about nature's inevitable decay in the world where "Beauty" loses the actual "lustrous eyes" the Lover's senses would engage as unchanging, where "new Love" can pine for them a moment, but not "beyond tomorrow," when that Lover "grows pale, and specter-thin, and dies." And so to the offices of fancy in an attempted escape: "Already with thee! tender is the night" in such an escape to that region where "haply the Queen-Moon is on her throne, / Clustered around by all her starry fays." Fanciful metaphor, indeed, a striving to believe the imagination to have gained an ascent into a larger reality. But then comes grim immediacy of circumstance, imagination crashing back into dark reality:

> But here there is no light,
> Save what from heaven is with the breezes blown
> Through verdurous glooms and winding mossy ways.

That breeze of reality blows as it listeth, leaving one in the "embalmed darkness" of nature decayed, thus drawn to be "half in love with easeful

Death." Stevens will have none of it, asserting that, since "we die for good," we must turn to the delight possible in the "happens to like" of intellect, in relation to how things "happen to fall," a delight in red, gray, gray-green to paint the moment's fiction in the accidents of being, including the accidental being of this responding intellect itself.

If none of these poets, Stevens or Williams or Pound, will entertain the question of immortality in its insistent eruption in intellect, whether the immortality of art or that of a rescue of the soul itself to its potential perfection—if they share in the secularized Pelagianism of our age, Williams values a proletarian empathy against Stevens's ascetic solipsism, which Stevens gives an Epicurean gloss. Neither will he consent to Pound's Pelagian-authorized intent to structure being in hierarchical society, Pound's continuing Classical Romanism as opposed to Eliot's late Christian Romanism, which neither Williams nor Stevens will accept either. Stevens will accept neither Williams's nor Pound's position, and most certainly not Eliot's, though there is in him a certain delight in the sophistications of hierarchy, most particularly a hierarchy of sensibilities. His delight is most apparent in those refinements of metaphor in which terms are drawn close to an identity, the most subtle differences proving the keenest delight to intellect.

Having made such distinctions among these poets, there remains a community of mind among them nevertheless, a community in principle: their acceptance of intellect as gnostic, though their intentional use of that principle makes them anarchists within the community of gnostic faith. That is a community Eliot found himself member of but with a growing restiveness. As that restiveness in Eliot became more conspicuous, his contemporaries who had elevated him as the principal poet of modernism found him more and more anti-modernist, and so more and more antagonist. Not in respect to prosody, of course, in which he is "modern" enough. It was that aspect of his art that seemed most baffling, for how could a traditionalist moving toward orthodoxy be so advanced in his prosody? Williams complains of Eliot's betrayal of poetry, making it hostage once more to the academy. Stevens insists that he and Eliot are direct opposites. But most clearly put, though seemingly most cryptic, is Pound's backhand to his companion poet, "Parson Eliot." For Pound saw early, by the time of *The Waste Land*, the direction Eliot was bound in, toward Purgatory Mountain and beyond. Their mutual concern to purify the dialect of the tribe shared a mutuality still, but a more limited one. Pound's view of the use of the "dialect" is at a level far short of Eliot's growing understanding of the word in its aspect as vortex. There will be for Eliot but one center at last to which may be attributed a description of the word as vortex "from which and through which, and into which, ideas are constantly rushing," in Pound's phrase. Ideas will be a pale insufficiency to Eliot as he moves beyond a Pelagian, Cartesian idealism, for it is the all of creation that concerns him as it relates to the All, the Word within the words and the concept. There is a bearing "presence" in reality and so in intellect which Eliot declares at last to be the Word within the word, the Word in the desert.

16

The Progress of Doubt to Habit

If there is a mistrust of metaphor by the "Romantic" poet through an intuitive recognition of metaphor's deceptiveness when attributive in its nature, such a wariness is warranted, given the poet's growing recognition of intellectual confusion inherited from Cartesian idealism. But the particular solutions to the problem by Pound or Williams or Stevens are not suitable to it. For to each in different ways, attribution is taken as a means sufficient to order so long as intellect itself exercises an authority through will. Given Decartes's use of "doubt," we remember as pertinent Aristotle's observation in his *Metaphysics* that doubt is a rarity among men and is itself a sign of intellectual cultivation. Our highly sophisticated intellectualism is founded on doubt, though largely focused upon precedent intellectuals as naive believers in doubt. Doubt as an initial agnostic address to a question becomes an article of faith held beyond particular questions, lest intellect be required to an assent that appears reductive of intellectual authority.

That is why we must recall that Aristotle advises us to "doubt judiciously." It is this refinement of doubt that Eliot moves toward out of the extreme skepticism he admits as his early position. We have heard him say in his "Second Thoughts About Humanism" that an intellectual consent, a sort of willing suspension of intellectual disbelief, allows intellect to entertain possibilities without embracing them, this being a species of judicious skepticism. He adds that "intellectual freedom is earlier and easier than complete spiritual freedom," the meaning of *freedom* by the time of his statement very close to that spoken in the *Prayer Book*'s collect addressing God, "whose *service* is *perfect* freedom." What is indicated by the collect's words is a full subservience to God which results paradoxically in freedom made perfect in the soul, from which follows at last an intellectual freedom far beyond the pretended freedom of skepticism.

That is the context in which St. Augustine promises that if we love God we may do what we will, the will itself made perfect by love.

But such are theological sophistications, unnecessary to the simple soul in that open love which a skeptical world will not abide. The skeptic can see such freedom only as contradictory, not as paradoxical. For the skeptic it is an enslavement, not a liberation of the soul in its potency. And so, between that position of "perfect freedom" and the alternative assumption of intellectual action as autonomous lies skepticism's dilemma. It is a dilemma made the more disturbing to the degree that the skeptical intellect senses itself forced by its desire for autonomous existence to an address of existence as possible only through attribution, which is a relation to accidents that proves discomforting. In that dilemma, reflection, thought about things known, becomes a condition of intellect to be avoided. For the forcing of attribution as the rescue of intellect to the freedom of autonomy will serve only as a temporary stay against confusion. Yet intellect is unable to be stilled, or to be "still and still moving" in Eliot's phrase for the soul's gathering perfect freedom as dramatized in "Ash-Wednesday."

The forcing of attribution by the intellect is a momentary stay against intellectual confusion. In putting the difficulty in these words, we are deliberately echoing yet another "Romantic" peer of Eliot's, Robert Frost, who affirms poetry as precisely that, "a momentary stay against confusion." It is a momentary stay through an intellectual action directed against all save the acting intellect, that *all* which Frost summarizes as the "background in hugeness and confusion shading away from where we stand into black and utter chaos." That Frost does not waver from this view of existence is underlined by his deliberately placing as the final poem of his final volume a parable of a winter military expedition of a single "I" "Against the trees." The sniper "lays a maple low," having first "marked" it. The parable concludes:

> I see for Nature no defeat
> In one tree's overthrow
> Or for myself in my retreat
> For yet another blow.

One might take the parable only on its surface, as an account of a literal gathering of wood from a forest. Or one may take it as, in a constant Frostian metaphor, a game this New England rustic plays against "Nature." But Frost is wily in his sophistication, so that when "Nature" is seen as "black and utter chaos" and the only soldier acceptable is this particular intellect whom we call Robert Frost, we begin to recognize him as more Sartrean than it is generally comfortable to acknowledge. What he knows is that from his position, any intellectual action is but a momentary stay against his own intellect's confusion before metaphysical questions. The defense against such questions is a very accomplished poetry of attribution whose burden is very like that of Wallace Stevens's. Of course the milieu from which each gathers accidents of being for metaphors is quite different, preventing our general recognition of their kinship. This is especially so since we ourselves have been rather effectively conditioned to respond sentimentally to the accidents of being through fancy, thus granting attribution an unwarranted authority. We must, then, make Frost's position more certain.

Frost, sixty years old, speaks of his position to students at Amherst, and it is not a joyful view of existence he holds. Himself Pelagian, though he does not use the term, he must contend with doubt, and he does so through "form" of his own making. As for the world he inhabits, it is hardly an encouraging one: "The background in hugeness and confusion shading away from where we stand into black and utter chaos," the proper response to which is "any small man-made figure of order and concentration." He concludes: "To me any little form I assert upon [that chaos] is velvet, as the saying is, and to be considered for how much more it is than nothing. If I were a Platonist I should have to consider it, I suppose, for how much less it is than everything." The continuing general impression of Frost as traditionalist spirit overlooks this very dark center, out of which the whole of his poetry grows. Frost is a modernist, though usually presented as a traditionalist because of his prosody and his New England country imagery, an obverse of the traditionalist Eliot. He makes a figurative, attributive "little form," projected upon chaos as velvet, a jewel displayed in a manner that distracts attention from the black and utter clouds against which it is projected. (I have considered this aspect of Frost's mind and poetry at greater length in "Robert Frost: One Who Shrewdly Pretends," *The Men I Have Chosen for Fathers*, 1990.)

If poetry, or any intellectual act, is only a momentary stay, a rear-guard action defending intellect's control of chaos, then the poet is committed to a continuous making of a poem lest chaos ("Nature") win out. Imaginative acts are likely to become increasingly a desperate defense, not primarily directed against the chaos, though that is the pretended antagonist, but against an interior seed of despair that threatens to blossom into a darker presence than the imagined chaos as antagonist. The imaginative action is again and again discovered to be but fleeting in its effectiveness. The poem as Stevens's "means of redemption" or Frost's "momentary stay" is the opposite of another possibility to intellect: a momentary vision into reality effected through the things of nature in themselves. Eliot speaks of such moments, we have said, as "still points." And we have suggested something of their complexity. What intellectual reflection discovers is the presence in intellect of a preconceptual knowledge possessed anterior to the reflection and continuing in the contemplation that blossoms into vision out of reflection. This is the direction Eliot takes in his escape of entrapment by that idealism common to these poets under consideration. It is a recovery beyond the more or less desperate attempt of intellect to control event, to control the action of its own making in opposition to those threats against its autonomy from either existence seen as chaos or an interior despair as the deadly effect of desire unfulfilled and so stifling to intellect itself.

There can be no resolution by the secular Pelagian, the inverted Platonist such as Frost or Stevens for whom Idea emanates from human intellect, as opposed to being projected from the transcendent as by direct Platonism. Platonist or inverted Platonist, what the Thomist holds as substantial reality is for either position but shadow. From the Thomistic realist's perspective, as he opposes the inverted Platonist—that is, as he opposes the Cartesian Idealist—analogated perfections rest in the thing itself understood by that Thomist as real and not shadow. For the Thomistic realist, intellect may indeed be reduced to an effect in intellect as if "black and utter chaos," but that is the effect of its denials. Reality itself is not affected. For that realist intellect, the substantial reality of things must be taken one thing at a time, and especially so if by that taking intellect intends viable metaphorical concepts. Otherwise attribution distorts or obscures the actuality of things, the substantial reality of things. As Fr. Phelan remarks, analogated perfection "exists intrinsically in only one of the analogates (and is, therefore, univocal), and is applied by the mind proportionately to others on the basis of some relation of causality existing between the prime analogate and the minor analogates."

The ground to that causal relation is *being*, through which *essence* is determinate in the singular thing in itself. It is in failing to govern metaphor according to this rubric of essence in relation to being that metaphor itself, though not the things named by the terms of the metaphor (the analogates) becomes distorted. Thus metaphor so made becomes as sign a glass further darkened, in which reality can only be the more darkly seen. It is in his recognition of this possible danger, and in resistance to its temptations, that Williams writes his "Term." The paper bag is "like" a man only in the relation of accidental characteristics of bag and man which fancy divorces from the reality named by the terms taken separately. Those characteristics, liberated by the separation, are dissociated from the essential nature of the things themselves: the bag is "about the length / and apparent size" of a man, which says nothing of either *bag* or *man* essentially. That the paper bag "crushed . . . to / the ground" by a car rises and rolls on down the street as a man would not in the circumstances points with a surprised recognition to a Thomistic principle at the heart of the recognition, whatever our poet may choose to make of the recognition as afterthought: the perfections possible to the bag in itself—as intrinsic to essence, or adhering to essence—are not of the same order comparatively as those possible to a man. The seeming likenesses between accidents adhering *to* the bag and the seemingly similar one adhering *in* the man require any metaphorical articulation of the terms thus yoked as metaphor to be governed by the proportionality of each thing as resting significantly but separately in the analogates. Past that moment in which fancy holds sway, the initial articulation of likeness in unlike things, the bag's fundamental nature is glimpsed: unlike a man, it rolls on. (We have already commented on the ironic implications of saying the bag "rises" as the man would not. Death for Williams is a finality in this stage of his reflections on the nature of man.)

We appear to be laboring the obvious, but Williams's figure deploys the problem so simply and directly that it is more convenient than less obvious instances in which the poet, far from such simple directness, delights in witty obfuscation. If the danger to intellect and ultimately to the soul itself are real, as St. Thomas for one would hold, then perhaps the labor and laboredness is to a good end. For what is of concern is the poet's careless disregard of the limits of proportionality in his making of metaphor by attribution such as those makings that disturbed Dr. Johnson about metaphysical poetry. He charged the metaphysical poet, we remember, with a "voluntary deviation from nature in pursuit of something new and strange." That "deviation" leads the poet to yoke by metaphor "the most heterogeneous ideas . . . by violence together," by that violence of his fancy. This intellectual violence may be exercised upon analogates by a wit intent on serving wit's delight, and the poet may himself be quite aware in doing so that he practices a distortion of sign pretending to a reflection of reality. Such is metaphor as a mirror of reality, but of that limited reality of the poet's intellect busy in his playful distortion, his making of a "fiction" to delight kindred intellects. Certainly John Donne in a poem like his "Community" is quite deliberate in distorting sign from reality in this manner.

We recall that Donne's sense of *community* in this poem is that of "common property," and the common *property* his speaker addresses, in a strictly logical development from an orderly premise, is *woman*. Who would bridle too quickly at the premise? "Good we must love, and must hate ill, / For ill is ill, and good is good." The argument is thus lodged in the moral realm, principles of good and evil attaching to moral agents. But there are things "indifferent" in that realm, in that they are neither good nor evil—like fire or water or air, and so on. It is improper for a moral agent to either hate or love these indifferent things in themselves, as if in themselves they were capable of willful good or evil. The bold turning follows. "Indifferent" things are therefore to be used "As we shall find our fancy bent." Then, before one can question *fancy*, the clever lawyer forces the argument ahead. It becomes impossible to stop him, except perhaps by an action I shall subsequently recommend as appropriate to the level of his argument. What happens rapidly is the assertion that woman is herself an "indifferent," neither good nor bad. The evidence is that since *good* is as "visible as green" (and this metaphor, trading on accident, is part of the argument's deliberate absurdity), if woman were good it would be as apparent as that green fields are green. If they were evil, they would no longer even exist, since "Bad doth itself and others waste." Having advanced these "self-evident proofs," the conclusion is that woman, being "indifferent," is to be used as "fruits" by man. Changed loves, then, are but "changed sorts of meat," and the kernel et, one logically flings away "the shell."

One hears without even bothering to listen our contemporary feminist's outrage, but that outrage is but a gullible submission to Donne's deliberate intent: to provoke just that sort of outrage by the argument's absurd audacity. Or rather, by his *speaker's* audacious intent, not Donne's. For to charge John Donne as chauvinist for such a display is to miss the point entirely, as any intellectual is likely to miss it who lacks wit or humor appropriate to a response, whether a feminist or some other. At the level of the poem's intentional absurdity, the argument has rushed along in such a way, with so many flaws in it, as to leave a riposte difficult if not impossible. The interlocutor, surely intended to be a woman, and probably one understood to have rebuffed the speaker, is left (or so the intent) in a sputtering rage. The only riposte suited to the level of the argument as argument, I now suggest, is that lady's using a heavy skillet over the perpetrator's head. If that did not refute the argument itself, it would be an appropriate rebuff to the man deporting himself in such false calm reasonableness, which contains and hides an angry hurt perhaps.

But then I do not intend to take the speaker's part here, and even less so the outraged feminist's as one might encounter it in the 1990s. I intend rather to take Dr. Johnson's side, but not without remarking that the poem, in itself, is something of a gem. It is only that gems may sometimes distract us from things of more worth, being themselves one of the "indifferents," for all the ecstasy and agony spent upon them in the course of literary history. There is, for the poet and even for the unwary reader a necessary caution in the face of such sparklingly made things. The danger in such distortion by reckless, if clever, attribution (and this is Dr. Johnson's concern) is that the violation of reality by such absurdities may by its very success tend to become habitual in intellect. The consequence to the poet may be that he gradually loses the authority proper to metaphor as authorized by reality. Some readers of Wallace Stevens may suspect that this happens to Stevens as poet, as Johnson thought it to happen to the metaphysical Poets. Certainly Donne sets out in his poem from just such an authority, his speaker very quickly distorting that authority in such a way that we might well deduce its poet trained in the law if we did not know that fact about Donne already.

The manipulative use of metaphor arrogates the accidents inhering in things. Such a strategy of metaphor allows "minor analogates" (*green* to *good, fruit* to *woman*) to shift intellect's attention to the new and strange as attached by metaphor to the centering analogate (*good, woman*). This shifting of the primary interest to a whim of the fancy, to the play of wit for its own sake, may establish bad habits in intellect which the poet may come to regret. This is so, whether the manipulation is the deliberate, knowing distortion by a poet like Donne or out of a desperation rising in our century's "Romantic" poets to maintain a momentary stay against confusion. In the end, the habit of desperation, too, exacerbates the disjunction of intellect from reality. Eliot was shocked into a recognition of this possibility at about the time of *The Waste Land*. Figurative language, if forced to conceptual presumptions of authority by the easiness of attribution acquired as habit, makes intellect's relation to reality more and more tenuous. When Eliot comes presently to set Lancelot Andrewes over John Donne as divine, it is largely because he sees in Donne's sermons and meditations the effects of such intellectual habits as Johnson had objected to in the poetry. There "hangs the shadow of the impure motive" in those sermons and meditations, leading Eliot to conclude that Donne was "the Reverend Billy Sunday of his time."

17

Grandeur's Charge Against Skeptical Denial

The desire in intellect for order, or a fear that disorder is the nature of existence itself, may turn intellect inward upon itself as the only arbiter of order. Thus the intellectual action of attribution may be used not only aggressively but defensively as well. In either posture, it is an action eroding the relation of intellect to being, most crucially to its own being. By that habit of turning inward, intellect may easily become victim of its own perverted existence, for such is one of the possibilities of its freedom. The habit of action, proper to its nature, may establish through perverse habit its own disjunction, making more and more difficult an openness to being. To summarize our argument in this way makes it seem rather theoretical, seemingly unanchored in experiences of our intellectual deportment toward being. And for that reason we have been concerned along the way to encourage reflection on our own actual experiences, as made somewhat more measurable through the testimony of other discrete intellects in signs directed to us toward that very purpose. For although the truth of how things stand lies in each intellect's specific experiences of reality, in which truth lies hidden, the testimony of other intellects supports and often clarifies for us our own experiences. When St. Thomas advises us that the purpose of our study of such testimony is not merely to learn what others have thought but to learn how the truth of things stands, he is defining the nature of philosophy itself.

In our own pursuit of the truth of things, we have been at pains to use those signs bequeathed us, not only by philosophers, but by those poets whom we have designated "Romantic" poets, intending by that designation no explicit historical limitations, though we have dwelt on nineteenth century poets. We rather intend a manner of intellectual deportment toward the problem of the truth of things, toward the nature of reality as intellect must engage it in any time or place. And we have welcomed poets as witnesses for two reasons at least. First, it is the poet who appears to us most intensely concerned for the relation of the sign to the thing signified, whereby he would take the sign as a means to an immediacy with the thing signified. He is likely to be less committed to the rational deportment of intellect through sign to that reality than to an "emotional" engagement through the sign, through what we hear Keats characterize as "negative capability."

We do not say that such a "Romantic" poet is more concerned than the philosopher is or ought to be, of course. But there is a difference between the poet's and the philosopher's deportment toward intellectual problems, though the deportments are often (and I think desirably) complementary in any intellect when it achieves at last its proper orientation to reality. Still, the philosopher is more likely than the poet to engage his questions from a bearing of detachment, requiring a careful use of term which must be carefully established and constantly justified. The poet is rather inclined to a carelessness in this respect, his action being more direct and immediate to the reality about which question hovers. This is to say that he is less likely than the philosopher to make a *rational* address through a cautionary deportment. He responds to what moves him to response in a manner the philosopher would sometimes characterize as "emotional." We have emphasized, however, that in that response he may not always recognize that not only the "object" moves him to response but an intuitive desire in him. This is to suggest that emotion in the poet is an ambient effect in him consequent to both his intuitive desire and his gesture out of that desire toward grasping some desired thing. Desire, moving intellect to an openness to reality, initiates that proper openness, in relation to which the emotional effect must be considered at last of a peripheral importance, however powerfully ambient of action. The difficulty he must overcome, indeed, is his disinclination to govern that intuitive desire by rational intellect, under the seductive influence of emotion, just as the philosopher's difficulty is the obverse: a disinclination too often to value his own intuitive desire in a proper relation to his rational engagement of that "object" for which he establishes a careful term, the establishment of which term may itself place a barrier between his intuitive desire to see into the truth of things and the thing into which he would see.

Having said these things about the philosopher and the poet as active intellects, we may better appreciate that "Romantic" poet who was initially, he supposed, a philosopher. In his beginnings he was somewhat

disoriented by inclination to serve both offices. I mean T. S. Eliot. We
have seen that he set out formally to train his intellect as philosopher, but
in the course of that preparation began to turn to the writing of poetry.
The intellectual context, the milieu of mind, within which Eliot developed
was largely determined by a community closed in its thinking about intellect's relation to being. Such was the intellectual community's Cartesian
and Darwinian heritage at Harvard at the turn of our century. But Eliot
was also—or so he supposed himself—a skeptic, separate from both that
intellectual climate and from its alternate which emerged in contention as
Humanism. Eliot puts his own position, while still pursuing a career as
philosopher, as an extreme skepticism. Now the formal deportment of
philosophy as Eliot encountered it at Harvard was more likely to describe
itself as *objective* rather than *skeptical*. *Objective* seems to carry connotations of *neutral*. We rather strangely take *objectivity* as the highest virtue
of intellect, as if that habit of intellectual detachment must be constantly
maintained, rather than as may be proper, seeing detachment as an initial
address to a question out of which one must come to some conclusion,
some commitment no longer to be described as "objective."

Eliot, it turns out (and he is quite open about this in his early letters) is
suspicious of philosophy as a discipline of intellect, finding it inadequate
because inevitably turning philosophy into sophistry. One might antici-
pate this as an inevitability to that profession of "objectivity" which eschews commitment to any truth which intellect may discover. It is for
this reason that Eliot abandons his formal preparations as philosopher,
although to a degree that he himself may not have appreciated, he continued a philosopher, turning that attitude of mind more and more upon
poetry. Thus as poet he uses the philosopher's "objectivity" to maintain
a detached position from the poetry he writes and the criticism he makes
about poetry. We have pointed especially to his arguments about the
"personality" of the poet in relation to his poems. It is a detachment
which dictates in his poetry the aloofness of irony and in his criticism a
rhetorical detachment which gives to that early criticism what he himself
will later speak of as a "juvenile" manner. (He applies the term specifically
to his "Tradition and the Individual Talent.") Thus Eliot in this early
turning maintains, though he is not able to maintain it for long, a detachment from the philosopher on the one hand and from the "Romantic"
poet on the other. He cannot maintain it for long, since he is himself both.
He is suspicious of his own inclination to sophistry, which means that he
does have a concern for the truth of things. And in the tension between
the two inclinations in himself, we observe an intrusion of the sardonic
into his ironic deportment. At the same time, he is fearful of the pull

through poetry into an immediacy to the truth in things, especially wary of the sensual nature required for such immediacy. He speaks with hauteur of Wordsworth's concern for "emotion" in poetry, in that essay he later characterizes as "juvenile." Like Joyce, he fears emotion as a loss of intellectual control and a submission to sentimentality, and not inappropriately. What is inappropriate, however, is to eschew as valid to intellect the initiating cause of the emotional danger, *desire* as it moves intellect to an openness to being. That Eliot is not able to exorcise desire is evident in his poetry up through *The Waste Land*, that first part of his *Collected Poems* dominated by the theme of desire in its mysterious relation to memory. The resolution of that mystery proves the "key" opening intellect to reality, as the final section of *The Waste Land* explicitly dramatizes.

And so for a time Eliot maintains a perilous balance, up to the point when he must at last surrender in an openness to being which all along he has most feared. That openness has been the alternative to a skepticism which could only be maintained at an extremity, a dogmatic detachment of intellect from all save itself, which we suggest means in the event a collapse of intellect in that its own reality is thus eroded. That is the destruction awaiting the "self-love" he dramatizes in "Prufrock." What has been forcing Eliot to an openness all along is his intuitive nature, and the turning point is memorialized in those "key" lines of *The Waste Land*, beginning with that giving of the self commanded by the heart (intuitive intellect) against the skeptical defenses of the head (rational intellect). The openness is recognized at once as no matter of spectacle for Eliot, in contrast to the actions of a Shelley or a Pound that make them figures of a drama of the poet as "Romantic." It is an action "not to be found in our obituaries." And it is a costly action, being "The awful daring of a moment's surrender / Which an age of prudence can never retract."

Eliot's early flight inward, then, is in defense of the *self* against the strangeness, the seductiveness of, the *other*. It leaves him with memory in spite of the willful turning of the key to lock out that other, a locking of the self unto the self. This self as "monad" finds its safe chamber from the larger sea of being (to adapt Prufrock's images associated with this condition of intellect), but this little room of the self is haunted still by the everywhere of existential reality, a most disturbing confusion in it, interior to intellect itself. That little room appears to be mirror walls, reflecting the intellect to itself as fragmented into a thousand insubstantial images. The testimony borne by these images, in spite of their insubstantiality, is that "consciousness" or "awareness" or "intellect" or "soul," against its most resolute turning inward, has failed to eradicate from its knowing the actualities of its experiences of that which is not itself. It cannot eradicate the context of its being as conditional to its existence, however tightly it lock itself away. And it cannot because it bears in itself a reality of its own nature: it already possesses as a gift of grace despite its attempted refusal *truths* from its encounter with things in themselves. The mirror walls of the self, self-isolated, may for a time obscure this reality of its own existence. It could not do so indefinitely for Eliot, and so there occurs that event of his return to the actual world in an openness, his "nervous breakdown," which was in actuality a spiritual crisis, testified to in *The Waste Land*, and in ways that Eliot himself would only gradually come to understand.

In such a summary of Eliot's intellectual history between his "Preludes" and *The Waste Land*, we have indicated as part of his difficulty the extreme pressure upon him as a would-be philosopher exerted by those about him whose skepticism was focused antagonistically upon the intuitive intellect, elevating thereby rational intellect as absolute in authority. The advocates of the rational intellect, we remember, were vigorously opposed by some of Eliot's undergraduate mentors at Harvard, such men as Babbitt and Santayana. But the rationalist tide was at the flood, and among its victims was figurative language itself, considered as little more than etchings of sad "Romantic" wishfulness upon intellectual shores being swept level by the rational flood-tide. The address of this emerging intelligentsia to language would eschew figurative language as distortion of reality, which reality for this new intellectual authority is existence as mechanistic accident. Nor would this ascendant intellectualism patiently abide any suggestion that there lies something substantial beneath the word, hidden beneath but supportive of, figurative language as St. Thomas insists is true. Words are rather convenient labels, stuck on ideas, and in that combination of idea and label constituting "reality." What is overlooked in that reductionism Eliot will come to discover through the shock of his spiritual crisis: image, idea, concept depend from the complexity of reality, independent of intellect as agent. When intellect disjoins these from dependency in being, they become abstract shadow of being, though given an illusional substantiality by the authority of willful intellect. Intellect is thus bound to discomforts that require more and more radical rejections of reality.

We have but briefly characterized the intellectual climate ascendant at Harvard at the turn of the century, nor have we perhaps sufficiently regarded its effects on other poets contemporary to Eliot, who show the same effects of that milieu. We have seen the effects in Robert Frost and in Wallace Stevens, both of them touched by Harvard at this early period of their careers. In effect, we have been presenting that climate as an extreme version of empiricism, as the new "science" usurping the offices proper to philosophy, and it is to the point that pragmatism emerges as victorious in this period of our intellectual history, despite the opposition of the "humanists." What the poet may sense out of these circumstances is that the new intellectual authority grows fat on the poet's decaying imagination. For as imagination surrenders authority in relation to the nature of reality, reality appears more and more vulnerable to the ravagements of empiricist intellect. That address of intellect, unmodified by any other mode of address to reality, is committed to a materialistic literalness not unlike that we saw in Wallace Stevens's sense of reality: existence at most supplies a sort of prime matter for the culturing of abstractions. The literal, the nominalist, address to that reality exorcises the essence of things, reducing essence to *form* from nature, whether form taken from intellect itself or from stones and trees and nightingales. Such is the address that led Wordsworth to cry against it that it murders to dissect. But the irony that escapes such empirical exorcists is that essence is not thereby effected. The change is only a denial of reality by the exorcist. His is a dogmatic insistence upon his own illusion as reality.

We have suggested that such a strict literalness, whereby existence is reduced to the letter of formulae, turns out in the end to be but another species of the figurative, to the dismay of this practitioner of intellect on discovering as much. For when actual existence is reduced to the letter, the letter becoming the thing by that illusion, there yet remains the shadow of the new thing (the letter). Miracle of miracles—the attempted erosion of existence through reductionist abstraction does not *effect* reality, but neither does it *affect* reality by making it not to be. *There* it still *is*, beyond intellectual operations upon it. But perhaps it may be accounted (since accounting is the necessity to abstractionism) a shadow of the reality held by intellect in its decreeing formulae as being, a residue of abstractionism like the residue in that technology famous in Chicago whereby all of a pig is made use of except its "squeal"? Yet still, the tree shouts a continuing presence more insistently than the dying pig: it stands beyond all analysis, on the bank of the Wye or of the Ganges as the case might be. As for the absolute destructiveness of technology, out of intellectual abstractionism—the death of "nature"—that fear is spoken to in the miracle of life's return at Mount Helena after its eruption. There were predictions dark and contrary to life, refuted as if by miracle, for hardly had the dust settled before life sprang up.

Creation continues, Hopkins insisted, out of his faith that is contrary to modernist presumptions of autonomous power over being. For the world is one "charged with grandeur" which suddenly flames forth to the bafflement of gnostic intellect. Though generations trod reality down, searing it with trade, with toil till it "wears man's smudge and shares man's smell," it is never "spent." For

> though the last lights off the black West went
> Oh, morning, at the brown brink eastward, springs—
> Because the Holy Ghost over the bent
> World broods with warm breast and with ah! bright wings.

Always, this is to say, the Lord and Giver of Life sustains beyond finite intellect's attempt to reduce existence to its own power, that pale gnostic version of man as lord and giver of life, whether as poet or as empirical scientist bent on reductionisms to the pleasures of autonomy.

When the reality is assumed shadowy, and the actual as but a shadow of the reality of formulae, collapse of intellect itself is near at hand, a collapse heralding hope for intellectual recovery. There has been a sort of poetry at work in the so-called hard sciences of late, and particularly in that increasingly softening hard science, physics. Physics' practitioners themselves are not always aware of that softening in what used to be confidently understood as the cutting edge of all science, sharpened by the very cutting. Still, in the post-World War II world it has been the physicist, even more than the poet, who must increasingly turn to a recognition of "mystery" as a term signifying more than "the as yet not known." Thus the physicist outdistances the poet more often than not in recognizing a return to reality as guided by intuitive intellect. Increasingly the mystery of reality is being acknowledged by intellect at its limit as yielding only partially to either empirical precisions or imaginative speculations, though recognizing as well that reality offers itself to intellect through the mutual support of science and poetry, or in our older terms, the intuitive and rational, or in St. Thomas's terms, the intellectual modes of the *intellectus* and the *ratio*. The province of particle physics has been most amenable to this companionable concern for the truth of things. It is with amused irony, then, that one might observe, in *Science News*'s record of the developments in particle physics in the 1970s and 1980s how often the headlines to an account were taken from Eliot's *Four Quartets*. (See my "The Poet and the Man of Science: Eliot and the Particle Physicist," *Southern Review*, Summer 1974.)

18

Growing Accustomed to Flowering Wholeness

Particle physics's concern for the truth of things, then, initiates a turning in our thought about things, slowly leading to a development of that thought as at once frightening and exciting, though our poets have not, perhaps, yet recognized how important to their own calling is this turning. We will discover at last, I think, that this turning is neither new, nor should it be frightening. The wholeness toward which it tends may be of a nature somewhat beyond even the physicists' visionary expectations at this moment of their explorations. What is certainly true, however, is that the prospect is intellectually exciting. For what is being gradually recovered in this emerging vision of existence is the nature of things to intellect. Each thing in itself and in concert as the whole of creation as "seen" by science undermines the old presumption of intellectual autonomy in relation to being, whether the being of the intellect itself or that of "things" not the intellect. What proves no longer tenable, through more or less impirical discoveries by intellect, is the presumption of existence as uncaused, accidental, mechanistic, closed universe. Let us pursue the matter, since it is of so central an importance to the question of intuition as intellectually valid. For we now recognize that the intuitive has proved no less valid to the rational scientist than to the poet.

We are fascinated, at a popular level, by reports of sympathetic responses of seemingly gifted persons to things, that sort of response we speak of as "psychic response." Such a person solves mysteries of lost objects or persons at a distance, through contemplation of artifacts associated with those persons or things. It becomes increasingly a fare at the newsstands, placed at checkout registers of grocery stores, or on prime time television programs catering to our residual sense of existence as

169

bordering upon the unknown in a haunting mystery. To know this mystery requires an action of intellect other than the rational deportment required by nineteenth century science. Recently an episode on the popular "Unsolved Mysteries," the television program mostly devoted to solving crimes and apprehending murderers and con men of various stripes, devoted a segment to the "mystery" of sympathetic responses of one identical twin to the other's experience of distress. (The literature studying this sympathetic affinity in identical twins is, of course, quite extensive.) The episode reconstructed an abduction of one twin, "seen" by her twin while the seer was in the presence of their father at home. The concrete details of that abduction the "seeing" twin reported as it was happening, to her father's disbelief. But at a point, the "seeing" twin announced her sister safe, having seen the car bearing the abducted twin wrecked, then pulled out of a ditch by a farmer and his tractor. The seeing twin relaxed, and then after an interval the missing sister appeared dishevelled but more or less whole. The father at once, telling the abducted twin to give no details, took both of them in search of the accident spot, guided by the "seeing" sister. So guided, they found the exact spot, confirmed by the victim, and by a farmer who had pulled the wrecked car out of the ditch with his tractor. That was the first of many "psychic" experiences in the sympathetic relation between these sisters.

Now, such fare proves exciting to our imagination. The skeptic (in this instance the father) at first took it merely as an excitement of fancy. But what are we to make of certain observations at the level of physics turned upon particles as reported in advancing this new science? In presenting the case for this new science at an accessible level, but more dependable than one might find it presented at a checkout counter in a mall, John Briggs and E. David Peat, have given us their *Looking Glass Universe*, follow with *Turbulent Mirror* (1989). The subtitle at once engages our attention, following what we have said of Frost and Stevens as poets: *An Illustrated Guide to Chaos Theory and the Science of Wholeness*. Given such a paradoxical title, one isn't surprised to find our authors taking recourse to Stevens's own poem "Connoisseur of Chaos," which appeared in the collection *Parts of a World* (1942), following *Ideas of Order* (1936). The poem sets two propositions formally as the theme of the poem, being also theme of the two collections of poems we at last realize:

A. A violent order is disorder; and
B. A great disorder is an order. These
Two things are one. (Pages of illustrations)

It is some 45 years later that Briggs and Peat give us their pages of illustrations of Stevens's counterpointing *greatness* and *violence*, in which the greatness supercedes the violence. Their illustrations are not from the poets but from their fellow scientists.

They move, for instance, from a rather generally known mystery in physics, what they speak of as the confusion to our understanding effected by a "schizophrenically" acting light: in one aspect light acts as a wave; in another as particles. What is required is a new beginning to science if this paradox is to yield to reason: a nonlinearity speculation about the nature of existence in contrast to what our authors call "the reductionist dream" of linearity out of Newton. That new approach leads to the "theory of chaos," but it is a strange *chaos* indeed, in that the parts of the whole of this chaos indicate sympathetic relationships. Thus even to speak of the *whole of chaos* is to speak paradox. As to the mystery in such paradox: physicists show us "that if two quantum 'particles' are separated by several meters with no mechanism for communication between them, they will nevertheless [remain] correlated in some mysterious fashion. As recent experiments show, a measurement performed on one such particle is correlated instantly with the result of a measurement on its distant partner." Sympathetic affinity, then, seems evident in more things of nature than merely identical twins. Such is a shocking rebuff to that physics which reduces existence to mechanics, as it is to thought reduced to mechanics—to the presumed operation of neural elements in the physical brain as sufficient grounding of "thought" in the physical world. We have already cited the shocking discovery of neurologists studying the physical brain in relation to "intelligence" which has revealed highly intelligent individuals (one of them with an I.Q. of 126) whose physical brains are largely water. The mathematics student with high I.Q., we noted, is discovered to have a brain far below the normal expectations, those expectations founded in the science of knowledge as determined by the functions of the physical brain. Even though this discovery of particle affinity remains (as *Science*'s report of the topic says) "speculative," it is of interest that science treats speculative intellect more tolerantly than it used to do.

High-speed computers have opened up this "chaos theory" to intensely serious scientific speculation in pursuit of the theory's "laws," to speak of which is to speak paradoxically. For what can be made of such a concern: the *laws* of *chaos*? Still, what seems to be revealed is that "everything in the universe is connected," giving rise to an "emerging science of wholeness" whose controlling metaphor is the "theory of chaos." This new approach, says the blurb for *Turbulent Mirror*, is "turning our perception of the world on its head." What is being turned on its head, we

might say from our Thomistic exploration of modernist thought as descended from Descartes and Bacon, whose positions are more or less
brought together in Newton, is the presumption of closed, linear systems
evolved by a reductionist science. In the nineteenth century, our authors
observe, Poincaré (before Einstein) "had thrown an anarchist's bomb into
the Newtonian model of the solar system," though the explosion was
delayed until an ignition out of particle physics as advanced by high-
speed computers. What we are fast approaching is a recognition of existence as indivisible in one aspect, but divisible by the necessity of discursive rational and specualtive intellectual actions in response to that
unity in another aspect. David Bohm's phrase for this paradox has creation a "flowing wholeness" in which the observer (intellect) and observed flowing wholeness cannot be extricated from each other. (That
insight was initiated, we might remember, by Heisenberg's uncertainty
principle.)

In the course of this new theory of chaos now emerging as the latest
science, our observation of discrete things becomes dependent upon the
discretion of the observer, whether an observation of parts in particle
physics or the proposed autonomy of intellect in the post-Newtonian but
pre-Chaotic world. In that post-Newtonian thought, analysis is dependent upon closed physical systems naively taken. Now, our authors suggest, the "relativity" that has extended in a trickle-down effect from science to politics and to individual morality must be considered only
"relatively autonomous" in respect to closed systems of thought. For
those systems are destructive of the openness of existence itself. What is
curious from a Thomistic perspective is that this emerging science of a
chaotic "flowing," which is yet a wholeness, should be so long delayed
from recognitions of the depths of mystery within the paradoxical language it is forced to use. In that language, the scientist is more and more
led to assume the offices of the poet, in that both the poet and this new
scientist recognize the necessity to their intellectual confusions of the aid
of the philosopher. What is being more and more required is metaphysics.

This science of chaos, an imaginative perception of reality, sees more
and more an indivisible wholeness in which parts are mutually affective,
speaking an order which the term *chaos* does not solve any more than
does the term *wholeness*, given the residual implications in those terms
collected about them since the late Middle Ages through the emerging
triumph of modernism. There is a necessity, more and more discovered
in our pursuits of parts by science, of a conclusion of a unity to which
science *as science* cannot adequately speak. What is rapidly confronting
scientific awareness, out of its analytical dissections of things, is that exis-

tence is somehow a simple wholeness. Clearly, then, what is needed is a metaphysics. A metaphysics of being? Undoubtedly. Our point from the outset has been that such a metaphysics is already available, not as a set of abstract rules, but as an orientation of intellect to the nature of being itself. It is from such orientation that the discoveries of science yield understanding, and understanding yields wisdom about this mystery of the one and the many, of the seeming chaos of the many which points to the necessity of a vision of simple unity as the rescue of intellect. It is through this vision that the rescue of the soul becomes possible, as Thomas said it would: through intellect's engagement of reality—actual existences perceived as essences through sensual apprehension, held in intellect as truth.

Our attention to the emerging "theory of chaos," in relation to the sense of dislocation of intellect out of such theory, might justify a final word here about that connoisseur of chaos so resolutely bent on order by the authority of imagination: that is, Wallace Stevens. How advanced he sounds, in relation to creation as turbulent mirror, when he speaks of a certain violence possible to intellect in its yoking of opposites, the violence of imaginative action. In Section II of his "Connoisseur of Chaos" he remarks that "a law of inherent opposites / Of essential unity, is as pleasant as port, / As pleasant as the brush-strokes of bough." What the metaphor of tree-bough does is bring into an essential unity the opposite natures of the actual tree's *bough* and the artist's *brush strokes* in imaging the bough. There is an essential disparity, Thomistically speaking, which is reconciled by the imaginative attribution whereby the painting and the reality are unified by intellectual act. For after all, he begins Section III, "After all the petty contrast of life and death / Proves that these opposite things partake of one." And then, as if recalling Donne's poem that reduces Death to death ("Death, be not proud") on the scholastic's authority, Stevens adds that "that was the theory when bishops' books / Resolved the world. We cannot go back to that. / The squirming facts exceed the squamous mind." The intellect's vertigo in that old way of thinking about the world must be resolved by the violence of imagination, not by bishops' books. Thus the imagination serves intellect as dramamine serves the squamous body with its car or plane sickness. Therefore, "suppose the disorder of truths [the "squirming facts"] should ever come / To an order, most Plantagenet, most fixed . . . / A great disorder is an order."

But not an order such as that supposed by the theory of chaos, which Stevens at last falls short of, though in a sense he may be the Moses to the New Canaan of this new science. The "great" order he "supposes" is contained by his own imaginative awareness. Thus the propositions A and

B are not "like statuary, posed / For a vista in the Louvre. They are things chalked / On the sidewalk so that the pensive man may see." This, though the rains of disorder should wash them away. But having somewhat seen, on those busy city streets "the way things happen to fall," the "pensive man" will from his pensiveness see "that eagle float / For which the intricate Alps are a single nest." That eagle of imaginative soaring through supreme fictions reduces the "Alps" of reality to a dependence upon the Eagle of the Imagination. The imagination may nest a moment before soaring once more, fed by the accidents of Alps.

One cannot resist here juxtaposing another poet's eagle, summoned in similar speculative circumstances, but to quite different ends. This time it is an "aged eagle" we see associated with the speaker in "Ash-Wednesday," who asks why that eagle should "stretch its wings," since so much reduced from the "vanished power of [its] usual reign" over a closed world of Alps. For Eliot, the initial circumstances are those of Gerontion, who has also lost the "infirm glory of the positive hour"—his existence in time and place through the course of years. The Alps are now surrendered as it were, in "Ash-Wednesday" as they must be in "Gerontion." But now the surrender is rather a spiritual one, and wonder of wonders the surrender restores the eagle. Even the actual senses are somewhat restored to a degree not possible to that "little old man" Gerontion. In our juxtaposing these poems of Eliot's and Stevens's, we note Stevens has reached 60 years, Eliot only 40. The point: Eliot, as with "Prufrock," once more projects himself as older than his personal history; Stevens in contrast holds to that youth of imagination which would escape the impinging realities of earthly years, so that he imagines himself still soaring above those ambiguous Alps reduced to a unity by the soaring of imagination and thereby imagines he has made them manageable.

Yet one word more: Stevens concludes his *Collected Poems* with one addressing a theme of William Carlos Williams's which we explored: Stevens calls his poem, "Not Ideas about the Thing but the Thing Itself" (1954). What we notice in the poem is a chink in the armor of presumptuous power of the imagination, or at least some loss of feathers for soaring. In mood the poem is akin to that opening mood of "Ash-Wednesday." And there is an address to the thing in itself that is not usual to Stevens. But though the poem pays homage to the thing itself, it does so only tentatively, as if a tribute paid by a somnambulant eagle not able here to spring airborne. It is March, and there comes a "scrawny cry from outside," some bird just before light, a "chorister whose c preceded the choir." There is not the same sense here of a complete isolation from the bird's cry (though it is outside and in the dark) as there is in Eliot's "Preludes" when we hear "sparrows in the gutters." For our speaker in Stevens's final poem to his selection from the "whole of harmonium" "knew that he heard it" though it is "outside" and before the first light of this very day. By an act of faith in having perceived the thing itself (and compare as well Keats's reaction to the nightingale, which he hears also but does not see from within his gloomy mossy ways) Stevens's voice declares that thing itself, the bird cry, "part of the colossal sun" for all its scrawniness. It is itself, and as such for the moment of his perception the center of a Ptolemaic universe, being "surrounded by its choral rings, / Still far away. It was like / A new knowledge of reality." One may only speculate, perhaps, out of hope, that this "new knowledge of reality" is the beginning of a new recognition in Stevens of unity dependent less on the power of imagination than on grace.

Put another way, one sees as possible here, and perhaps even probable, that this aging eagle in that bed at St. Francis Hospital experienced this larger world in a recovery such as Eliot describes for himself as aged eagle in "Ash-Wednesday." Recovering from "broken wings," the "lost heart" as it stiffens from response to this world, yet "rejoices / In the lost lilac and the lost sea voices" and "quickens to recover / The cry of quail and the whirring plover," even finding that "smell renews the salt savor of the sandy earth." This is the time between dying for three score years and a birth beyond that death. Certainly Father Arthur Hanley's account of Stevens's last days, where he attended Stevens at his worldly death, suggests as much. "Everything," Stevens says at his end, "has been created. There is only one uncreated." Baptized, he said to Fr. Hanley with some comfort, "Now I'm in the fold." And so gathered, he is no longer Eliot's exact opposite as he had so long insisted. The "theory" of the "bishops' books," long rejected, seems to have "Resolved the world" for Stevens at his end—or rather at his beginning.

19

Concept: The Lonely Tenor of Our Intellectual Way

The intellect as conditioned by Modernism is plagued by difficulty, whether we speak of the "Romantic" poet's intellect or that of the emerging "Romantic" scientist who is in pursuit of an *essential* unity of creation through his theory of "chaos," which we suggested supplied by Thomas's concept of being. The attempt is to rescue intellect to reality. The difficulty, increasingly recognized even by Stevens in the end, is an ambiguity which finite intellect has difficulty accommodating to. This ambiguity in the *appearance* of reality is at least as ancient as Plato's *Parmenides*, that ambiguity whereby existence to the glance appears as *many*, in the next glance as *one*. The singular intellect may seize one "viewing" of reality or the other and advance it with a dogmatism that denies an alternate, an alternating, view to the discursive intellect. Others, Plato among them, recognize that the singular intellect itself may be subject to such disparate views, confused by disparity if not at last reconciled by a more steady vision than the blinking of the eye allows. That is a problem to the philosopher, but it is also, by extension, a problem to the literary critic, especially when he does not establish his more specific concern as critic in a philosophical vision sufficient to his specialization as a "scientist" of art. The *one* and the *many*. When the ambiguity is reduced to the more local, specialized concern for *likeness* in *unlike* things, for metaphor, by that very reductionism he is likely to lose a proper orientation in the larger complexity to thought that must engage the mystery of the *one* and the *many* beyond local manifestations.

Concerning the modernist's difficulty with metaphor, then, we might relate the classical-scholastic terms "prime analogate" and "minor analogate" to equivalent terms made popular in modern criticism under the

influence of I. A. Richards. For those older terms have the virtue of deriv-
ing from a metaphysical view of the physical realities of the *one* and the
many that challenge philosophy itself. Now Richards's bent as critic turns
toward the scientific, especially so if one count psychology as developed
in the first quarter of our century as scientific. Richards's address to the
uses of poetry in the 1920s may seem at this late date more historical,
more antique and even primitive, than is actually true of it, especially as
we discover his lingering presence in the literary criticism of the 1990s.
For in his address to the sign, to the text, lies the beginning of a dislocation which grows out of the "New Criticism." After World War II, certain of the New Critics prove to have made a way for the destroyers of
literature's anchor in the reality of our experiences of existences, through
which relation alone literature is to be recovered. That recovery is not, of
course, as an alternate to religion but servant to it, as Eliot was to conclude. With a specialized intensity focused on the *text*, with a growing
disregard for literature's *context* of reality, criticism issues into "structur-
alism" and "post-structuralism" and thence into "deconstruction," in a
progressive separation of the significance of sign to any reality proper to
sign, to the meanings of words that lie hidden under words themselves, as
St. Thomas puts it.[13]

In Eliot's concluding lecture of his Charles Eliot Norton series at Harvard, "The Modern Mind" (March 17, 1933), Richards is Eliot's principal
antagonist, against whom he plays Maritain, especially Maritain's *Art and
Scholasticism*. He takes immediate issue with Richards's statement that
"Poetry is capable of saving us," asking what, in Richards's thought, is it
to be saved. Eliot quotes from Richards's "Science and Poetry" the charge
that "For centuries . . . countless pseudo-statements—about God, about
the universe, about human nature, the relations of mind to mind, about
the soul, its rank and destiny—have been believed; now they are gone,
irrecoverably; and the knowledge which has killed them is not of a kind
upon which an equally fine organization of the mind can be based." Richards's statement, says Eliot, is itself a pseudo-statement "if there is such a
thing." And what it reveals to Eliot is that Richards, like Arnold before
him, would "preserve emotions without the beliefs with which their history has been involved." Thus Eliot has said (a few paragraphs earlier),
"Mr. Richards is much occupied with the religious problem simply in the
attempt to avoid it," the difficulty for him lying in that, as a rationalist
intent on organizing the mind, he would do so by logic justified by those
systems of knowledge that have (for Richards) destroyed traditional beliefs.

The problem: the justifiers—psychology evolved from deterministic

Darwinism, for instance—are not comfortable allies to Richards, not promising "an equally fine organization of the mind." What is implied in this logic is precisely what Eliot says is there: a "belief" on Richards's part in the necessity of pseudo-statements to the organizing of mind, to the building of supreme fictions of order by logic, rather than through metaphor as with Wallace Stevens. There is in this climate of Richards's thought interesting echo of that controversy of Modernism within the Church itself which occupied theology at the close of the nineteenth century and extends late into the twentieth. One cannot but muse upon the irony of "religion's" role in literary matters as "religion" is secularized by the Modernist theologians of that controversy.

George W. Rutler gives us some account of the controversy, in "Tyrrell on Liberalism and Modernism," *Christ and Reason* (1990). Modernism within the Church, says Fr. Rutler, attempts what Matthew Arnold longed to do in order to rescue mind, to establish a "morality touched by emotion," which for Arnold meant poetry as salvific. Modernism as theology, grown within Rome itself (and still within the Church), would have the character whereby "the mystical desire for God and the modern expectation of what God must be" in the light of the latest science are made compatible. While "Liberal Protestantism wanted a Gospel without a Church," says Fr. Rutler, Catholic Modernism "wanted a Church without a Gospel." Antagonists to each other, these two species of Modernism confuse the climate of thought within the intellectual community of which Eliot became a part. In sum, the Liberal Protestant, the Catholic Modernist, the agnostic or atheistic rationalist share a common gnostic address to reality, intent on shaping being to its present desire, a desire supposed justified rationally, though the rational had long since become restricted to the province of materialistic determinates. Where that leaves such a rationalist as Richards is shown most pathetically in his remark in *Practical Criticism* that perhaps "Something like a technique or ritual for heightening sincerity might well be worked out." A psychological conditioning is here called for, in whose service poetry is central, replacing the sacrificial rituals that Modernism so facilely dismisses by the term "primitive."

The effect of our latest criticism is the disjunction of poetry, of the text, from its vital service to intellect whereby sign restores a relation of intellect to reality through its recovering a vision of proper proportionality. It may do so through the art of concept enlarged by sign, since through sign intellect approaches reality, an experience modifying concept. Such is the reciprocal nature of the growth of intellect in its potential. The problem in the disjunction through modernist presumptions, conspicuously represented by "Deconstruction" as a literary method, has been an extreme pluralism among intellects whose only commonality is the principle of intellectual autonomy. In this newest criticism each "critic" is at once his own poet and by being both poet and critic he constitutes a "school." The community of intellects is reduced to a dialogue of intellect with itself. Criticism and its literature, then, becomes an extended "Self-Love Song of Whoever." To such a poet-critic as a revolving, self-contained world, the proposition of the necessity of a community of intellect in being is most repugnant, for reality is the significant enemy to an anarchist intent pursued as if merely pluralistic, even as if merely "democratic." Only by an intellectual pluralism bound toward the necessary end of intellectual anarchy is it possible for that lone intellect to maintain its pretense to absolute autonomy, a pretense implicit but seldom announced.

Having thus put I. A. Richards as at least mediate father to present critical confusions, if not their founding father, let us turn to the question of metaphor as Richards presents it in a famous distinction, that between *tenor* and *vehicle*. There is a certain clarity afforded through his distinction, and it has the virtue of helping one learn to read signs. That is a beginning recovery of intellectual craft which was much decayed when he came upon the scene. But in his position metaphor is still left independent of any purchase upon the true ground of likeness in unlikeness. It is necessarily isolated since his concern, as Eliot pointed out, is "emotions without belief." The concern is with a state of mind and not with a state of mind in relation to existence not the mind itself. The true ground of similitude is discovered through perceptions of existences understood by intellect out of such perception. The scholastic insistence is decisive to such an assertion: *nihil in intellectu nisi quod prius in sensu*. In concept, out of perception through the senses, the existent thing has a presence as a "subject" as it were, designated by sign as opposed to the "object," the actuality existing independent of perception. It is this operation of concept in intellect that Wordsworth attempts to formulate when he speaks, in "Tintern Abbey" of "all the mighty world / Of eye, and ear,—both what they half create, / And what perceive," through which a "language of the sense" responds to "nature." Thus might thought be purely anchored to the health of "heart" and "soul" of ones "moral being." But in a disjunction from reality, thought finds itself focused in concept, with an insufficient justification of concept itself by reality. It will then appear to thought that the "presence" of the thing is within the concept and its sign, which are thus easily mistaken for the object itself. A closure of mind against reality is the result. That knowledge of the *essence* of the thing, borne through perception to intellect as the *truth* of a *thing*, becomes thus lost by a locking of intellect upon concept.

This means that, in the modernist manner of specific sciences, against which the current revolt is from the scientist himself, concept is taken as the measure of truth, rather than truth the measure of concept. But in the sciences it has become more and more evident, and especially in the development of nuclear physics since Bohr, that the immanent danger to scientific thought is specialized language exercised in a Nominalistic way. That procedure demonstrably affords a limited access to aspects of reality, which have been intellectually siphoned from reality, after which the largeness of reality may be set aside. Such a procedure is of some limited legitimacy as intellectual action, of course, so long as the operating intellect recognizes the importance of the term *limited*. But our world's agony over the Bomb is a sufficient evidence of the neglect of limit. The danger lies in an inclusiveness of Nominalistic reductionism, practiced upon reality as if that limited intellectual procedure where not precisely that—a limited reductionism—but rather a metaphysical principle sufficient unto itself. Bruce Gregory in his recent *Inventing Reality: Physics as Language* (1990) addresses this confusion.

Gregory is careful to caution against such presumptuous confusions of the limits of intellect: "What is not given to physicists by nature, but is rather invented by them, is what they say about these outcomes, i.e., about the outcomes of their 'talk about experimental arrangements and observations.' " What physics "invents" is "the language they use to talk about nature," so that in "the final analysis, physics is only indirectly about the world of nature." Gregory recognizes the distinction necessary: "In the realm of most religions the appeal is to authority; in the realm of science the appeal is to observations and experiments." What Gregory distinguishes here is that in the realm of religion, authority at least purports to be exercised in relation to the largeness of nature and natures, rather than in relation to isolated aspects of existence such as science talks about. Science is necessarily, since only thereby can it be effective, reductionist by its very nature as intellectual action.

In granting the existence of "realms" explored by intellect that are larger than the reduced arenas proper to those sciences such as physics, Gregory is not antipathetic to the view of this same concern as it is held by St. Thomas, though he is not necessarily sympathetic to it. (That he is at least a skeptic is indicated by his ironic appropriation of St. John to his opening chapter, "In the Beginning Was the Word," by which he means only that intellect itself creates language and by it creates a certain level of reality, though not inclusive of reality, by the authority of its made signs.) St. Thomas in the *Summa* (I, Q57) distinguishes the knowledge called *wisdom* from the knowledge called *science*. Wisdom, he says, differs from science, in respect to knowledge, in that science is dependent upon different habits of differing sciences, distinctive from each other and required to be distinctive through the different kinds of knowable matter. But *wisdom* is a "knowing" which is singular, in contrast to the knowings of science which are plural. Wisdom is the habit of intellect whereby all knowledge is ordered toward the first Cause of all things, including knowledge itself, so that through wisdom intellect is itself proportionately ordered to its Cause and End by the relation of the variety of "knowledges" available to the rational intellect. Thus the structure of reality is discovered through wisdom, and though wisdom cannot fully comprehend, it nevertheless understands beyond the inevitable reductionisms upon which the sciences necessarily depend. Physics, as Bruce Gregory argues, cannot purport to be in itself an understanding vision of reality. It is at best, and at its best, a *saying* about reality, where understanding and the wisdom out of understandings are a *seeing* of reality.

In St. Thomas's view, it is at the level of wisdom's inclusive understandings that the sciences are reconciled to each other, insofar as they may be so reconciled by finite intellect. The reconciliation is in relation to being itself. And the key to that possible reconciliation is that fundamental recognition by intellect itself which Thomas expresses thus: it is wisdom to "know the believed things in themselves, by a kind of union with them" through the actions of that initiating movement of intellectual act, its intuitive response to being. The intuitive response is supported by the discursive labors of rational intellection. This is the "knowing" which "pertains to the gift of wisdom." We have considered earlier a very recent attempt to recover this wisdom in relation to being, for such is that intellectual habit which we hear Keats call "negative capability."

Having said all this, we may consider that it is the poet's concern, through intuition, to recover the proper relation between intellect and being, a relation which is that we term wisdom. The "scientific" analysis of the poet's attempt to more fully understand his own "science" through analysis—his attempt to know the limits implied by "tenor" and "vehicle" as pertinent to a metaphor of primary and secondary analogates—contributes at last to wisdom beyond its limit as science. To recover at least an understanding, if not wisdom, on this point is to recognize that "literary criticism" as a science is subordinate: its very nature requires actions of reductionism in which it is not safe for intellect to find its end. Intellect may not continue at rest in the reductionism of any of its sciences, lest it confuse itself as determinate of the mystery of being itself, as if that mystery were ever truly reduced to science.

20

Our Lot Crawling Between Dry Ribs, to Keep Our Metaphysics Warm

Keeping in mind our concern that the poet's desire is stirred by an intuitive inclination to participate in reality according to his nature, let us follow briefly Richards's distinction between *tenor* and *vehicle* in metaphor, in the interest of our recovering the ground lost to analogy by attribution, lost by our having abandoned St. Thomas's insight into the mystery of reality characterized by him in the concept of proper proportionality. For that reality must govern concept and so must govern sign. And here we must bear in mind Thomas's warning to us about the actuality of things in relation to our concepts about things and signs representing those concepts. What is required is a deepening of concept through knowing "believed things" in themselves, by a kind of "union with them." There are, says Thomas, "many kinds of things that hide inwardly and that the apprehension of man must penetrate as if intrinsically. For the substantial nature of things lies hidden under accident; the meanings of words lie hidden under words; figured truth lies hidden under similitudes and figures" (*Summa*, II-II, Q8, 1).

Richards defines *vehicle* as that term of a metaphor which carries the principle of comparison, of what Thomas calls "similitudes." The *tenor* is the subject to which *vehicle* refers. His illustration of the distinction is Hamlet's metaphor, "What should such fellows as I do crawling between earth and heaven?" The *crawling*, says Richards, might apply literally, that is by the sign's explicit reference to things in relation to a specific action by Hamlet—if for instance Hamlet should be reduced to moving on his belly by crawling motions. But there is in the term "an unmistakable reference to other things that crawl." It is to this species of reference

183

(spiders, insects, and the like) that Richards applies the term *vehicle*, Hamlet as man being the *tenor*.

Richards's *tenor* then we might relate to Thomas's *prime analogate*, his *vehicle* to *minor analogate*. But what is so clearly different between the two approaches to metaphor becomes clear with some attention given to Richards's illustration. Richards's position rests in his primary commitment to the psychological dimension in metaphor, understood to be based only in a biological entity, Hamlet (or Hamlet as representative of man). Mind itself is taken as but an extension of that limited perspective upon human existence which is held by Richards. It is a recognition of this inadequacy in Richards's position that led Eliot, late in his career as poet, to express grave reservations about Richards as critic. For Richards reveals no poetic or philosophical foundation sufficient to his analysis of metaphor. Eliot comes to a radical separation from Richards, we observed, in consequence of his own break with modernist conceptions of intellect. We cited Eliot's final lecture at Harvard, his "The Modern Mind," in evidence. As Eliot then (1933) recognizes, Richards has committed himself only to the furthest reach of logic, by which logic he manipulates language independent of reality. It is a manipulation not only of language but it is attributive in concept. It therefore denies any believed reality independent of intellect. It is, in brief, Richards's modernist position that Eliot rejects, a position which accepts only intellect as determinate. For logic isolated from a governance by reality can be but attributive since its sole anchor is autonomous intellect. Such a position may seem sufficient to Richards, since his concern, in Eliot's words for it, is "to preserve emotions without the beliefs with which their history has been involved." But this makes Richards's attempt, despite his denials, a sort of "rear-guard religious action," *vehicle* much truncated.

To make such a judgmental assertion about Richards's position somewhat clearer, let us look again at the *Hamlet* quotation with which he establishes his terms *tenor* and *vehicle*. What is evident from the context of this quotation, and from the tone emerging in Hamlet's words in consequence of context, is quite un-Richardsonian. That is a point of importance to the dramatic effect of the words as spoken in the play. And dramatic effect, in any final justification of art as an imitation of the reality of the action of intellect, rests in our own immediate knowledge of reality which we bring to the occasion from our own experiences. It is experience at the most elementary level: our experiential knowledge of such creatures as spiders that crawl in relation to persons we know such as ourselves. Here there is an inadequacy in the very metaphor Hamlet speaks, which is precisely the issue for him and the reason he deliberately makes such an inadequate metaphor. That is, Hamlet through his metaphor expresses a sardonic response to the complexity of his own circumstances, to a reality he recognizes as somehow independent of anything he might effectively "say" about it. And so with intellectual deliberateness, he indicts circumstances, coming perilously near to an indictment of the Cause of circumstances, that transcendent cause of spiders and man, God Himself. It is a dark moment of alienation indeed. "Such fellows" as Hamlet in his present circumstances finds himself unnaturally reduced to "crawling," and he protests an injustice to his nature as man, from his position now entrapped by natures—that is, as located "between earth and heaven."

The implication in his words, given Hamlet's sardonic irony as tonally reflected, is that this particular fellow Hamlet is less than a *fellow*, less than man, and he is so in his own view through some reductionism whose cause is difficult to locate. There is a grave injustice operative, whose source he has yet to identify. His protest bears at least a residual sense of the proper proportionality in things, necessary to a vision of the truth of things which should prevent such reduction and yet does not. For it is a violation of that proportionality which has somehow resulted in this injustice to him as a "fellow." Such is not proper to his nature. He should not be reduced to "crawling," since by nature he would walk upright, his head toward the clouds and toward heaven. Now an attributive fancy might propose such alternative figuring as in "crawling," toward testing proper proportionality by imaginative actions of intellect. In such moods as Hamlet's, attribution becomes most tempting, out of an uncertainty in his intellect. So often in such a "state of mind" one takes recourse to irony, and in acute instances to sardonic irony, as is here present in Hamlet's words, as they are more conspicuously present in Prufrock's conclusion that he "should have been a pair of ragged claws" scuttling the floors of silent seas. In such a moment, intellect senses an intolerable isolation, whose cause must prove ultimately its own, insofar as it approaches understanding. But in the moment, it is far from an understanding. Even so, understanding may be insufficient to a resolution. In that state intellect is likely not only to have a strong sense of an injustice visited upon it, but suspect some agent other than itself as the cause of the injustice, and the most handy cause for Hamlet is God. For Prufrock, a God to blame is not convenient to his thought.

As St. Thomas says, however, "the substantial nature of things lies hidden under the accidents," here the created accidents of attribution by intellect. Such accidents are thus too easily taken as substantive, if taken by "fancy." Thereby intellect imposes by means of words upon the circumstances external, as if to force words to a reality. Still, the true "meanings of words lie hidden under words" even in such instances. That is, even when words are wrongly used, they bear a certain true witness, and that is the nature of dramatic irony specifically. What dramatic irony reveals is the agent's *miss-taking* of his circumstances. And within conceptual structure raised by intellect as well "figured truth lies hidden under similitudes and figures" such as those conceptually proposed through signs. Which is to say that actual, communal likeness among things is always resident in the nature of the particular thing itself, though intellect may *miss-take* its own apprehension of *essences*. Through a perception of this truth, and through it alone, is it possible for intellect to discover a just measure of likeness in unlike things, of a relation of *fellow* to *crawling things*. It is in Shakespeare's remarkable gift to such discovery that Keats stands in awe of Shakespeare. Shakespeare's is that gift of "negative capability" which Thomas expresses as the wisdom of knowing, whereby one knows believed things by a kind of union with them. Or as Thomas puts it in his own words, it is an act through which the "understanding apprehension" of intellect "penetrates to the essence of the thing" and knows it for "what it is," in and of itself. It will also know it in that same act as dependent in being, a knowledge whereby intellect orients itself in its nature as existing "between earth and heaven" as Hamlet would do. Such is the tensional complex to the poet's imaginative act of metaphor, that intuitive movement of intellect that is exercised by "right reason about certain works to be made" such as the works of metaphors. And that is the exercise required in his making, to be acquired through the habit of practical intellect.

In such a perspective, one must take metaphor as complex beyond the merely biological-psychological dimensions of intellect, though including those as well. That is a larger dimension to metaphor than I. A. Richards is prepared to grant or to engage as a possibility even. Prufrock, in Eliot's poem, is himself unable to resolve this tensional activity in his own intellect, retreating behind attributive metaphors akin to Hamlet's own, as if after crawling to the tea party he should then discover himself "penned and wriggling" by words. Prufrock's elected arena is considerably reduced from that of Hamlet, for Hamlet yet concedes his as lying "between earth and heaven." Still, the sardonic irony in both Hamlet and Prufrock threatens to dissolve intellect into the despair of isolation. Eliot is uncomfortably aware, at the time he wrote "Prufrock," that somehow there is a meaning to existence which has yet to yield to his figures and similitudes. The irony in his poetry is itself already a signal that the poet who is making the ironic texture of a consciousness such as Prufrock's is attempting to move beyond modernist reductionism. The action of attribution is never quite so simple as it may seem on the instant. Attribution as a device in the making implies a maker not simply free of that action but engaged by it, and it is an engagement which (in a recognition which may or may not come) speaks an inclusiveness in being beyond the moment's sense of isolation that may trouble intellect. Intellect through attribution is attempting to force order upon being in an exercise of power over being. But in a recognition of that relationship, the forcing intellect can not indefinitely ignore the prior existence of that upon which it would force order. Thus *being* may be discovered as lying *fundamentally* active in reality, within the nature of things as they are. Those natures perceived through accidents yet bear intellect's "seeing" into that reality, a seeing into the life of things. That is a recognition far removed from Prufrock, of course, as it was also from Eliot at that time. And it is also far removed from Richards as literary critic, as Eliot at last becomes aware.

We touch here upon that most central battleground in which modernism would route the truth of reality and substitute its own. It is an attempt which will reveal itself as just this by intent, again and again, and conspicuously so through the *manner* of the particular intellect's address to analogy. It is a manner which proves inescapable in the tonal qualities of the signs used, speaking the presence of the particular maker of those signs. That is why a person's words, and most particularly his similitudes and figures, reveal him most nakedly, a realization which made Eliot at the close of his career as poet quite uncomfortable with some of his earlier work, both his poetry and criticism.

It is in recognition of this importance of words to truth that made such a "Romantic" poet as Pound dogmatically concerned with the image. He fears particularly the threat to image through a figurative language carelessly taken. In his memoir, *Gaudier-Brzeska* (1916), a tribute to his sculptor friend killed in World War I, Pound says, concerning the problem of "metaphor":

> The pine-tree in mist upon the far hill looks like a fragment of Japanese armour.
> The beauty of the pine-tree in the mist is not caused by its resemblance to the plates of the armour.
> The armour, if it be beautiful at all, is not beautiful *because* of its resemblance to the pine in the mist.
> In either case the beauty, in so far as it is a beauty of form, is the result of "planes in relation."
> The tree and the armour are beautiful because their diverse planes overlie in a certain manner.
> The Poet, whatever his "figure of speech," will not arrive by doubling or confusing an image.

Pound establishes "Beauty" as lying in the poet's craft as its primary cause, in the execution of which he overlays planes in relation, thus structuring a thing whose effect is an intentional "Beauty." There is an inescapable presence in his words of his confidence in the authority of his own intellect in respect to being itself, a confidence he underlines by his embrace of Confucius. Nevertheless, he reveals himself aware of a problem to be overcome, a certain arbitrariness in attributive metaphor which allows an abuse by fancy, by the "Amygists." Thus the problem seems to lie more in the possible failure of the poet as autonomous maker than in that principle of making as he embraces it. It is more an irresponsibility of autonomous practice than a failure of vision into the truth of things. But that is precisely where the problem is located as seen from a Thomistic perspective. And so one concludes Pound beseiged intellectually by modernism, whose ally he has proved, leading to the spectacle of his incarceration in that open-air cage at Pisa.

Lest I appear to condemn the attributive action of intellect as suited to poetry, we have argued it an aspect of intellectual action implicitly possible to intellect by its own limited nature. Such an action of nature the poet certainly imitates. Our concern is that he must know what he is about. Burns knows when he says his love is like a "red, red rose." One being playful in such metaphor might speak of his love as simply "like a rose," and go on to thorns, perhaps to infecting aphids in season, or to the inclination of that plant to be pliable, or to grow in random profusion. And in making such suggestion of audacious attribution, one well recalls a most remarkable poem, Hugh MacDiarmid's *A Drunk Man Looks at a Thistle*, which is an extraordinary play with metaphor that MacDiarmid governs by a sense of proper proportionality, even as his protagonist speaking the poem is not always so governed. There is yet another very long, magnificent poem devoted centrally to the principle of proper proportionality as it allows a praise of things in themselves, David Jones's *Anathemata*. Much of our argument in these pages finds support in these two important poems. Especially revealing, I believe, would be a critical reading of Pound's *Cantos* in comparison to Jones's *Anathemata*. Such a consideration might well lead to the elevation due Jones's great poem, which has been in part overshadowed by the *Cantos*. It seems evident to me that Pound himself came to see, though late and perhaps only fleetingly, the Thomistic principle, in his experiences at Pisa, waiting transportation home to stand trial for treason.

It is in the cage at Pisa that for a moment at least Pound recovers beyond the modernism that has closed upon him. He regains a capacity of intellect to enter into the life of things and thereby recovers similitude beyond intellect's attributions:

When the mind swings by a grass-blade
an ant's forefoot shall save you
the clover leaf smells and tastes as its flower

And Brother Wasp is building a very neat house
Of four rooms, one shaped like a squat indian bottle.

One must be insensitive in the extreme not to discover in such lines an opening of the poet's intellect to a recovery of things in themselves, and with a growing sense of proportionality, a tenderness toward attribution as inadequate. It is a moment of recovery not to "Imagism," but to that state of the soul in creation which we think of in relation to St. Fancis of Assisi.

As we have said, William Carlos Williams reacts to the dislocation of figurative language by Imagism, made by the Imagist at a fundamental level of intellectual knowledge about things. He turns to "Objectivism." In defining Objectivism for the *Princeton Encyclopedia of Poetry and Poetics*, Williams says the movement "arose as an aftermath of imagism" in response to the weakness of that movement in not being "specific enough." Objectivism "concerned itself with an image more particularized yet broadened in its significance. The mind rather than the unsupported eye entered the picture." Another way of putting this would be to say that Williams had come to recognize that the accidents of things are insufficient to the thing in itself, and it is to get back to the thing itself that occupies him more and more. He takes that direction more from Husserl than from St. Thomas, of course, but it is movement in a direction Thomas would recognize, in which "mind" enters the picture as if to get below the picture to that which the picture hides. In this sense, art for Williams must turn back, through intellect, to its proper moorings of its act of "reason in making," however reluctant that Romantic poet Williams may be to use such a term as *reason*. What Williams wishes to accomplish as poet, an end intuitively desired from early in his career, he states in "A Sort of Song":

—through metaphor to reconcile
the people and the stones.
Compose. (No ideas
but in things) Invent!

Williams is, like Pound, quite wary of metaphor as a technical device attributively manipulated, as we have seen. In "A Sort of Song" there is his concern to recover the thing itself to an intellectual union through perception, and with an immediacy of union beyond analytical obfuscations. It is as if Williams would recover that knowledge of the known but forgotten gift to knowing which St. Thomas insists upon in saying that intellect already possesses a knowledge of the nature of things through perception, in a pre-conceptual state of intellect in its relation to the things of the senses.

Neither Williams nor Pound, however, established himself with a sufficient firmness in that ground, within which image itself is supported by the analogy of proper proportionality, the ground lying in that relation between *essendo* and *esse*, between Thomas's *being* and *existence*. It is an attempt to regain the truth of things through bringing the mind into the picture in support of the sensual eye that Williams advocates in his "Objectivism." It is a support to the "eye" against the Cartesian confusions about mind which keep getting in the way of the Romantic's intuitive desire. It is to this confusion of "mind" that Fr. Phelan speaks in observing of attributive analogy that it involves an "ontological univocity coupled with a logical use of the univocal term after the manner of true analogy." Such analogy is then *logically* valid, and from the Cartesian point of view it seems to establish the authority of intellect itself as decisive. But it is incapable of bearing "the weight of metaphysical or transcendental predication." Thus it is typically an idealist's analogy that results, used to "maintain the necessary distinction between the Absolute and the Relative," but only on the authority at last of finite intellect. It is an analogy thus inevitably attributive only, and so a dead end to metaphor. For, Phelan adds, "idealism either explicitly or implicitly reduces metaphysics to logic and erroneously applies procedures valid in dealing with the *entia rationis* of logic to the *entia realia* of ontology." This is what Gilson objects to in his *Methodical Realism* as the idealist's attempt to extract an ontology from thought.

As for the poet, as opposed to Gilson's philosopher, here too lies the locus of Samuel Johnson's objection to the Metaphysicals, though Johnson does not put it in Scholastic terms. For those poets, in "yoking by violence disparates together" in their metaphorical games, end by having yoked "the most heterogeneous ideas" by that violence, at the expense of reality. In consequence Johnson finds that their "courtship was void of fondness and their lamentation of sorrow" as witnessed by the poetry itself. It is very much to this point that Eliot, in his early celebration of John Donne and his own early dependence upon him in reaction to cloyed Romanticism, is at that same point declaring himself a relativist, though adding that "One can be a relative idealist or a relative realist"

(Letter dated January 6, 1915). When Eliot later discovers Lancelot Andrewes, he sets Andrewes beside Donne and finds Donne severely wanting, and for reasons akin to Johnson's demurrer to metaphysical poetry, though it is Donne as Divine that Eliot faults. "About Donne," says Eliot, "there hangs the shadow of the impure motive; and impure motives lend their aid to a facile success." As Divine, Donne is "the Reverend Billy Sunday of his time."

But that is a judgment of Donne late in Eliot's career, at the time of "Ash-Wednesday." That is at a time when Eliot has largely recovered himself as poet in order to be governed at last by a reality discovered through rational expositions of his intuitive "seeing" of reality. In a sense, the discovery means an end of Eliot as poet, though it has been as poet that he made the necessary journey which has led him to the place from which he set out. Now enabled by that journey, he is confident that he "sees" that place for the first time, and with a joyful, though not a "happy," recognition that "all manner of thing shall be well."

Endnotes

1. Such figurative address to the nature of intellect is constant in poetry from Homer to Frost. Frost's poetry is metaphorically ordered, almost without exception, by the antithesis of head and heart, whether lyric or monologue. See for instance "On the Heart's Beginning to Cloud the Mind" which puts the metaphor's paradigm as Frost uses it generally. Or consider "After Apple-Picking." So, too, "The Death of the Hired Man" and, a darker engagement of heart and head, "Home Burial."

2. In a filmed interview Frost remarked, "When you talk about your troubles and go to somebody about them, you're just a fool. The best way to settle them is to make something that has form, because all you want to do is get a sense of form." (Quoted in Sohn and Tyre, *Frost: The Poet and His Poetry*, 1967.) To talk about one's troubles with a priest or to God in prayer makes one a fool in Frost's judgment. He sees himself as making the only possible rescue from troubles, a "making." There is a Prufrockian dimension in Frost himself, reflected in his poetry and in such remarks, in that he protects himself against a vulnerable openness. Don't show too much feeling, for the "strong are saying nothing," as one of his poems puts it.

3. I have paid tribute to this remarkable thinker Eric Voegelin in "Eric Voegelin as Prophetic Philosopher," reservations given in "On Fides, Intellectus, Ratio," Afterthought VII, to that essay, in *The Men I Have Chosen for Fathers* (1990). An extended reservation would address Voegelin in relation to grace. While not specific to that concern, a word on our modern difficulties with grace as a reality and as a concept, and its role in relation to the battle between hope and despair that is the typical theme of our century's principal poets and a theme of our present discourse: I am acutely aware of the awkwardness that occurs whenever the concept of *grace* is introduced into intellectual concerns. It is as if the presence of that concept is a violation of propriety and indeed it is, given the current climate of intellectual address to the nature of reality. It is so, because the present intellectual community is so heavily affected by Pelagianism, that ancient heresy which Voegelin characterizes as "modern gnosticism." My own position

193

194   *Endnotes*

is that the awkwardness is an indication of just how deeply Western thought has
become Pelagian. One may discuss the condition of intellect more or less accept-
ably in relation to Descartes or to Kant, as opposed to Augustine or Thomas,
since the apparent arena thus agreed upon is comfortably within the Pelagian
territory. In that limited territory, a question such as the relation of the gift of
grace to our intellectual isolation is not the sort of question one would deal with.
My own contention is that one can avoid the reality of grace only at peril to
intellect and its actions. One may do so by denying any sense to the obvious
experience to intellect itself that it is a given, already active upon givens by the
time it becomes committed by will to intellectual action. What is desired by will,
in opposition to the reality of grace, is the self-creation of intellect by will, which
requires the denial of any given, though a sort of reluctant, even sentimental,
acknowledgment of a materialistic given, the amorphous world of "nature," is
common enough. Unwilling to credit itself as created by aught but itself, intellect
nevertheless seems willing enough to credit its material locale as not of its own
making. The biological ground of intellect may be acknowledged as precedent,
because one has pride of intellect: intellect is risen above its material origins as
proposed by Darwinian materialism. It is an intellectual attitude compatible with
the common, if mystical, acceptance of Progress. Mystical, in that the teleological
questions attendant upon a faith in progress are always intellectually vaporous.
Progress *versus* grace: that seems the religious antithesis. Intellect may deny the
reality of grace by willful rejection only, and in the interest of itself as self-saviour.
What is inescapable in that refusal of all givens in being is an inevitable isolation
of intellect from being. Such has been the history of intellect in Western thought
since the Renaissance, as it is the history of thought in specific intellects that make
such rejections of being in any time or place. There comes a point to the individual
intellect, however, in which its sense of isolation raises the shadow of despair,
despair itself the ultimate sin against operative grace and as such a sure evidence
of grace as external to intellect and its operations. Despair may be resisted by the
agitations of spirit characterized as *acedia*, a more or less frenzied busy-ness of
intellect whose attempt is to keep despair at bay. I myself would contend that the
shadow of despair falling on intellect in its growing isolation unto itself is itself
an action of grace. One is not inclined to embrace despair except at a final extremity of spirit, so that the shadow of despair may be said to serve as turning intellect
toward the light of hope.

    4. I am much indebted to John Hittinger's meticulous exploration entitled
"Reason and Intellect in Two Texts of St. Thomas Aquinas," a dissertation on the
subject submitted to the philosophy faculty at the Catholic University of America
in 1978. The two texts centering the concern are *Expositio super librum Boethii
'De trinitate'* and *Quaestiones disputatae de veritate*, with attention to relevant
arguments in other of Thomas's works. We might remember that our own argument does not say that Thomas establishes our terms beyond reflective consideration, and it is to that point that Josef Pieper speaks in his *Guide to Thomas
Aquinas* (1962): Thomas's *disputatio* is the "free" discussion of questions, free

discussion in that only significant meaning to "academic freedom," a concept so far decayed as seemingly beyond rescue, at least by our current academy. It is in the free and open pursuit of truth that Thomas develops the procedure of the *articulus*, the structural element in the *Summa* and *Quaestiones disputatae*, though other of his work uses the essay, the extended argument. The *articulus* is admirably suited to teaching, of course. The form demands an intellectual orderliness between teacher and student, as sonnet form makes such demand upon poet in his making. As Pieper says, the *articulus* is very much the Platonic dialogue in small. The argument advanced is put succinctly, but its defender is required to formulate objections to it in a public recapitulation in order to demonstrate that he understands the possible objections. Only then is he justified in answering the objections, since he and the objector are thus in agreement as to nature of the particular objection. Thomas's *quaestiones*, says Pieper, "are really questions, dilemmas, dubieties," and "they make no claim to offering comprehensive answers, but throw open the gates to an infinitude of further seeking." That is a truth about Thomism seldom recognized, at least partly the fault of Thomists who find the *articulus* an end rather than as it was for Thomas himself, a starting point.

5. What we are here concerned to maintain is a continuing mystery in existence, and especially the mystery of intellectual encounter with existences. One is well struck by the likeness in unlikeness among creative intellects in respect to discoveries beyond method or process. In 1952 Brewster Ghiselin edited *The Creative Process*, an anthology of recollections by a variety of minds ranging from physicist and mathematician, to poet and painter, in which collection one is reminded of the continuing mystery of intellect's acts of making. One well reads such anecdotes alongside such work as that of Oliver Sacks, particularly his *The Man Who Mistook His Wife for a Hat*, or the speculative works of Michael Polanyi, *The Tacit Dimension* and *Personal Knowledge*. To do so is to have restored a sense of the unknown, since we are disproportionately fascinated with what is known, especially since ours is such a lively intellectual century in which technological advantages to knowledge tempt us to dogmas that would obviate mystery. Indeed, the unjustified confidence in rationality as an object of faith, born in the Enlightenment and now seemingly justified by sophisticated technology, makes us not merely C. P. Snow's "Two Cultures" in respect to intellectual community, but a multitude of cultures founded in certainties antipathetic to each other or as yet unreconciled to each other. It is this condition of intellectual community which led Eric Voegelin to say our age very much requires a new Thomas Aquinas.

If Sacks presents arresting mystery in relation to neurological actions of intellect, John Lorber, a British neurologist, presents equally arresting concerns for physiological reductions of intellectual action. Concerned with hydrocephalus, Lorber reports: "There's a young student at this university [Sheffield] . . . who has an I.Q. of 126, has gained a first-class honors degree in mathematics, and is socially completely normal. And yet the boy has virtually no brain" (*Science*, Dec. 12, 1980). He adds: "I can't say whether the mathematics student has a brain weighing 50 grams or 150 grams, but it's clear that it is nowhere near the normal 1.5 Kilograms . . . and much of the brain he does have is in the more primitive deep structures that are relatively spared in hydrocephalus."

6. C. S. Lewis, in his essay "On Ethics" (*The Seeing Eye*) engages the modernist use of *instinct* as an attempt to justify a present responsibility to the future as the "preservation" of our species. If there were such an instinct binding present and future, he argues, "it would not do the work which those who invoke instinct in this context demand of it." Again, "You may vivisect your grandfather in order to deliver your grandchildren from cancer: but, take away traditional morality, and why should you bother about your grandchildren?" Again, "Let me ask anyone . . . who is a father whether he has a spontaneous impulse to sacrifice his own son for the sake of the human species in general." Or we might intensify the difficulty by another question: whether a father would sacrifice his son for his grandson. What concerns Lewis is a use of *instinct* to designate "Behaviour as if from knowledge" while denying knowledge. For "we refuse to attribute conscious design and forknowledge to the agent" in act and so declare that "it has acted 'by instinct.' " And thus the idea of preservation of species is bootlegged into the question as a pseudo-metaphysical speculation restricted to the physical arena of existence, the spiritual thus denied. Thus instinct becomes the "god" necessary if a rationalist order is to be justified as complete when it must on principle consider only the physical dimension of existence. As I suggest elsewhere, *instinct* as a cold, rational reduction of existence gives way to a warmer personification of "Nature," whereby an aura of benevolence is maintained. Maintained at least until one must, as Tennyson at last was forced to do, come to terms with "Nature red in tooth and claw," which the concept of preservation of the species does not answer to the satisfaction of intellect's desire. Intellect's intuitive knowledge speaks of preservation of a *species*, but it is that species, the specific, discrete soul, a species unto itself.

7. On these three sorts of vision, see Dom Hudleston's "Introduction," pages xvi following, in his edition of Dame Julian's *Revelations of Divine Love*. London: Burns Oates, 1927.

8. In another work as yet in manuscript, I treat in detail the relation of "The Hollow Men" to "Ash-Wednesday," with attention to the ambiguity of the "shadow" which seems to cause spiritual stasis, a work called "T. S. Eliot and the Still Point of Consciousness: An Excursion into the *Four Quartets*."

9. I have explored at length this aspect of Eliot's poetry in *T. S. Eliot: An Essay on the American Magus* (1970) and *Eliot's Reflective Journey to the Garden* (1979).

10. Concerning this point about the New Critics, see my "Cleanth Brooks and the Life of Art," *The Men I Have Chosen for Fathers*, 1990.

11. Gilson, in *The Spirit of Thomism*, formulates the first question intellect must deal with, the question at least from which it must set out: "What is being?" We have already used this passage, but it is central and warrants emphasis. For intellect, aware of its existence, cannot escape the question, *what is it to exist*? And so, says Gilson, "if we want to philosophize, it is really *the* problem of problems."

He then summarizes St. Thomas's answer to that question, taken from *Quaestiones disputatae de potentia* (Q7, Art. 2, ad 9m): "In Thomas' technical language, actual existence, which he calls *esse*, is that by virtue of which a thing, which he calls *res*, is a being, an *ens*. It is the being-hood or being-ness of being. It is *be* in being. It is *to be* that makes a certain thing to be a being. *Esse* is defined by its essence, namely that which the thing is."

12. Who could, or would, wish to deny the pleasure of intellectual entertainment Stevens's art gives one. If he is nearly always "preaching" his own position on the virtues of imaginative play, one takes a delight which is denied by Pound as a Preacher of his own position. Pound seems too often more nearly akin to one of those severe Puritan fathers of New England, though sermonizing on a "religion" which is widely removed from their sort of Gnostic inclination. Stevens assumes a sophisticated intellect is to be entertained, his own, and so by extension intellects like his if they so desire. Consider, for instance, the delightfully witty and intricate explication of his theory of the imagination in "Someone Puts a Pineapple Together," a poem constituting one of three "Academic Pieces," the others in prose, in his collected essays, *The Necessary Angel*. Or that expression of "paganism" in "Sunday Morning" or "The Man with the Blue Guitar," both argumentative expositions of his theory of the imagination and its uses through poetry.

13. On the destructive nature of this critical movement, see Gerald Graff's *Literature Against Itself*. See also my own *The Trouble with You Innerleckchuls*, and on the necessity of care in charging all the New Critics with current critical chaos, my "Cleanth Brooks and the Life in Art," *The Men I Have Chosen for Fathers*.

Index

accidents of being, xiii, 52, 68–69, 115; attribution and, 72, 154; insufficiency of, 189; mistaking for substance, 89–90, 91, 98; penetrating, 65; relation to essence, 100; relation to image, 143; sign and, 80

advertising, 112

agent, 51, 52, 58

ambiguity, 177

analogates, 183, 184

analogy, xii–xiii, 13, 80, 97; attributive (*see* attribution; attributive analogy); nature of, 77; proportionate, 9; reality and, 98; true, 91, 96, 97, 115; use by intellect, 119; use in poetry, 96

Andrewes, Lancelot, 125, 126, 159, 191

apprehension, 53

Aquinas, St. Thomas, xii; on art, 29; *articulus* and, 195n4; on being, 196–97n11; *On Being and Essence*, xiii, 63; concern for others, 16; on intellect, 15, 20; on intellectual habits, 25; on knowledge, 29–30, 54; on mystical knowledge, 113; on natural light, 16 (*see also* natural light); on the personal, 37; on play, 108; on proper proportionality, 2, 65 (*see also* proper proportionality); refutation of Averroists, 111; on sign, 135;

on soul, 69; on understanding, 15, 53–54; on wisdom, 29–30, 53–54, 182

Aristotle: on art, 31; on doubt, 153; on poets, 114; on possible/probable in art, 51; on testing concepts, 98

Arnold, Matthew, 179

art, xii, 29–31; attitude toward, 95–96; defining, 75–76; distinction from reality, 56; effect of, 184; as end, 44–46, 108; as evidence of soul, 59; feeling in, 33–34 (*see also* emotion); good, 108; as intellectual response to creation, 15; metaphysics of, 57; nature of, 32; objectivity in, 35; personal in, 57–58; as reason in making, 14; relation to intellect, 11; role in discovering gifts as makers, 13; as salvific, 46, 48, 49, 95, 109, 150; transcendence via, 46; understanding of nature of, 15; as wishful thinking, 136–37. *See also* made thing; making; poem; poetry

art work, 14, 30

artist, 30; as creator, 13–14; as maker, 72; man as, 44; as spiritual mediator, 46

Astrophel and Stella, 3–4

attribution, xii, xiii, 13; distortion by, 159; effect on intellect, 1; errors of,

199

poem, 1, 10–12, 14, 35, 49; relation
to society, 46, 47–48; responses to
sign/reality, 124; role of, 53, 61, 90;
Romantic (*see* Romantic poets);
seeing of likeness by, 12, 103, 114;
understanding of own nature, 51,
53, 55; as witness, 161–62
poetry, 91; actualities in, 131; bad, 34;
Cartesian Idealism and, 83–84;
medieval, 101; movements in, 116;
poet's relation to agent, 51, 52;
power of, 67, 148; purpose of, 149;
reason's role in, 33–34, 36; relation
to reality, 34–35, 178; revisions of,
32; as salvific, 142, 179; science of,
42; sign and, 116–17; spontaneity in,
31, 32–33; as stay against confusion,
154, 155. *See also* art; made thing
point of view, 51–52, 57
Pound, Ezra, 28, 61, 151; attribution
and, 72–76, 141–42, 147–53; on
beauty, 107–8, 188; on false witness,
112; Imagism and, 133, 138; on language and image, 187; metaphor
and, 147, 149; metaphysics, 81–82;
on poet's role, 48–49; recovery of
intellect, 188–89; on use of sign,
134, 139; on Wordsworth, 19, 126;
on Yeats, 48
practical intellect. *See* rational intellect
preconceptual knowledge, 83, 114, 156;
of being/thing, 78, 104; of essence,
xii, 5, 6, 103, 190; as preliminary to
intellectual action, 15
presence: in existence, 84–85; language
and, 147; in made thing, 82; of
maker, 45–46, 49, 55–56, 187; resonance of in art, 45–46, 52
proper proportionality, xiii, 2, 59, 63,
65, 183; in analogy, 97; attributive
making and, 157; likeness and, 100;
poet and, 77; in poetry, 188; revelation of, 90; sign and, 179; understanding of, 52, 62; understanding
structure of reality by, 94

prudence, 25, 75, 107
psychic experiences, 169–70

randomness, 115
ratio, 5, 20
rational intellect, xi, 4–5, 42; attribution by, 61; incompleteness of, 113;
preliminary necessity for, 15; understanding and, 68
rationalism, 165
rationality, 195n6
Realism, Thomistic. *See* Thomistic
Realism
reality: analogy and, 98; appearance of,
177 (*see also* accidents of being);
common experience of, 80–81; concept and, 183; denial of, 166, 184,
187; dislocation from, 44, 120; distinction from art, 56; distortion of
sense of, 14; intellect and, 98, 173;
intuition and, xii; nature of, xi, 96,
193n3; order of, 40; poet and poem
within, 12; rationalist view of, 166,
167; recovery of, 17; restriction of
freedom by, 13; seeing (*see* seeing);
self-exile from, 44; sign and (*see*
sign); structure of (*see* structure of
reality); Thomistic Realist view of,
156; violation of, 1, 61, 87–88, 115.
See also being; *esse;* existence
reason, 104–5; beauty and, 108, 109.
See also intellect; rational intellect
reductionism, 39–43, 101, 103, 130; effect on reality, 166; Imagism and,
142; in science, 181
reflection, 25, 123, 154, 156
response, spiritual, 45
Richards, I. A., 178–79, 187; on metaphor, 180, 183–84, 186
Romantic poets, xi, 19, 67, 161–62; discomfort with metaphor, 116–17,
119, 153; mysticism and, 83; sign
and, 77. *See also individual poets'
names*

About the Author

Marion Montgomery, professor emeritus of English at the University of Georgia, has published poems, short stories, and essays in a variety of periodicals over the past forty years. Among his many books are collections of poems and essays, novels, and critical studies, including *T. S. Eliot: An Essay on the American Magus* and *The Reflective Journey Toward Order: Essays on Dante, Wordsworth, Eliot, and Others*. His critical trilogy is *The Prophetic Poet and the Spirit of the Age*: Vol. I, *Why Flannery O'Connor Stayed Home*; Vol. II, *Why Poe Drank Liquor*; Vol. III, *Why Hawthorne Was Melancholy*. His latest collection of essays is *The Men I Have Chosen for Fathers: Literary and Philosophical Passages*. He lives in Crawford, Georgia.

DATE DUE

MAY - 7 1999	

UPI 261-2505 G